T0305777

Financial Crisis, Corporate Governance, and Bank Capital

In the aftermath of the 2007–8 financial crisis, senior policymakers and the media have blamed excessive risk taking by bank executives in response to their compensation incentives for the crisis. The inevitable follow-up to this was to introduce stronger financial regulation in the hope that better and more responsible behavior could be induced. Despite the honorable intentions of regulation, such as the Dodd-Frank Act of 2010, it is clear that many big banks are still deemed "too big to fail." This book argues that by restructuring executive incentive programs to include only restricted stock and restricted stock options with very long vesting periods and financing banks with considerably more equity, the potential of future financial crises can be minimized. It will be of great value to corporate executives, corporate board members, institutional investors, and financial policymakers, as well as graduate and undergraduate students studying finance, economics, and law.

SANJAI BHAGAT is Provost Professor of Finance at the University of Colorado, Boulder. He has worked previously at the US Securities and Exchange Commission, Princeton University, and the University of Chicago. He is a board member of ProLink Solutions, an enterprise software company; Integra Ventures, a venture capital company; and the National Association of Corporate Directors, Colorado Chapter. He has advised US government agencies and Fortune 500 companies on corporate governance and finance issues and has submitted several *amici curiae* briefs on class action litigation to the US Supreme Court that have been cited in the High Court's decisions.

Financial Crisis, Corporate Governance, and Bank Capital

SANJAI BHAGAT
University of Colorado, Boulder

CAMBRIDGE
UNIVERSITY PRESS

CAMBRIDGE
UNIVERSITY PRESS

University Printing House, Cambridge CB2 8BS, United Kingdom

One Liberty Plaza, 20th Floor, New York, NY 10006, USA

477 Williamstown Road, Port Melbourne, VIC 3207, Australia

314-321, 3rd Floor, Plot 3, Splendor Forum, Jasola District Centre, New Delhi - 110025, India

79 Anson Road, #06-04/06, Singapore 079906

Cambridge University Press is part of the University of Cambridge.

It furthers the University's mission by disseminating knowledge in the pursuit of education, learning and research at the highest international levels of excellence.

www.cambridge.org
Information on this title: www.cambridge.org/9781107170643
10.1017/9781316756669

First published 2017

A catalogue record for this publication is available from the British Library

ISBN 978-1-107-17064-3 Hardback

to
Rohun, Akil, and Leena
for the lessons on intellectual capital and incentives...

Contents

List of Figures   *page* ix
List of Tables   xi
Preface   xiii
Acknowledgments   xv

1   Introduction   1

2   Mortgage Public Policies and the Financial Crisis   12

3   Precrisis Executive Compensation and Misaligned
    Incentives   24

4   Managerial Incentives Hypothesis versus Unforeseen
    Risk Hypothesis   30

5   Bank CEOs' Buys and Sells during 2000–8   35

6   Executive Compensation Reform   73

7   Director Compensation Policy   101

8   Are Large Banks Riskier?   117

9   Bank Capital Structure and Executive
    Compensation   154

10 Why Banks Should Be Mostly Debt Financed: Parade
of Non Sequiturs   168

11 Conclusion   174

Appendix A: Credit-Rating Agencies and the Subprime
            Mortgage Securitization Process   179
Appendix B: Data Used in This Book: Available Online   183
Notes   203
Bibliography   228
Index   241

Figures

2.1   (A) Real Standard & Poor's (S&P) 500 Index and real
Case-Shiller Home Price Index, 1890–2013. (B) Real
S&P 500 Index and real Case-Shiller Home Price
Index, 1960–2013.   *page* 13

2.2   (A) The growing and important role of Fannie Mae
and Freddie Mac in the US residential mortgage
debt market during 1992–2008. (B) The growing and
important role of Fannie Mae and Freddie Mac in the
US residential mortgage debt market during
1992–2008.   14

2.3   (A) Total holdings of US mortgages by type
of financial institution. (B) Market- and bank-based
holding of home mortgages.   15

2.4   Enterprise housing goals and performance.   17

2.5   Subprime mortgage originations.   18

2.6   Distribution of MBS issuances by issuer.   20

2.7   Subprime originations and securitization rate.   21

5.1   Relative portfolio returns of bank portfolios,
2000–8.   44

5.2   CEO net trades for 14 TBTF banks and 37 No-TARP
banks.   56

5.3   Value of CEO and insider net trades for 14 TBTF
banks.   61

6.1   Ratio of bank CEOs' net trades to beginning holdings,
2000–8.   79

6.2   (A) Impact of stock sales restrictions on net CEO payoff.
(B) Impact of stock sales and salary restrictions on
net CEO payoff.   86

7.1   (A) Relationship between dollar board ownership
      by quartiles and industry-adjusted return on assets
      for the subsequent two years for the 1,500 largest
      US companies, 1998–2012. (B) Relationship between
      dollar board ownership by quartiles and industry-adjusted
      return on assets for the subsequent two years for the
      1,500 largest US companies, 1998–2002. (C) Relationship
      between dollar board ownership by quartiles and
      industry-adjusted return on assets for the subsequent
      two years for the 1,500 largest US companies, 2003–5.
      (D) Relationship between dollar board ownership by
      quartiles and industry-adjusted return on assets for
      the subsequent two years for the 1,500 largest US
      companies, 2006–8. (E) Relationship between dollar
      board ownership by quartiles and industry-adjusted
      return on assets for the subsequent two years for
      the 1,500 largest US companies, 2009–12.   110
7.2   Probability of disciplinary CEO turnover among the
      worst-performing largest 1,500 US companies during
      1998–2012, sorted by director ownership quartiles
      (Q1–Q4).   113
9.1   Balance sheet of a large bank.   161
10.1 Relation between ROE and ROA for a bank.   171
A.1   Securitization process of mortgage-backed
      securities.   180
A.2   Moody's quarterly revenues from rating various
      securities.   181

Tables

2.1	Loan Characteristics at Origination	*page* 22
5.1	Selected Descriptive Statistics	37
5.2	Trades by CEOs during 2000–8	40
5.3	CEO Payoffs, TBTF Institutions	46
5.4	CEO Trading and CEO Holdings	55
5.5	Trades by All Insiders, Including Officers and Directors, 2000–8	58
5.6	Fama-French-Carhart Four-Factor Abnormal Return Regressions	62
5.7	Risk Factors, *Z*-Scores, and Write-Downs	65
5.8	Determinants of CEO Trading	68
6.1	Restricted Equity Proposal's Impact on Net CEO Payoff	83
7.1	Director Stock Ownership Requirements for S&P 500 Firms during 2003 and 2005	105
7.2	Examples of Ten S&P 500 Firms with Director Ownership Guidelines (2005)	106
7.3	Firm Performance and Director Dollar Value of Holdings	108
7.4	Bank CEO Net Trades and Bank Director Ownership during 2000–8	114
8.1	Summary Statistics	131
8.2	Correlation Coefficients for the Main Regression Variables	132
8.3	Firm Size (Total Assets) and Risk-Taking	135
8.4	Two-Stage Least-Square (2SLS) IV Regression of Firm Size on Risk-Taking	141
8.5	Size and Risk-Taking across Financial Crisis Periods	146

8.6	Decomposition of *Z*-Score	150
9.1	CEO Trading and Bank Capital	164
B.1	TARP Recipient Information	184
B.2	CEOs during 2000 and 2008 by Firm	187
B.3	Net CEO Payoffs, 2000–8, L-TARP and No-TARP Firms	192
B.4	Variable Definitions and Data Sources for Chapter 8 Analysis	201

Preface

Despite the honorable intentions of the Dodd-Frank Act to make "too-big-to-fail" banks a thing of the past, investors and policymakers believe that many big banks are still too big to fail. This issue has come up repeatedly in the 2016 US presidential campaign and among senior policymakers in the United States and Europe. We propose a solution to the too-big-to-fail problem that can be implemented with minimal or no additional regulations, only the intervention of corporate board members and institutional investors in these big banks.

While some have argued that incentives generated by executive compensation programs led to excessive risk-taking by banks contributing to the 2008 financial crisis, there are more important causes of the financial and economic crisis that started in 2008. For example, public policies regarding home mortgages whose goal was to increase home ownership by those who could not otherwise afford it are perhaps the single most important cause of the financial and economic crisis of 2008.

Our focus in this book, however, is on whether incentives generated by bank executives' compensation programs contributed to excessive risk taking. We recommend the following compensation structure for bank executives: incentive compensation should consist only of restricted stock and restricted stock options – restricted in the sense that the executive cannot sell the shares or exercise the options for one to three years after his or her last day in office. We contend that this incentive compensation package will focus bank managers' attention on the long run and discourage them from investing in high-risk, value-destroying projects. We discuss and provide solutions to many of the caveats that arise, specifically regarding under-diversification and loss of liquidity. Also, we discuss and comment on two recent executive compensation reform proposals – one by six US federal agencies and another by the UK Prime Minister's office.

Similarly, we suggest that director incentive compensation be constructed along the same lines as the one for the executives proposed in the preceding paragraph. Specifically, all incentive compensation for directors should consist only of restricted equity (restricted stock and restricted stock option) – restricted in the sense that directors cannot sell the shares or exercise the options for one to three years after their last board meeting.

Our recommendation for executive and director compensation is based on our analysis of compensation structure in banks. However, our recommendation for executive and director compensation is fully applicable to other industries in the nonfinancial sector.

The aforementioned equity-based incentive programs lose their effectiveness in motivating managers (and directors) to enhance shareholder value as a bank's equity value approaches zero (as they did for the too-big-to-fail banks in 2008). Additionally, our evidence suggests that bank CEOs sell significantly greater amounts of their stock as the bank's equity capital (tangible common-stock-to-total-assets ratio) decreases. Hence, for equity-based incentive structures to be effective, banks should be financed with considerably more equity than they are being financed currently. Greater equity financing of banks coupled with the aforementioned compensation structure for bank managers and directors will drastically diminish the likelihood of a bank falling into financial distress; this will effectively address the too-big-to-fail problem and the Volcker Rule implementation that are two of the more significant challenges facing implementation of the Dodd-Frank Act. Our recommendation for significantly greater equity in a bank's capital structure is consistent with the spirit of the Financial CHOICE Act recently proposed by the US House Financial Services Committee.

Acknowledgments

We thank conference participants at Yale University, Northwestern University, Vanderbilt University, New York University, the US Securities and Exchange Commission, the US Department of Treasury, the US Federal Reserve Board, the Council of Institutional Investors, the National Association of Corporate Directors, and The Clearing House for constructive comments on presentation of parts of this book.

This book partly draws on our prior research, which stresses different aspects of the restricted-equity executive incentive compensation proposal, including

Bhagat, S., and B. Bolton. 2014. "Financial Crisis and Bank Executive Incentive Compensation." *Journal of Corporate Finance* 25, 313–41.

Bhagat, S., and H. Tookes. 2012. "Voluntary and Mandatory Skin in the Game: Understanding Outside Directors' Stock Holdings." *European Journal of Finance* 18, 191.

Bhagat, S., Bolton, B., and Romano, R. 2014. "Getting Incentives Right: Is Deferred Bank Executive Compensation Sufficient?" *Yale Journal of Regulation* 31, 523–64.

Bhagat, S., Bolton, B., and Lu, J. 2015. "Size, Leverage, and Risk-Taking of Financial Institutions." *Journal of Banking and Finance* 59, 520–37.

Passages from these articles are used with permission.

I   Introduction

The financial crisis that started in 2008 has inflicted a large cost on the US economy and an even larger cost on US workers and families. Hall (2014) estimates the shortfall of output at the end of 2013 as 13.3%, or $2.2 trillion. The labor force participation rate is currently at 62.8% – the lowest it has been for more than three decades. Hall (2014) estimates that the labor force participation rate in 2013 was 1.9% below the 1990–2007 trend. This 1.9% figure translates to 4.4 million *additional* US adults who are unemployed as of 2013.

We write this book because despite the honorable intentions of the Dodd-Frank Act to make "too-big-to-fail" (TBTF) banks a thing of the past, many investors and policymakers still believe that many big banks are TBTF.[1] This issue has come up repeatedly in the 2016 US presidential campaign and among senior policymakers in the United States and Europe. We propose a solution to the TBTF problem that can be implemented with minimal or no additional regulations, only the intervention of corporate board members and institutional investors in these big banks.

In the wake of the global financial crisis, attention has often focused on whether incentives generated by bank executives' compensation programs led to excessive risk-taking. Broadly speaking, postcrisis compensation reform proposals have taken one of three approaches: long-term deferred equity incentive compensation, mandatory bonus clawbacks on "inappropriate" risk-taking, accounting restatements or financial losses, and debt-based compensation. Governments worldwide have, in particular, regulated bank executives' compensation by requiring deferral of incentive compensation, mandating clawbacks, and in some instances even restricting compensation amounts.[2] In earlier work we recommended the

1

following compensation structure for bank executives, with which these government initiatives are only partially consistent: incentive compensation should consist only of restricted stock and restricted stock options – restricted in the sense that executives cannot sell the shares or exercise the options for one to three years after their last day in office; we refer to this as the *restricted equity proposal*.[3] We contend that such an incentive compensation package will focus bank management's attention on the long run and discourage investment in high-risk, value-destroying projects.

Equity-based incentive programs such as our proposal may lose effectiveness in motivating managers to reduce excessive risk-taking as a bank's equity value approaches zero. There is a moral hazard or agency cost of debt in this context arising from shareholders' potential preference to take extreme risks when close to insolvency. This is because shareholders gain from the upside of a positive outcome, albeit low in probability, while limited liability leaves the losses, should the gamble fail, on creditors. The moral hazard problem when equity value approaches zero may well be more severe for banks, as their creditors have less interest in monitoring against risk-taking activity because the government not only stands behind retail depositors but also often bails out other creditors as well.[4] Properly aligning management's incentives in this context therefore calls for focus on the interaction among bank capital structure, bank capital requirements, and bank executive incentive compensation – whereas the extant literature analyzes compensation reform in isolation.[5]

Incentive compensation reform proposals that advocate linking bank executives' compensation to debt are directed at this moral hazard concern, although the tendency for broad-based creditor bailouts complicates the efficacy of such an approach compared with using debt-based compensation to address the phenomenon in nonfinancial firms. We contend that equity-based incentive pay is still decisively preferable to debt-based pay in motivating managers to maximize bank value. In our judgment, the appropriate approach to mitigate the insolvency-related moral hazard problem is to combine a properly structured equity incentive scheme with a capital structure that contains considerably more equity than currently required.

Our focus is incentive compensation not because we believe that it was the most important contributing factor to the crisis. We doubt that to be the case. We believe that public policies regarding home mortgages, whose goal was to increase home ownership by those who could not otherwise afford it, was the primary cause of the financial crisis; we discuss this in detail in Chapter 2. Our focus is on bank executive incentive compensation because it is an area in which legislators and banking regulators worldwide have implemented regulatory reforms, though the appropriateness of pay structures is still a matter of contentious debate. It is also the factor most within the control of bank corporate boards and shareholders, so the private sector could undertake further beneficial changes without the need for coordinated government action.

Although we believe that the restricted equity proposal is superior to the approach regulators have taken to compensation, our proposal is directed to boards of directors because we recognize that it is unrealistic to expect regulators to substitute it for their recently adopted initiatives, especially at an international level, given the arduous process of obtaining multinational consensus. The complementary proposal for increased equity capital could also be implemented by financial institutions without regulatory action. But because deposit insurance and creditor bailouts have resulted in the market not requiring banks to hold substantially higher equity capital than current levels, short of the market believing that postcrisis resolution initiatives will be effective at limiting future bailouts, we think it improbable that our proposal would be voluntarily adopted given the sustained and strong opposition by bank managers with regard to increasing equity capital. Although the restricted equity proposal's effectiveness would be further optimized if it were combined with an increase in equity capital requirements, it does not require such a regulatory change. It would, we assert, reduce the probability that a bank will be near insolvency, the zone in which the need for increased capital requirements is most critical.

Greater equity financing of banks coupled with the aforementioned compensation structure for bank managers and directors will drastically diminish the likelihood of a bank falling into financial distress. This will effectively address two of the more significant challenges facing implementation of the Dodd-Frank Act:

1. *The too-big-to-fail problem.* Regulators and their critics have observed that implementation of the Dodd-Frank Act may have institutionalized the TBTF aspect of the largest US banks.[6] Policymakers note that TBTF banks are here to stay and are proposing explicit or implicit taxes on banks above a certain threshold size. The major problem with the TBTF banks is exactly that – they are "too big to fail"; that is, these large banks have to be bailed out with taxpayer funds (when faced with insolvency) to prevent "alleged" significant disruption to the national economy. We placed alleged in quotation marks here because whether or not insolvency of one or more large banks might cause significant disruption is an open question. We are not aware of any empirical evidence that documents significant disruption to the national economy resulting from the recent insolvency of few large banks. Under our proposal (of greater equity financing of banks coupled with a compensation structure for bank managers and directors that discourages managers from undertaking high-risk investments that are value destroying and instead focuses their attention on creating and sustaining long-term shareholder value), managers (and directors) would not want to grow the bank to a size (or manage a bank of a size) that jeopardizes the solvency/financial viability of the bank, for that would also jeopardize the value of their restricted stock and restricted stock options that they own and cannot sell until some years after they leave the bank. Furthermore, greater equity capitalization of the banks would provide a cushion against investments that ex ante were value enhancing but ex post were value-reducing.

2. The Volcker Rule essentially prohibits/discourages proprietary trading by TBTF banks. The problem in implementing the Volcker Rule is in defining and identifying trades that are proprietary (where profits/losses accrue to the bank) versus the market-making trades a bank makes in its normal course of business to serve a particular client. Under our proposal (of greater

equity financing of banks coupled with the aforementioned compensation structure for bank managers and directors), managers (and directors) would not want to engage in proprietary trades that jeopardizes the solvency/ financial viability of the bank, for that would also jeopardize the value of their restricted stock and restricted stock options that they own and cannot sell until some years after they leave the bank. Furthermore, greater equity capitalization of the bank would provide a cushion against proprietary trades that do not turn out well for the bank. Regarding the market-making trades – to the extent that the market-making trades were value-enhancing for the bank, the bank managers would have the incentive to continue to engage in such market-making trades.

Professor Anat Admati of Stanford University is waging a heroic campaign to get the banks to significantly increase their equity capital; see her coauthored book (Admati and Hellwig 2013) and her website (www.gsb.stanford.edu/news/research/Admati.etal .html). We view this book as complementary to the efforts of Professor Admati and her colleagues.

Also, we study the effect of size on the risk-taking of US-based financial institutions. Using data on the size and risk-taking of financial institutions from 2002 to 2012, we investigate whether cross-sectional variation in the size of banks is related to risk-taking. Our measures of risk-taking are comprehensive. They include two model-based measures (namely, the Z-score, and Merton's distance to default [Merton DD]), a market-based measure (volatility of stock returns) and an accounting-based measure (write-downs). We document four important facts. First, bank size is positively correlated with risk-taking, even when controlling for endogeneity between size and risk-taking. Our second finding: the decomposition of Z-score reveals that bank size has a consistent and significant negative impact on the bank common-stock-to-total-assets ratio; we do not find a consistent relation between bank size and return on assets or earnings volatility. *These findings suggest that banks engage in excessive risk-taking mainly through increased leverage.* They also suggest that economies of scale do not exist for banks. Regressions with volatility of stock return as the dependent variable indicate that size-related diversification benefits may not exist in the financial sector because size is positively associated with return volatility. Third, we find that our recently developed corporate governance measure (Bhagat and Bolton 2008), calculated as median director dollar stockholding, is negatively associated with risk-taking. This has important policy implications, to wit, policymakers interested in discouraging banks from engaging in excessive risk should focus on bank director compensation and stock ownership. Finally, we document that the positive relation between bank size and risk was present in the precrisis period (2002–6) and the crisis period (2007–9) but not in the postcrisis period (2010–12). Perhaps the intense scrutiny put on bank risk-taking by the bank regulators, senior policymakers, and the media in the postcrisis period may have curbed the appetite and ability of large banks to engage in high-risk investments.

This book is organized as follows. Chapter 2 highlights how public policies regarding home mortgages "caused" the financial crisis. Chapter 3 briefly overviews precrisis compensation packages and how they might have led to misaligned incentives. The next two chapters present the evidence of such misalignment of executive compensation incentives. We find that TBTF bank CEOs were able to realize a substantial amount on their common stock sales in the precrisis period (2000–7) compared to the large losses the executives experienced on their equity stake during the crisis (2008). Additionally, stock sales by TBTF bank CEOs were significantly greater than stock sales by other bank CEOs (defined in Chapter 5) in the precrisis period. Finally, several different bank risk-taking measures suggest that TBTF banks were significantly riskier than other banks. Our results are mostly consistent with the argument that incentives generated by executive compensation programs in the TBTF banks are positively correlated with excessive risk-taking by these banks in high-risk but value-decreasing investment and trading strategies. Also, our results are inconsistent with the argument that the poor performance of the TBTF banks during the crisis was the result of unforeseen risk.

Chapter 6 states and discusses our restricted equity proposal, which we maintain will mitigate bank managers' excess risk-taking incentives (but maintain their incentives to invest in value-increasing strategies), and explains why it is preferable to both compensation reforms that governments have implemented and debt-based compensation proposals. An aspect of our restricted equity proposal needs emphasis: this proposal, unlike most other executive compensation reform proposals, does *not* place a ceiling on executive compensation. The proposal only limits the annual *cash* payouts an executive can realize. The *present value* of all salary and stock compensation can be higher than bank managers have received historically because the amount of restricted stock and restricted stock options that can be awarded to a bank manager is essentially unlimited per our proposal, though, in practice, the award amounts should and need to be anchored to the current practices in the particular company. Of course, the higher value would only be realized were the banks to invest in projects that lead to value creation that persists in the long term, in which case we have a win for long-term investors and a win for managers. Also, a focus on creating and sustaining long-term shareholder value would minimize the likelihood of a bailout, which would be a win for taxpayers.

Chapter 6 concludes with a discussion of some recent public policy developments regarding executive compensation. On April 21, 2016, six US agencies (Federal Reserve System, Federal Deposit Insurance Corporation, Federal Housing Finance Agency, Office of the Comptroller of the Currency, National Credit Union Administration, and the Securities and Exchange Commission) jointly proposed new regulations, *incentive-based compensation arrangements*, to prohibit incentive-based compensation that would encourage "excessive" risk-taking by banks. We support the essence of the April 2016 incentive-based compensation arrangements regulations proposed by the six US agencies. The deferral, forfeiture, and

clawback provisions in the proposed regulations are focused on discouraging "inappropriate" risk-taking by banks. A critical question:
What is *inappropriate* risk-taking by banks? From a financial viewpoint, the risk of a project or trading strategy would be inappropriate if
the net present value (NPV) of the project or trading strategy is negative. However, the measurement of such risk (and associated cash
flows) is subject to both manager biases and estimation errors; we
discuss this in Chapter 3. Our evidence in Chapter 5 suggests that
enforcing deferral, forfeiture, and clawback provisions can lead to very
large potential losses for managers. Given the potential losses of tens
or hundreds of millions of dollars, affected managers are likely to
litigate the occurrence of a particular trigger event or the measurement of the "inappropriate" risk. Given the inherent uncertain outcome of any litigation, the disciplining effect of the April 2016
regulations on bank manager inappropriate risk-taking behavior
would be muted. The restricted equity proposal has an inherent clawback (and deferral and forfeiture) feature that renders unnecessary
intricate mechanisms requiring repayments (forfeiture) of bonuses
on income from transactions whose value proved illusory.
The automatic clawback inherent in the restricted equity proposal is
simpler to administer than the specified regulatory clawbacks, avoiding definitional and, consequently, litigation pitfalls.

We note a second concern with the April 2016 regulations,
which cover bonuses but do not cover compensation derived from
the sale of stock. Our evidence in Chapter 5 suggests that TBTF
bank managers' compensation derived from sale of their banks'
stock is usually twice as large as, or greater than, their compensation
from salary and bonus. Hence, even if the April 2016 regulations are
successful in discouraging some inappropriate risk-taking by banks,
the adverse incentives from compensation derived from the sale of
stock remains a potent problem. Our restricted equity proposal would
address this problem as well.

On June 23, 2016, the United Kingdom voted to leave the
European Union – the Brexit vote. Subsequent to the vote, the

United Kingdom elected a new prime minister. Prime Minister May has noted that reforming executive incentive compensation would be one of her government's priorities. On July 21, 2016, Prime Minister May proposed making annual shareholder votes on executive compensation binding. Despite the obvious attractiveness of "say on pay" (on the surface, allowing shareholders a voice on management compensation appears to be a sensible proposition), there is no consistent evidence supportive of "say on pay" in either the United States or the United Kingdom. Instead of focusing on "say on pay" regulations, we believe that public policymakers (as well as corporate board members and institutional investors) should focus their efforts on an "optimal" executive compensation policy. The restricted equity proposal (that incentive compensation of executives should consist only of restricted equity – restricted in the sense that the individual cannot sell the shares or exercise the options for one to three years after his or her last day in office) is our suggestion for the most important component of an optimal "pay" policy in "say on pay" regulations.

Chapter 7 outlines our proposal for director compensation; this would be complementary to the restricted equity proposal for managers. Chapter 8 focuses on the relation between bank size, bank risk-taking, and bank leverage.

Chapter 9 presents our approach to bank equity capitalization reform, which is complementary to the restricted equity incentive compensation proposal. We advocate that banks hold significantly higher equity capital (tangible common-stock-to-total-assets ratio) than presently required; specifically, bank equity capital should be, at least, 20% of bank total assets; we recommend against any risk-weighting of bank total assets. In our judgment, combining the restricted equity proposal with bank equity capitalization reform is a better mechanism for reducing the probability of banks taking on excessive risk and contributing to another financial crisis. We note that the restricted equity proposal and the bank equity capitalization proposal rely only on the private incentives and actions of bank managers, bank directors, and bank institutional investors. More specifically, our proposals do *not* rely on additional regulations.

We conclude Chapter 9 with a discussion of some recent public policy developments regarding bank capital. On June 2, 2016, two Federal Reserve Board governors signaled that big banks will be required to hold more equity. We applaud the efforts of these Federal Reserve Board governors. We hope that the Federal Reserve requires bank capital to be calibrated to the ratio of tangible common equity to total assets not the risk-weighted capital (i.e., to total assets independent of risk) and requires the denominator to include balance-sheet assets and off-balance-sheet assets (of structured investment vehicles).

On June 23, 2016, the US House Financial Services Committee released a discussion draft of the Financial CHOICE (Creating Hope and Opportunity for Investors, Consumers, and Entrepreneurs) Act. The Financial CHOICE Act allows banks that have a leverage ratio of at least 10% to elect exemption from Basel III capital and liquidity standards and the Dodd-Frank Act Section 165 heightened prudential standards. The denominator of this leverage ratio would include total balance-sheet and off-balance-sheet assets; importantly, these total assets would be independent of risk. We applaud this proposal of the Financial CHOICE Act.

The *Wall Street Journal* in its on July 29, 2016, op-ed noted that both the Republican and Democratic Party platforms called for reinstating the Glass-Steagall Act of 1933, which separated commercial banking and investment banking businesses. In a similar vein, the Volcker Rule of the Dodd-Frank Act attempts to prevent/discourage commercial banks from risky securities trading. As noted earlier, the problem in implementing the Volcker Rule is in defining and identifying trades that are proprietary (where profits/losses accrue to the bank) versus market-making trades that a bank makes in its normal course of business to serve a particular client. The *Wall Street Journal* suggests, "The better solution is to shrink the taxpayer safety net, raising capital standards high enough so that banks that take insured deposits can better withstand trading or lending mistakes." We support the *Wall Street Journal* proposal; this proposal is consistent with our bank capital proposal (restricted-equity-more-equity-capital proposal).

Chapter 10 highlights fallacies in the popular arguments for financing banks with mostly debt. Chapter 11 presents our conclusions.

2 Mortgage Public Policies and the Financial Crisis

Government policies promoting subprime risk-taking by government-sponsored enterprises (GSEs, e.g., Fannie Mae and Freddie Mac) dominating the residential mortgage market so as to increase home ownership by those who could not otherwise afford it are the most likely "cause" of the financial crisis of 2008.[1] We place *cause* in quotation marks because causation has always been and is likely to continue to be notoriously hard to prove in a strict statistical sense. We highlight the careful and detailed evidence presented in Peter Wallison's recent book, *Hidden in Plain Sight: What Really Caused the World's Worst Financial Crisis and Why It Could Happen Again.* Wallison's (2015) evidence is consistent with the hypothesis that mortgage public policies intended to increase home ownership by those who could not otherwise afford it is the most likely "cause" of the financial crisis of 2008.

Figure 2.1 highlights the dramatic increase in inflation-adjusted real estate prices (measured by the Case-Shiller Home Price Index) during 1995–2005. Prior to this period, for more than a century, namely, from 1890 to 1995, inflation-adjusted real estate prices, while exhibiting volatility from year to year, were basically unchanged.

Figures 2.2 and 2.3 highlight the growing and important role of GSEs in the US residential mortgage debt market during 1992–2008. Why did the GSE's role in the US residential mortgage debt market increase so significantly during 1992–2008?

The US Congress passed the Federal Housing Enterprises Financial Safety and Soundness Act in 1992 (the GSE Act) with the worthy goal of helping low-income families buy homes. The GSE Act initially established a goal for Fannie Mae and Freddie Mac – that at

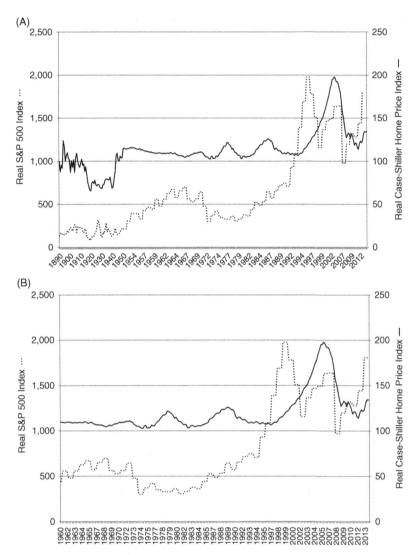

FIGURE 2.1 (A) Real Standard & Poor's (S&P) 500 Index and real Case-Shiller Home Price Index, 1890–2013. This panel highlights the dramatic increase in inflation-adjusted real estate prices (measured by the real Case-Shiller Home Price Index) during 1995–2005. Prior to this period, for more than a century, namely, from 1890 to 1995, inflation-adjusted real estate prices, while exhibiting volatility from year to year, were basically unchanged. (*Source:* Robert Shiller, www.econ.yale.edu/~shiller/data .htm.) (B) Real S&P 500 Index and real Case-Shiller Home Price Index, 1960–2013. (*Source:* Robert Shiller, www.econ.yale.edu/~shiller/data .htm.)

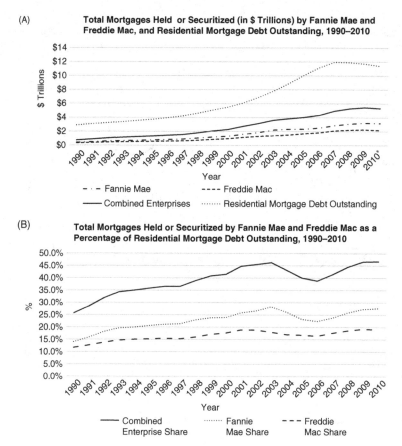

FIGURE 2.2 (A) The growing and important role of Fannie Mae and
Freddie Mac in the US residential mortgage debt market during
1992–2008. (*Sources:* Enterprise Financial Statements, 1994–2010;
Mortgage Debt Outstanding: Federal Reserve Board's Flow of Funds
Accounts of the United States, Annual Flows and Outstandings,
March 11, 2010.) (B) The growing and important role of Fannie Mae and
Freddie Mac in the US residential mortgage debt market during
1992–2008. (*Sources:* Enterprise Financial Statements, 1994–2010;
Mortgage Debt Outstanding: Federal Reserve Board's Flow of Funds
Accounts of the United States, Annual Flows and Outstandings,
March 11, 2010.)

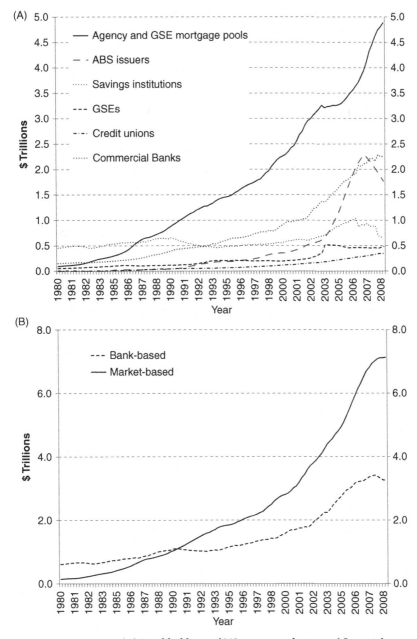

FIGURE 2.3 (A) Total holdings of US mortgages by type of financial institution. (*Source:* Adrian and Shinn 2009.) (B) Market- and bank-based holding of home mortgages. Market-based holdings refer to the holdings of GSE mortgage pools, private-label mortgage pools, and GSE holdings. Bank-based holdings refer to holdings of commercial banks, savings institutions, and credit unions. Market-based suppliers of credit have become increasingly important during 1995–2008. (*Source:* Adrian and Shinn 2009.)

least 30% of all mortgages they bought needed to be from borrowers/ homeowners who were at or below the median income level of the area in which they lived. The thinking was that the liquidity provided to banks and other mortgage originators would enable and encourage them to extend mortgage loans to low- and moderate-income home-buyers (whose incomes were below the median income for the area).

Prior to 1992, most mortgages were prime mortgages, that is, mortgages offered to homebuyers who had good credit histories, were able to put 10% to 20% as down payment on the house, and whose loan-payment-to-income ratios were below 33% (after the mortgage was closed). Families/individuals unable to meet these underwriting criteria were usually unable to buy a home. The aforementioned underwriting criteria had been developed by mortgage originators over several decades and reflected the payment and default experiences they had with their borrowers. In other words, these underwriting standards would lead to a sustainable mortgage market and had done so up to that time. Government policies that required Fannie Mae and Freddie Mac to ensure that a certain percent of all mortgages they bought were from borrowers/homeowners who were at or below the median income level of the area would eventually put pressure on mortgage originators to lower these underwriting standards. If these mortgage originators could readily sell these subprime mortgages (which did not meet the aforementioned underwriting standards) to Fannie or Freddie, then the mortgage originators would not be concerned with lowering the underwriting standards. Of course, Freddie and Fannie owned the credit risk of those mortgages to the extent that they decided to retain those mortgages in their portfolios. Finally, if the US Treasury had to bail out Freddie and Fannie from insolvency (due to losses from these subprime mortgages), then the credit risk of these subprime mortgages would ultimately be borne by US taxpayers.

Figure 2.4 illustrates the GSE housing goals for low- and moderate-income borrowers during 1996–2008 and the performance of Fannie Mae and Freddie Mac with respect to these goals. The GSE housing goal for low- and moderate-income borrowers was 40% in

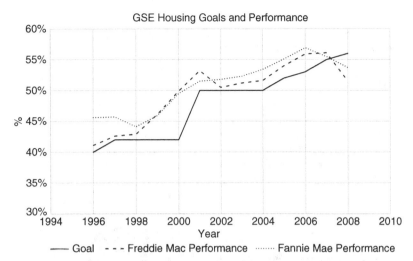

FIGURE 2.4 Enterprise housing goals and performance. GSE housing goals for low- and moderate-income borrowers during 1996–2008 and the performance of Fannie Mae and Freddie Mac with respect to those goals. The GSE housing goal for low- and moderate-income borrowers was 40% in 1996 and was rapidly increased to 56% by 2008. Fannie and Freddie were able to meet or exceed these goals for every year except for 2008. (*Source:* FHFA 2010.)

1996 and was rapidly increased to 56% by 2008. Fannie and Freddie were able to meet or exceed these goals for every year except for 2008. Figure 2.5 illustrates subprime mortgage originations during 1996–2008 and subprime's share of the entire mortgage market. The years 2000–6 witnessed a rapid increase in subprime mortgage originations. Coincidentally, the GSE housing goal for low- and moderate-income borrowers was 42% in 2000 and was rapidly increased to 53% by 2006. The increase in the GSE housing goals for low- and moderate-income borrowers and the increase in subprime mortgage originations during 2000–6 are consistent with the following argument: *government housing policies reflected in GSE housing goals for low- and moderate-income borrowers likely fueled the subprime mortgage originations during 2000–6.*[2]

Subprime mortgage products were initially intended for low- and moderate-income borrowers who did not have good credit histories

Subprime Mortgage Originations

In 2006, $600 billion of subprime loans were originated, most of which were securitized. That year, subprime lending accounted for 23.5% of all mortgage originations.

IN BILLIONS OF DOLLARS

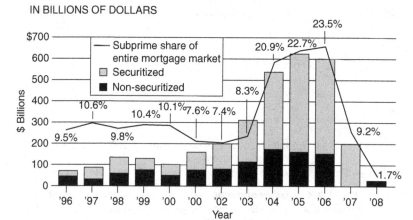

NOTE: Percent securitized is defined as subprime securities issued divided by originations in a given year. In 2007, securities issued exceeded originations.

FIGURE 2.5 Subprime mortgage originations. The years 2000–6 witnessed a rapid increase in subprime mortgage originations and the securitization of these mortgages. (*Source:* FCIC 2011.)

and/or were unable to put 10% to 20% as down payment on a house and/or whose loan-payment-to-income ratios were above 33%. However, over time, prospective homebuyers who were *not* in the low- and moderate-income categories and who could qualify for a prime mortgage for a (less expensive) home started using subprime mortgage products to purchase more expensive homes or put less money down. Consider a prospective homebuyer who had $30,000 as a down payment. He or she could purchase a home valued at up to $300, 000 and still qualify for a prime mortgage because his or her down payment would be more than 10%. However, if the homebuyer chose to put down only 5% as a down payment, then he or she could purchase a home valued at $600,000. Of course, the mortgage for the $600,000 house would be subprime. According to the US Department of Housing and Urban Development (HUD), 37% of mortgage loans bought by Fannie Mae in 2007 and 32% of mortgage loans bought by Freddie Mac in 2007 were made to borrowers *above* the median income level who put down less than 5% as a down payment (see HUD 2008). Also, in 2007, the National Association of Realtors reported that 45% of first-time homebuyers put no money down; furthermore, of those who did put down a payment, the median amount was 2% of the purchase price (*USA Today*, July 17, 2007). Additionally, Barth et al. (2008) document that "during the period January 1999 through July 2007, prime borrowers obtained thirty-one of the thirty-two types of mortgage products ... obtained by subprime borrowers." This evidence suggests that GSE housing goals for low- and moderate-income borrowers led to lowering of mortgage underwriting standards not just for low- and moderate-income borrowers but also for *all* borrowers.

ROLE OF BIG BANKS IN THE FINANCIAL CRISIS

The big banks played two important roles related to the financial crisis. First was their large and growing role in the issuance of mortgage-backed securities (MBSs), especially during 2004–6 (see Figure 2.6). MBSs issued mostly by big banks were known as *private-label securities* (PLSs). As Figure 2.6 indicates, PLSs were more than 50% of the issuance of MBSs for each of the years 2004, 2005, and 2006. More important, PLSs for each of the years 2005 and 2006 were valued at more than $1 trillion. The ability of the big banks to issue such a large volume of securities enabled them to earn significant fees. However, more important than these fees was the phenomenon of these big banks investing massively for their own portfolio in the top-rated (AAA) tranches of the MBSs they were issuing. A question arises: Why were these big banks investing in the (top-rated AAA tranches of the) MBSs they were issuing?

Historically, banks have been intermediaries between depositors and borrowers. However, the process of securitization changed the role of banks to intermediaries between investors. Banks would pool mortgages into MBSs. MBS owners would receive the principal

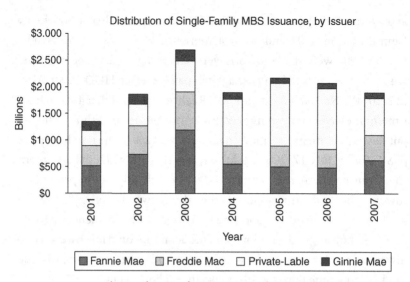

FIGURE 2.6 Distribution of MBS issuances by issuer. PLSs (MBSs issued by mostly big banks) were more than 50% of the MBS issuance for each of the years 2004, 2005, and 2006. PLSs are denoted by the unshaded part in each vertical bar in the figure. (*Source:* OFHEO 2008.)

and interest from the underlying mortgages. MBSs were structured into tranches based on risk. The most risky tranche offered the highest return but would be the first to have its promised payments defaulted if the principal and interest payments from the underlying mortgages were insufficient. The least risky tranche offered the lowest return but, correspondingly, would be the last to have its promised payments defaulted if the principal and interest payments from the underlying mortgages were insufficient. These tranches would be rated, and the least risky tranche would almost always receive the AAA rating. These tranches would be sold to institutional investors in the United States and abroad. Figure 2.7 illustrates the growing importance of securitizations during 2004–6 and the increasingly dominant role of subprime mortgages in these securitizations.

During 2004–7, most of the large banks started investing (holding as assets in their balance sheets) heavily in the AAA-rated tranches of the MBSs they (or other big banks) had securitized. These banks

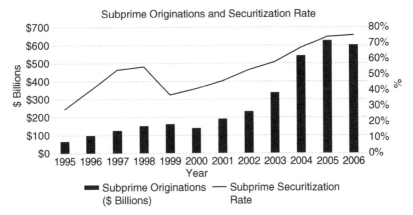

FIGURE 2.7 Subprime originations and securitization rate. The subprime originations and securitization rate of the subprime mortgages was growing in importance during 2004–6. (*Source:* Raboy 2009.)

would borrow short term, often overnight, at close to the London Interbank Offered Rate (LIBOR) and use the funds to invest in the AAA-rated tranches. The banks would invest mostly in the AAA-rated tranches because regulatory guidelines/requirements required them to not hold additional (equity or retained earnings) capital if the additional investment was in safe AAA securities. The yield on the AAA-rated tranches was more than the LIBOR: *the banks would book the difference as profit.* Just because the banks booked it as "profit" did not make it so! These "profits" were not profits in the traditional net-present-value sense but were merely an accounting artifact of the difference between the AAA tranche yield and the LIBOR. As is taught in any Finance 101 class in this country and across the globe, if security A offers a higher expected return than security B, then A is riskier than B. Borrowing at the LIBOR and investing in AAA-rated tranches did not mean that the risk of the AAA-rated tranches had been eliminated (or reduced to the level implied by the LIBOR). Somebody had to bear the risk of these AAA-rated tranches – they were the bank's bondholders and stockholders and, ultimately, US taxpayers. Indeed, this risk was not notional.

Table 2.1 *Loan Characteristics at Origination*

	Prime loans				Subprime loans			
	2004	2005	2006	2007	2004	2005	2006	2007
Percent default in first 12 months	2%	2%	4%	5%	11%	16%	24%	25%
Percent default in first 18 months	4%	8%	8%	7%	16%	24%	35%	34%
At 12 months since origin								
Loan sold to GSE	74%	71%	72%	83%	4%	6%	9%	40%
Loan sold to private securitizer	19%	24%	23%	11%	91%	92%	89%	55%
Loan held on portfolio	7%	6%	5%	6%	5%	2%	3%	5%

Source: Federal Reserve Bank of Chicago 2010.

As the US real estate market stalled and then real estate prices started heading downward during 2005–8, homeowners (who had little or no equity in their homes) began defaulting on their mortgages. Table 2.1 documents that subprime loans were defaulting at extremely high rates: 35% and 34% default rates 18 months after origination during 2006 and 2007, respectively; more important, a very high percentage of subprime mortgages originated during 2004–7 were sold to the big banks (private securitizers) for securitization purposes. Ultimately, these defaults by homeowners led to defaults of the AAA-rated tranches, leading to substantial losses by the big banks that had invested in these tranches. In many cases these losses were large enough to potentially lead to bank insolvency. Banks and their allies publicly argued that their insolvency would severely and adversely affect the US financial system and the economy. Whether or not insolvency of some of these big banks would have been catastrophic for the country is debatable; regardless, the banks and their allies were able to convince the key policymakers in the United States – hence the "need" for US taxpayer bailout of these banks. Tsesmelidakis and Merton (2012) estimate the value of the implicit guarantees that led to massive wealth transfer (via the taxpayer-funded bailout) from US taxpayers to bank shareholders and debtholders as $365 billion during October 2008–June 2009. Acharya, Anginer, and Warburton (2015) estimate that these implicit guarantees afforded the big banks a funding advantage of 30 basis points during 1990–2012. More recently, Gandhi, Lustig, and Plazzi (2016) provided evidence of the implicit guarantees provided by US taxpayers to the big banks. This documented large wealth transfer from US taxpayers to the big-bank investors makes this an important issue in the ongoing national debate on the economy.

Regarding the "profits" (difference between the AAA tranche yield and the LIBOR), the banks were booking – this was the source of substantial compensation to bank employees (and their managers) involved in the securitization process and related transactions. Some of this compensation involved cash bonuses. Perhaps more important – to the extent that bank analysts were unable to discern the source of the bank's higher earnings (via the "profits") – bank stocks were overvalued.[3] Bank managers could sell these overvalued shares and/or exercise their options to take money off the table before the analysts and other market participants realized the source of these "profits." As we will see in the following chapters, most managers of the big banks did just that.

3   Precrisis Executive Compensation and Misaligned Incentives

Precrisis executive incentive compensation packages often did consist of an equity portion that was deferred, typically with a two- to five-year vesting requirement, most often granted for meeting annual performance targets.[1] But many lower-level employees, whose activities could nonetheless cause disastrous losses and who were highly paid, did not receive such incentive compensation. For example, individuals trading for the bank's proprietary account often received straight cash bonuses at year end, pegged to the booked profits of their trades (even though the trades were open and initial profits could, as it turned out in the crisis, generate crushing losses).[2] Further, banks' risk officers were often paid low or flat salaries compared to other executives, and their authority and ability to control risk-taking varied considerably across institutions.[3] These organizational incentives no doubt worked at cross-purposes with senior executives' ability to manage their firms' risk and performance as the global crisis unfolded.

How might the incentives generated by incentive compensation programs in banks lead to excessive risk-taking and benefit executives and traders at the expense of long-term shareholders? Consider the stylized example in Bhagat, Bolton, and Romano (2014): an investment project or trading strategy that in any given year can lead to six cash flow outcomes with equal probability. One could think of the six outcomes of this investment project as the outcome from rolling a fair die. Five of these are a positive $500 million, and the sixth is a random loss that increases over time (until a certain future period), denoted by the following time-varying random variable:

Sixth outcome $= -\$(0.5 + \varepsilon) \times (t)$ billion, for t between years t_1
and t_2, and

Sixth outcome $= -\$(0.5 + \varepsilon) \times (t_2)$ billion, for $t > t_2$ years $\qquad$ (3.1)

where ε is an error term with mean zero and standard deviation σ.

Given these payoffs, the expected cash flow from the investment project or trading strategy is positive for the first few years. However, after these initial years, the expected cash flow from the investment project or trading strategy turns negative. Additionally, the life of the project is such that its net present value (NPV) is negative.[4] The probability, the magnitude of the cash flows of the six outcomes, and the life of the project are known only to the bank executives. Given the information available to or processed by the investing public, were the project or strategy announced in advance, they would not perceive that the sixth outcome's loss is increasing over time, and therefore the stock market would have a different – positive – valuation of the trading strategy from bank management, as indicated in Example 3.1.

How should the individual decision-maker – a bank executive or trader – respond to this investment project or trading strategy if he or she were acting in the interest of long-term shareholders? As indicated in Example 3.1, because the NPV of the investment project/trading strategy is negative, this investment project or trading strategy should be rejected.[5]

But will the individual undertake the investment project or trading strategy? To answer this question, we have to consider the compensation structure. For convenience, we will refer to the decision-maker in the example as the bank CEO. Assume that the CEO owns a significant number of bank shares. Furthermore, these shares are unrestricted – that is, they have either vested or have no vesting requirements. If the bank adopts this trading strategy, and given the belief of the stock market about this investment project or trading strategy, the bank's share price will increase.

Example 3.1 *Expected Cash Flows (Executives Know True Probabilities)*

	Expected cash flows	
	Belief of bank executives	Belief of investing public
Outcome 1	+$500 million	+$500 million
Outcome 2	+$500 million	+$500 million
Outcome 3	+$500 million	+$500 million
Outcome 4	+$500 million	+$500 million
Outcome 5	+$500 million	+$500 million
Outcome 6	$-\$(0.5 + \varepsilon) \times t$ billion, for t between years t_1 and t_2; $-\$(0.5 + \varepsilon) \times (t_2)$ billion, for $t > t_2$ years	$-\$500$ million
NPV	Negative	Positive
Investment decision	Do not invest	Invest

In any given year, there is a very high probability (5/6 = 83%) that the trading strategy will generate a very large positive cash flow of $500 million. If the realization from the trading strategy is one of the positive cash flow outcomes (and there is an 83% probability of this), the bank share price will rise; the bank, in response, will award incentive compensation to key employees, including the CEO, and the CEO can then liquidate a significant part of his or her equity holdings at a profit.[6]

To be sure, in this stylized example, the bank CEO knows that the expected cash flow from this trading strategy will be negative in the later years. There is also some probability (17% in this example) that in any given year the trading strategy will lead to a negative cash flow outcome. Additionally, the magnitude of the negative outcome increases over time. What then? In the textbook corporate finance paradigm, the bank's share price will decline, and depending on the bank's equity capitalization, the bank will be insolvent or close to insolvent and subject to corrective action or government takeover.[7] This insolvency or close-to-insolvency scenario will certainly have a significantly negative impact on the value of the CEO's bank stock-holdings. However, if during the first few years of this trading strategy the cash flow outcomes have been positive and the CEO has liquidated a significant number of shares, then despite the CEO experiencing large losses on his or her remaining holdings as the bank faces large losses or possibly insolvency in a future year, the CEO's net payoff from employment in the bank (salary, bonus, and proceeds from the sale of stock) in the earlier years may well still be positive and even possibly substantial. In addition, during the global financial crisis, governments did not permit the largest banks to fail, so a rational CEO may have a further impetus to take on the risk: if it is a too-big-to-fail (TBTF) bank, even his or her equity may be preserved when the bank is bailed out.

It is not necessary to assume, as does our stylized example, that bank CEOs intentionally undertook or encouraged employees to undertake negative NPV projects or trading strategies to suggest that precrisis compensation packages could have produced misaligned incentives. An alternative scenario that could produce a similarly distorted investment outcome would occur if a CEO misperceives the probabilities of a project's negative cash flows such that a value-destroying project appears to be value creating. If, for instance, executives have a rosier picture of a project's outcome than warranted because, say, they are overconfident in their abilities to manage it or they are overly optimistic about the future, then we do not have to posit managers who intentionally seek to rip off shareholders. We would only be acknowledging human nature "as we know it" – that individuals quite often believe that they are more talented than most and therefore are overly confident and more optimistic regarding the success of their endeavors than the objective situation would warrant (in this instance, the executive is overconfident with regard to project selection or trading ability and hence overly optimistic about projected cash flows).[8] Precrisis compensation packages could again produce misaligned incentives because they could exacerbate the impact of optimism by not inducing executives to focus diligently on estimating more accurately all of a project's cash flows or the risks associated with those cash flows. A similar misalignment could occur without behavioral assumptions of overconfidence and optimism if the CEO miscalculates a project's expected outcome due to inadequate internal organization information flows or simply sloppiness (e.g., lack of effort).

Consider the following emendation of our earlier stylized example in which the probabilities of the six possible outcomes are not equal. In addition, the bank executives do not know the true cash flows and probabilities. Because the executives' expected probabilities will differ from the actual probabilities, some investment decisions will be made that should not have been made.[9] As indicated in Example 3.2, this occurs in the example because the executives perceive the project to have a positive NPV when it actually has a negative NPV. This is so because the managers' calculation perceives the possible loss as more remote than is actually the case, as well as occurring much farther in the future (when they would expect, no doubt, either that the project would no longer be pursued or that they would no longer be with the firm).[10]

Of course, these cash flows and probabilities are hypothetical; the key is that there can be nontrivial differences between expected and actual future outcomes. These differences can drive the investment decisions of the bank, which can be problematic if the incentives of bank executives and shareholders are not properly aligned. If, as in Example 3.1, the executives' stock and stock options (awarded via their incentive compensation contract) can be liquidated in the near term, they might be able to benefit more on their stock sales than they lose on their equity holdings when the project's negative value is realized after the initial successes. The point of this second stylized example is that even if executives do not seek intentionally to mislead shareholders, but for a variety of reasons, including overconfidence,

Example 3.2 *Expected Cash Flows (Executives Do Not Know True Probabilities)*

		Expected probability	Actual probability
Outcome 1	+$500 million	18%	15%
Outcome 2	+$500 million	18%	15%
Outcome 3	+$500 million	18%	15%
Outcome 4	+$500 million	18%	15%
Outcome 5	+$500 million	18%	15%
Outcome 6	$-\$(0.5 + \varepsilon) \times t$ billion, for t between years t_1 and t_2; $-\$(0.5 + \varepsilon) \times (t_2)$ billion, for $t > t_2$ years	10%	25%
	Project NPV	Positive	Negative
	Investment decision	Invest	Do not invest

optimism, poor internal organization, or sloppy thinking, they misjudge the outcome, they could be rewarded for doing so because of their short-term incentive compensation. Because their compensation depends solely on the current (realized) year's cash flow, they will have little incentive to estimate more diligently the probabilities of the project's continuing cash flows. A longer-horizon incentive compensation structure should focus their attention on obtaining more accurate estimates of a project's expected future cash flows. Moreover, they could no longer benefit at the shareholders' expense from a project whose short- and long-term cash flows were so disparate because, not being able to sell their shares or receive cash bonuses in the early years of the project's life, they will bear the same ultimate net loss on their holdings as the outside long-term investors.

4 Managerial Incentives Hypothesis versus Unforeseen Risk Hypothesis

The *managerial incentives hypothesis* posits that *incentives generated by executive compensation programs led to excessive bank risk-taking.* As we argue in Bhagat and Bolton (2014), the excessive risk-taking would benefit bank executives at the expense of the long-term shareholders; that is, projects that led to the excessive risk-taking were ex ante value diminishing (negative net present value). As highlighted in Example 3.1, managers would engage in such behavior *if their compensation is heavily weighted toward short-term incentive compensation.* Also, as we illustrate in Example 3.2, even if executives do not seek intentionally to mislead shareholders (but for a variety of reasons, whether out of overconfidence, optimism, poor internal organization, or simply sloppy thinking, they misjudge the outcome), they could be rewarded for doing so if their compensation is heavily weighted toward short-term incentive compensation.

Fahlenbrach and Stulz (2011) document the significant value losses from holdings of stock and vested unexercised options in their companies of bank CEOs during 2008. The authors point to this wealth loss in 2008 as evidence "inconsistent with the view that CEOs took exposures that were not in the interests of shareholders. Rather, this evidence suggests that CEOs took exposures that they felt were profitable for their shareholders *ex ante* but that these exposures performed very poorly *ex post*." This is the essence of the *unforeseen risk hypothesis*. Note that under the unforeseen risk hypothesis, the bank executives only invest in projects that, ex ante, have a positive net present value (NPV). In this case, we should not see the executives engage in insider trading that suggests that they are aware of the possibility of an extreme negative outcome especially in the later years of the project. The CEOs do not liquidate an abnormally large portion of their holdings because they do not anticipate large future losses from their banks' investment strategy. If the banks do suffer from the negative outcome due to risks associated with the investment that the executives could not anticipate, the CEOs will suffer as much as or more than the long-term shareholders.

The predictions of the unforeseen risk hypothesis are in contrast to the risk-taking incentives of bank executives – as per the managerial incentives hypothesis noted earlier. The managerial incentives hypothesis posits that incentives generated by executive compensation programs led to excessive risk-taking by banks that benefited bank executives at the expense of long-term shareholders. Bank executives receive significant amounts of stock and stock options as incentive compensation. If the vesting period for these stock and option grants is *long*, managers will identify more closely with creating long-term shareholder value. If the vesting period for these stock and option grants is *short*, managers will identify more closely with generating short-term earnings, even at the expense of long-term value.[1]

Managers who own significant amounts of *vested* stock and options have a strong incentive to focus on short-term earnings. If these short-term earnings are generated by value-enhancing projects, there would be no conflict vis-à-vis serving long-term shareholder interests. What if managers invest in value-decreasing (negative NPV) projects that generate positive earnings in the current year (and perhaps a few subsequent years) but lead to a large negative earnings outcome after a few years? If managers and outside investors have a similar understanding of the magnitude and probability of the large negative outcome, managers will be discouraged from investing in such value-decreasing projects because stock market participants will impound the negative impact of such projects on share prices of these banks. (The negative impact on share prices will have a similar, or greater, negative effect on the value of the managers' stock and option holdings.) However, managers have discretion over the amount, substance, and timing of the information about a project they release to outside investors.[2] Hence, given the information provided the outside investors, the stock market may underweight the probability (and timing) of a very negative outcome – and view a value-decreasing project as value enhancing.

How might managers behave if they were presented with a value-decreasing (negative NPV) project that generated positive earnings in the current year (and perhaps a few subsequent years) but leads to a large negative earnings outcome after a few years? If these managers were acting in the interests of long-term shareholders, they would not invest the bank's funds in such a project. If the managers were not necessarily acting in the interests of long-term shareholders but in their own self-interest only, and if they owned sufficient (vested) stock and options, they would have an incentive to invest in such a value-decreasing project. If the earnings from the project are positive in the current and next few years, the company's share price rises giving managers the opportunity to liquidate their (vested) stock and option holdings at a higher price. In other words, managers can take a significant amount of money "off the table" during the early years of the project. If the large negative earnings outcome occurs after a few years, the firm's share price will decline, and the managers will incur a wealth loss via their stock and option ownership. While these wealth losses can be large, they can be less than the money the managers have taken off the table in the earlier years. The end result is – managers make positive profits in spite of investing in a value-decreasing project; long-term shareholders, of course, experience a negative return because they did not have the knowledge to opportunistically liquidate their holdings as the CEO did.

This discussion suggests a way to empirically distinguish whether the unforeseen risk hypothesis or the managerial incentives hypothesis leads to a better understanding of bank manager incentives and behavior during 2000–8. The managerial incentive hypothesis predicts that manager payoffs (including cash compensation, sale of shares, and exercise of options and subsequent sale of shares) would be positive over a period of years, whereas long-term shareholders will experience a negative return over this same period. The unforeseen

Table 4.1 *Testable Implications of the Managerial Incentives Hypothesis and Unforeseen Risk Hypothesis: Testable Implication Regarding Net CEO Payoff*

	Manager incentives	Net CEO payoff during financial crisis and period prior to the crisis
Managerial incentives hypothesis	Acting in own self-interest sometimes dissipating long-term shareholder value	+
Unforeseen risk hypothesis	Manager consistently acting to enhance long-term shareholder value	–

Note: Net CEO Payoff during 2000–8 is (A) + (B) + (C), where (A) is CEO payoff during 2000–8 from net trades in their own company's stock, (B) is total cash compensation (salary plus bonus) during 2000–8, and (C) is estimated value lost by the manager from the decrease in value of his or her beneficial holding during 2008.

risk hypothesis predicts that *both* manager payoffs and long-term shareholder returns would be negative during this period. Tables 4.1 and 4.2 outline the testable implications from these two hypotheses.

However, there are other important reasons why CEOs might liquidate portions of their vested stock and option holdings. Theories of optimal diversification and liquidity (e.g., see Hall and Murphy 2002) predict that risk-averse and undiversified executives would exercise options and sell stock during 2000–7 regardless of whether they believed stock prices would fall in 2008. The manager incentive hypothesis suggests that manager trades of the shares of their bank's stock (sale of shares and exercise of options and subsequent sale of shares) are "abnormally large" during the financial crisis and the prior period. In contrast, the unforeseen risk hypothesis holds that some manager trades (reflecting the "normal" liquidity and diversification needs) are expected and "normal" during the financial crisis and the

Table 4.2 *Testable Implications of the Managerial Incentives Hypothesis and Unforeseen Risk Hypothesis: Testable Implication Regarding CEO's Net Trades*

	Manager incentives	CEO's net trades during financial crisis and period prior to the crisis
Managerial incentives hypothesis	Acting in own self-interest sometimes dissipating long-term shareholder value	Abnormally large
Unforeseen risk hypothesis	Manager consistently acting to enhance long-term shareholder value	Normal

Note: Normal CEO's net trades are with reference to CEOs of banks that did not seek government bailout funds. Additionally, we construct a Tobit model of expected CEO trading based on the extant literature on insider and CEO trading.

prior period. What is "normal" for manager trades of the shares of their bank's stock? We consider two benchmarks for normal managerial trading. First, trades of managers of other banks (that did not seek government bailout funds) would reflect the normal liquidity and diversification needs of bank managers. Hence we benchmark normal manager trades with reference to managers of banks that did not seek government bailout funds. Trades similar to this normal level would be consistent with the unforeseen risk hypothesis. In contrast, trades greater than this normal level would be consistent with the managerial incentives hypothesis (see Table 4.2). Second, we construct a Tobit model of expected CEO trading based on the extant literature on insider and CEO trading; we detail these results in Chapter 5.

5   Bank CEOs' Buys and Sells during 2000–8

5.1   SAMPLE SELECTION

The starting point for our sample is the list of 100 financial institutions studied in Fahlenbrach and Stulz (2011). From this list, as we detail in Bhagat and Bolton (2014), we identify the 14 firms studied in this analysis that were chosen due to their role in the US financial crisis prior to and during 2008. Nine firms are included because the US Treasury required them to be the first participants in the Troubled Assets Relief Program (TARP) in October 2008. These firms are Bank of America, Bank of New York Mellon, Citigroup, Goldman Sachs, JP Morgan Chase, Morgan Stanley, State Street, Wells Fargo, and Merrill Lynch, which was subsequently acquired by Bank of America.[1] Bear Stearns and Lehman Brothers are included because we suspect they would have been included in this first round of TARP funding had they been independent going concerns in October 2008. Bear Stearns was acquired by JP Morgan Chase in May 2008 and Lehman Brothers declared bankruptcy in September 2008. Mellon Financial merged with Bank of New York in July 2007; it is included to allow for consistency throughout the period under study. Countrywide Financial is also included for consistency and because it was one of the largest originators of subprime mortgages prior to the crisis. Countrywide was acquired by Bank of America in July 2008, so all of its investments and liabilities became Bank of America's investments and liabilities at that time. Finally, American International Group, or AIG, is included because of its central role in the crisis. While not a depository institution or investment bank, AIG was a trading partner with most of the other institutions in this study, and was involved in the real estate market by selling credit default swaps and other mortgage-related products to these institutions and other investors. AIG was also one of the largest recipients of TARP funds and was one of the last firms in the sample to repay the Treasury's TARP investment. In our discussion below we refer to AIG and the 13 other banks noted above as too-big-to-fail (TBTF) "banks."

Besides the 14 TBTF banks, for comparison purposes we consider two additional samples of lending institutions, comprised of the remaining 86 institutions listed in the appendix in Fahlenbrach and Stulz (2011). The first comparative sample includes 49 lending institutions that received TARP funds several months after the TBTF banks received their TARP funds; we refer to these 49 lending institutions as later-TARP banks or L-TARP. The second comparative sample includes 37 lending institutions that did not receive TARP funds; we refer to these 37 lending institutions as No-TARP, and note details of the L-TARP and No-TARP banks. Table 5.1 provides summary data on the size (total assets and market capitalization) of the TBTF, L-TARP and No-TARP banks. As expected, TBTF banks are much larger than L-TARP and No-TARP banks. L-TARP and No-TARP banks are of similar size.

5.2 DATA

The insider trading data come from the Thomson Insiders database. We rely on Form 4 data filed with the Securities and Exchange Commission (SEC) for this study. In addition to direct acquisitions and dispositions of common stock, we also consider acquisitions of stock through the exercise of stock options.[2] Many individual Form 4 filings are manually reviewed on the SEC website to ensure consistency of the data.

Director ownership data are from RiskMetrics, formerly Investor Responsibility Research Center (IRRC). The compensation data are from Compustat's ExecuComp. Individual proxy statements are reviewed to corroborate director ownership and compensation data. In some cases, for example, the ownership data used are slightly

Table 5.1 *Selected Descriptive Statistics*

	End of 2000		End of 2006		End of 2008	
	Assets (000's)	Market capitalization (000's)	Assets (000's)	Market capitalization (000's)	Assets (000's)	Market capitalization (000's)
TBTF Sample (*n* = 14)						
Mean	$326,499,343	$73,627,243	$733,089,630	$98,809,110	$1,072,356,700	$47,368,914
Median	281,093,000	48,122,194	670,873,000	80,444,709	872,482,500	33,746,034
L-TARP sample (*n* = 49)						
Mean	$23,088,619	$4,996,060	$48,612,142	$9,146,771	$43,454,635	$3,570,823
Median	5,919,657	1,472,203	11,157,000	1,959,887	13,552,842	1,413,087
No-TARP Sample (*n* = 37)						
Mean	$16,803,982	$2,776,577	$32,386,871	$5,117,365	$23,498,223	$1,694,581
Median	5,162,983	1,136,433	11,558,206	2,021,643	8,353,488	1,166,516

Note: This table presents the mean and median dollar amount of assets and market capitalization as of the end of 2000, 2006, and 2008 for each of the three primary samples: the 14 TBTF firms, the 49 L-TARP firms, and the 37 No-TARP firms. TBTF refers to the 14 too-big-to-fail financial institutions, including Bank of America, Bank of New York Mellon, Citigroup, Goldman Sachs, JP Morgan Chase, Morgan Stanley, State Street, Wells Fargo, Merrill Lynch, Bear Stearns, Lehman Brothers, and AIG. L-TARP includes 49 lending institutions that received TARP funds several months after many of the TBTF banks received the TARP funds. No-TARP sample includes 37 lending institutions that did not receive TARP funds.

different from the RiskMetrics data because of disclosures about the nature of the ownership provided in the footnotes of the proxy statement. For example, in the 2001 Bear Stearns' proxy statement, 45,669 shares of common stock owned by CEO James Cayne's wife are not included in his beneficial ownership; in the 2002 proxy, these same 45,669 shares (presumably) are included in his beneficial ownership. Manually reviewing the proxy statements and the relevant footnotes allows me to be more consistent across time and across firms. Further, manually reviewing the proxy statements allows me to distinguish and appropriately characterize securities such as unexercised options and restricted stock.[3]

Finally, stock price data are from Center for Research in Securities Prices (CRSP), and financial statement data are from Compustat. Again, individual financial statements are reviewed to better characterize the information in some cases.

5.3   VARIABLES

The primary variable used in this study is *net trades*. This variable subtracts the dollar value of all of an insider's purchases of common stock during a fiscal year from the dollar value of all of that insider's sales of common stock during the year. Exercising options to acquire stock is considered a purchase of common stock in the calculation of Net Trades$_{i,t}$, net trades of bank executive i in year t. This variable is calculated as follows:

$$\text{Net Trades}_{i,t} = \text{Stock Sales}_{i,t} - \text{Stock Purchases}_{i,t}$$
$$- \text{Option Exercises}_{i,t} \qquad (5.1)$$

We consider the posttrade ownership after each transaction. One information item disclosed on Form 4 is the "amount of securities beneficially owned following reported transaction." We multiply the number of shares disclosed on Form 4 by the transaction price of the stock from Form 4 to get the dollar value of ownership following the transaction. We also add back the value of shares sold or subtract the value of shares purchased to determine the pretrade ownership stake.

We consider *salary* and *bonus* for compensation data, which represent current cash considerations. We do not directly consider stock or option grants. We analyze any stock or option compensation only when the insider converts that into cash by selling the stock or exercising the option, which is captured in the net trades variable defined earlier.

We also calculate the *estimated value lost*, or the change in beneficial ownership for each CEO in 2008. This amount is estimated by subtracting net trades from *beginning beneficial ownership* in number of shares to get estimated shares at the end of 2008. This is multiplied by the ending stock price change and then subtracted from the beginning beneficial ownership in dollars to get the estimated value lost. We calculate the *estimated value remaining* at the end of 2008 using the preceding estimate of shares owned at the end of 2008 multiplied by the ending stock price. Note that this is not necessarily the same as beneficial ownership at the beginning of 2009 disclosed in a firm's proxy statement because it does not include stock gifts or compensation received during 2008. We do not include these values because doing so would not directly capture the effects of the financial crisis on the CEO's ownership stake during 2008.

5.4   NET PAYOFF TO BANK CEOS DURING 2000–8

Table 5.2 provides details on the CEOs' buys and sells of their own company stock during 2000–8. During this period, the 14 CEOs as a group bought stock in their companies 73 times and sold shares of their companies 2,048 times. During 2000–8, the 14 bank CEOs bought stock in their banks worth $36 million but sold shares worth $3,467 million.[4] In addition, CEOs acquired stock by exercising options at a total cost of $1,660 million.

Table 5.2 *Trades by CEOs during 2000–8*

This table presents the stock ownership, trading, and compensation information for the CEOs of the 14 identified firms during 2000–8. Panel A presents the trades by firm. Panel B presents the trades by year, summing all 14 firms' trades. The *value of buys* and *value of sales* represent the cumulative cash flows realized via stock acquisitions or dispositions during the period. The *value of option exercises* represents the cost of acquiring stock through exercising options and is calculated as number of options acquired multiplied by exercise price. The *value of net trades* is the value of buys and value of option exercises subtracted from the value of sales. The *value of net trading to posttrade Form 4 holdings* represents the ratio of stock traded to the amount of stock owned following each trade, based on the information disclosed on the Form 4 filing with the SEC.

Panel A: Trades by CEOs during 2000–8 by Firm

Company	No. of buys	No. of option exercises	No. of sales	Value of buys	Value of option exercises	Value of sales	Value of net trades: (sales – buys), 2000–8	Ratio of net trading to posttrade Form 4 holdings (average across years)
AIG	1	14	0	$10,568	$7,392,620	$0	($7,403,188)	0.0%
Bank of America	11	17	292	2,129,776	197,404,497	223,725,511	24,191,238	27.8%
Bank of New York	29	26	566	128,480	21,877,806	77,786,666	55,780,380	15.1%
Bear Stearns	0	0	15	0	0	243,053,692	243,053,692	4.2%
Citigroup	9	43	99	8,430,672	763,368,027	947,325,315	175,526,616	18.4%

Countrywide Financial	0	267	274	0	128,199,209	530,143,206	401,943,997	55.1%
Goldman Sachs	0	0	15	0	0	40,475,735	40,475,735	1.4%
JP Morgan Chase	8	12	24	11,069,195	60,518,375	101,074,462	29,486,892	11.9%
Lehman Brothers	1	15	304	19,272	150,274,172	578,502,379	428,208,935	24.2%
Mellon Financial	11	32	65	3,311,837	10,308,283	30,287,267	16,667,147	8.5%
Merrill Lynch	1	8	69	11,250,000	6,323,804	95,478,463	77,904,659	16.0%
Morgan Stanley	0	15	46	0	62,173,905	150,980,730	88,806,825	6.8%
State Street	0	6	178	0	13,500,127	37,995,090	24,494,963	18.3%
Wells Fargo	2	15	101	50,841	238,266,366	410,583,053	172,265,846	32.4%
All firms	**73**	**470**	**2,048**	**$36,400,641**	**$1,659,607,191**	**$3,467,411,569**	**$1,771,403,737**	**15.3%**

Table 5.2 (cont.)

Panel B: Trades by CEOs during 2000–8 by Year

Year	No. of buys	No. of option exercises	No. of sales	Value of buys	Value of option exercises	Value of sales	Value of net trades (sales – buys), 2000–8	Ratio of net trading to posttrade Form 4 holdings (average across years)
2000	2	45	81	$4,671	$707,882,633	$962,970,443	$255,083,139	38.6%
2001	2	22	43	14,968	35,859,131	153,851,211	117,977,112	9.2%
2002	6	20	83	585,334	60,407,064	124,253,270	63,260,872	4.3%
2003	5	42	213	23,361	92,537,722	295,147,013	202,585,930	8.6%
2004	5	41	240	22,674	98,441,507	265,625,885	167,161,704	11.0%
2005	9	110	529	187,256	102,993,845	577,315,758	474,134,657	15.3%
2006	11	84	430	2,912,955	428,598,544	575,492,859	143,981,360	14.3%
2007	9	100	399	485,323	119,857,907	428,158,406	307,815,176	14.1%
2008	24	6	30	32,164,099	13,028,838	84,596,724	39,403,787	31.2%
All years	73	470	2,048	$36,400,641	$1,659,607,191	$3,467,411,569	$1,771,403,737	15.3%

This table also notes the *value of net trades* for these CEOs in the shares of their own company; value of net trades subtracts the dollar value of all purchases of common stock from the dollar value of all sales of common stock. There is significant cross-sectional variation in the net trades of the CEOs during 2000–8. Lehman Brothers' CEO engaged in the largest dollar value of net trades of about $428 million, followed by Countrywide's CEO at $402 million, and Bear Stearns' CEOs at $243 million. On the low end, AIG CEOs engaged in net acquisitions of $7 million, while Mellon Financial and Bank of America CEOs engaged in net trades worth $17 million and $24 million, respectively.

Observers of US capital markets know that investors in these 14 banks fared poorly during 2008 (see Figure 5.1). Since these CEOs owned significant blocks of stock in their companies, they also suffered significant declines in the value of their stockholdings. As a group these CEOs suffered value losses (from stockholdings in their companies) in 2008 of about $2,013 million. Individually, these losses range from a low of about $3 million (Wells Fargo) to about $796 million (Lehman Brothers).[5]

Both bank CEOs and their shareholders experienced negative returns during 2008. This evidence is consistent with both the managerial incentives hypothesis and the unforeseen risk hypothesis. To distinguish between the unforeseen risk hypothesis and the managerial incentives hypothesis, one would need to consider their returns during a period prior to 2008. The managerial incentives hypothesis predicts that manager payoffs would be positive during the period, whereas long-term shareholders will experience a negative return over this same period. The unforeseen risk hypothesis predicts that both manager payoffs and long-term shareholder returns will be negative during this period.

To distinguish between the unforeseen risk hypothesis and the managerial incentives hypothesis, we need to consider manager payoffs for a period of years prior to 2008. What time period is implied by this "period of years prior to 2008"? Conceptually, this period

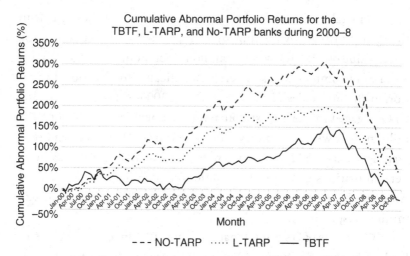

FIGURE 5.1 Relative portfolio returns of bank portfolios, 2000–8. This figure presents the relative cumulative portfolio returns from 2000 to 2008 of three different bank portfolios. The dashed line on top represents the cumulative portfolio returns of the 37 No-TARP institutions, or those that never received TARP funding. The dotted line in the middle represents the cumulative portfolio returns of the 49 L-TARP institutions, or those that did receive TARP funding, but only after October 2008. The solid line represents the cumulative portfolio returns of the 14 TBTF firms, or those designated as too big to fail. Monthly returns are used to form equally weighted portfolios. Shareholders in the TBTF banks fared significantly worse than shareholders in the No-TARP banks (smaller banks that did not receive taxpayer-funded bailout funds) during 2000–8. Shareholders in the TBTF banks also fared significantly worse than shareholders in the L-TARP banks (banks, smaller than the TBTF banks, that did receive taxpayer-funded bailout funds after October 2008) during 2000–8. (*Source:* Authors' calculations.)

includes the years when bank managers initiated or started emphasizing excessively risky investments or trading strategies. Chesney, Stromberg, and Wagner (2010) consider bank CEO incentives during 2002–5 arguing that "the vast majority of deals related to the subprime and mortgage backed security market originated in the early part of the decade." Figure 2.5 supports their contention. Bebchuk, Cohen, and Spamann (2010) consider the period 2000–8 in their case study of manager compensation in Bear Stearns and Lehmann. Consistent with this literature, we consider 2000–8 as our period for analysis. We include the longer period because we want our analysis to capture both the cash compensation and any liquidation of the CEOs' personal holdings during this period. As a robustness check, we consider two additional periods: 2002–8 and 2004–8.

Table 5.3 notes that as a group these 14 CEOs experienced a cash inflow of $1,771 million from their net trades during 2000–8. In addition, these 14 CEOs received cash compensation worth $891 million during this period. Combining these two numbers – as a group, CEOs of the 14 banks experienced cash inflow worth $2,662 million; we refer to this as *CEO Payoff*. Compare this with their estimated combined losses from beneficial stock holdings in 2008 of $2,013 million.[6] The *CEO Payoff* sum of $2,662 million for the 14 CEOs as a group can be considered as money these CEOs took "off the table" as their banks continued with the high risk but negative net present value trading/ investment strategies during 2000–8. However, the high risk but negative net present value trading/investment strategy would ultimately lead to a large negative outcome – namely, the large loss of $2,013 million in 2008. The sum of net trades and cash compensation for 2000–8 is greater than the value lost in 2008 (from beneficial stock holdings) by $649 million for these 14 CEOs as a group – we refer to this as the *Net CEO Payoff*. The data for the CEOs of the 14 companies as a group are consistent with the *Managerial Incentives Hypothesis* and inconsistent with the *Unforeseen Risk Hypothesis*, based on the predictions in Table 4.1.

Table 5.3, Panel A, also provides data on the net trades, cash compensation, and value losses in 2008 for CEOs of each of the 14 companies. The net CEO payoff is positive for CEOs in 10 of the 14 sample firms; Bank of America, Goldman Sachs, Lehman Brothers, and State Street are the exceptions. The net CEO payoff ranges from $221 million for Citigroup and $377 million for Countrywide to losses of $126 million for Goldman Sachs and $311 million for Lehman Brothers. However, even for Goldman Sachs and Lehman Brothers, CEO payoffs for 2000–8 are quite substantial at $132 million and $485

Table 5.3 *CEO Payoffs, TBTF Institutions*

This table presents the cash flows realized by each firm's CEO during the relevant period via stock trades and cash compensation, as well as the estimated value lost in 2008 and the estimated value remaining in 2008. Panel A presents cash flows for 2000–8. Panel B presents cash flows for 2002–8. Panel C presents cash flows for 2004–8. The value of stock holdings at the beginning of each period represents the dollar value of stock beneficially owned by the CEO at that time. Note that this value only pertains to the owner who was CEO at that time; no adjustments are made to this number for subsequent CEO changes. This number is presented for perspective only and is not included in any calculations performed within this table. Column (A) shows the dollar value of total net trades made by each CEO during the period. Total net trades are sales buys and option exercises. Column (B) shows the dollar value of cash compensation the CEO received through salary and bonus payments. The "CEO Payoff" column is the sum of columns (A) and (B) and represents the realized cash gains to the CEO. The "Estimated Value Lost, 2008" is shown in column (C). This column estimates the dollar value of beneficial ownership each CEO lost during 2008. It is calculated by subtracting the net shares sold during the year from the number of shares beneficially owned at the beginning of the year to estimate the number of shares owned at the end of the year. This number is then adjusted by the decrease (or increase) in the firm's stock price during 2008. The "Net CEO Payoff" column sums columns (A), (B), and (C), or CEO payoff less estimated value lost in 2008. The final column shows the estimated value remaining at the end of 2008, which is calculated by multiplying the estimated number of shares owned at the end of the year [based on the column (C) calculation] by the stock price at the end of the year. This number is based on the beginning of 2008 beneficial ownership adjusted by intrayear transactions and does not include stock gifts or compensation grants received during the year.

Because not all 14 firms were independent, going concerns throughout 2008, several assumptions are necessary. The following notes relate to unique situations concerning estimated value lost during 2008 and estimated value remaining at the end of 2008 at four firms:

1. For purposes of calculating estimated value lost and estimated value remaining, Bear Stearns' ending 2008 stock price is assumed to be $9.35, or the estimated price JP Morgan Chase paid per share on June 2, 2008.

2. Countrywide Financial was acquired by Bank of America in July 2008. Countrywide did not file a 2008 10-K or proxy statement. No information is available about cash compensation for CEO Angelo Mozilo for 2008, so it is set at $0 for the year. Estimated value lost is based on Mozilo's

3. Lehman Brothers filed for bankruptcy on September 15, 2008. For purposes of calculating estimated value lost and estimated value remaining, Lehman Brothers' ending 2008 stock price is assumed to be $0.

4. Mellon Financial was acquired by Bank of New York in July 2007. Mellon did not file a 2007 10-K or proxy statement. No information is available about cash compensation for CEO Robert Kelly for 2007, so it is set at $0 for the year. Estimated value lost is based on Kelly's estimated stock holdings at the beginning of the year and the change in Mellon Financial stock price through June 30, 2007. Estimated value remaining is based on Kelly's estimated holdings in Mellon as of June 30, 2007.

Panel A: 2000–8 CEO Payoff

Company	Value of stock holdings, beginning of 2000	Total net trades, 2000–8 (A)	Total cash compensation, 2000–8 (B)	CEO payoff (realized cash gains), 2000–8 (A)+(B)	Estimated value lost (unrealized paper loss), 2008 (C)	Net CEO payoff; 2000–8 (A) + (B) + (C)	Estimated value remaining, end of 2008
AIG	$3,288,184,509	($7,403,188)	$53,000,338	$45,597,150	($20,052,183)	$25,544,967	$554,943
Bank of America	42,931,341	24,191,238	41,645,833	65,837,071	(124,620,911)	(58,783,840)	64,557,116
Bank of New York	35,277,000	55,780,380	62,187,998	117,968,378	(13,609,007)	104,359,371	18,871,423
Bear Stearns (1)	299,219,861	243,053,692	83,528,081	326,581,773	(324,691,895)	1,889,878	38,385,395
Citigroup	1,217,275,401	175,526,616	85,156,839	260,683,455	(38,914,762)	221,768,693	11,487,816
Countrywide Financial (2)	66,775,746	401,943,997	90,211,728	492,155,725	(114,773,127)	377,382,598	104,005,498

Table 5.3 (cont.)

Company	Value of stock holdings, beginning of 2000	Total net trades, 2000–8 (A)	Total cash compensation, 2000–8 (B)	CEO payoff (realized cash gains), 2000–8 (A)+(B)	Estimated value lost (unrealized paper loss), 2008 (C)	Net CEO payoff,: 2000–8 (A) + (B) + (C)	Estimated value remaining, end of 2008
Goldman Sachs	371,469,755	40,475,735	91,489,574	131,965,309	(257,534,257)	(125,568,948)	166,334,884
JP Morgan Chase	107,767,012	29,486,892	83,361,250	112,848,142	(105,420,736)	7,427,406	274,250,479
Lehman Brothers (3)	263,173,216	428,208,935	56,700,000	484,908,935	(796,322,784)	(311,413,849)	0
Mellon Financial (4)	26,402,150	16,667,147	19,208,205	35,875,352	1,212,310	37,087,662	28,833,326
Merrill Lynch	199,120,374	77,904,659	89,407,692	167,312,351	(20,192,048)	147,120,303	6,583,385
Morgan Stanley	840,975,081	88,806,825	69,103,887	157,910,712	(144,474,839)	13,435,873	62,513,526
State Street	26,501,303	24,494,963	20,767,340	45,262,303	(51,530,173)	(6,267,870)	48,404,149
Wells Fargo	133,412,007	172,265,846	45,468,535	217,734,381	(2,758,746)	214,975,635	114,546,238
All firms	$6,846,638,948	$1,771,403,737	$891,237,300	$2,662,641,037	–$2,013,683,157	$648,957,880	$939,328,179

Panel B: 2002–8 CEO Payoff

Company	Value of stock holdings, beginning of 2002	Total net trades, 2002–8 (A)	Total cash compensation, 2002–8 (B)	CEO payoff (realized cash gains), 2002–8 (A) + (B)	Estimated value lost (unrealized paper loss), 2008 (C)	Net CEO payoff, 2002–8 (A) + (B) + (C)	Estimated value remaining, end of 2008
AIG	$3,594,451,657	($5,382,707)	$46,000,338	$40,617,631	($20,052,183)	$20,565,448	$554,943
Bank of America	91,786,388	23,366,558	32,612,500	55,979,058	(124,620,911)	(68,641,853)	64,557,116
Bank of New York	142,638,677	52,035,882	41,392,260	93,428,142	(13,609,007)	79,819,135	18,871,423
Bear Stearns (1)	430,959,258	217,312,893	62,189,373	279,502,266	(324,691,895)	(45,189,629)	38,385,395
Citigroup	1,644,100,384	11,947,821	47,685,677	59,633,498	(38,914,762)	20,718,736	11,487,816
Countrywide Financial (2)	113,447,815	399,466,126	78,693,417	478,159,543	(114,773,127)	363,386,416	104,005,498
Goldman Sachs	370,810,790	40,475,735	64,682,474	105,158,209	(257,534,257)	(152,376,048)	166,334,884
JP Morgan Chase	127,334,850	25,590,073	66,080,000	91,670,073	(105,420,736)	(13,750,663)	274,250,479
Lehman Brothers (3)	447,312,706	349,144,912	42,450,000	391,594,912	(796,322,784)	(404,727,872)	0
Mellon Financial (4)	39,351,461	8,367,088	14,833,205	23,200,293	1,212,310	24,412,603	28,833,326

Table 5.3 (cont.)

Company	Value of stock holdings, beginning of 2002	Total net trades, 2002–8 (A)	Total cash compensation, 2002–8 (B)	CEO payoff (realized cash gains), 2002–8 (A) + (B)	Estimated value lost (unrealized paper loss), 2008 (C)	Net CEO payoff, 2002–8 (A) + (B) + (C)	Estimated value remaining, end of 2008
Merrill Lynch	232,105,475	52,421,714	71,457,692	123,879,406	(20,192,048)	103,687,358	6,583,385
Morgan Stanley	344,463,808	43,321,434	47,328,887	90,650,321	(144,474,839)	(53,824,518)	62,513,526
State Street	114,098,116	19,329,608	16,106,995	35,436,603	(51,530,173)	(16,093,570)	48,404,149
Wells Fargo	194,214,701	160,946,349	35,603,535	196,549,884	-(,758,746)	193,791,138	114,546,238
All firms	**$7,887,076,084**	**$1,398,343,486**	**$667,116,353**	**$2,065,459,839**	**-$2,013,683,157**	**$51,776,682**	**$939,328,179**

Panel C: 2004–8 CEO Payoff

Company	Value of stock holdings, beginning of 2004	Total net trades, 2004–8 (A)	Total cash compensation, 2004–8 (B)	CEO payoff (realized cash gains), 2004–8 (A) + (B)	Estimated value lost (unrealized paper loss), 2008 (C)	Net CEO payoff, 2004–8 (A) + (B) + (C)	Estimated value remaining, end of 2008
AIG	$3,002,954,389	($3,064,736)	$32,500,338	$29,435,602	($20,052,183)	$9,383,419	$554,943
Bank of America	145,346,983	(3,429,732)	18,862,500	15,432,768	(124,620,911)	(109,188,143)	64,557,116
Bank of New York	164,790,978	44,119,270	28,898,240	73,017,510	(13,609,007)	59,408,503	18,871,423
Bear Stearns (1)	551,226,148	140,090,185	40,773,191	180,863,376	(324,691,895)	(143,828,519)	38,385,395

Citigroup	84,295,049	1,889,769	39,081,666	40,971,435	(38,914,762)	2,056,673	11,487,816
Countrywide Financial (2)	465,597,033	376,914,498	46,730,652	423,645,150	(114,773,127)	308,872,023	104,005,498
Goldman Sachs	407,201,420	40,475,735	57,228,974	97,704,709	(257,534,257)	(159,829,548)	166,334,884
JP Morgan Chase	173,500,840	21,587,849	48,400,000	69,987,849	(105,420,736)	(35,432,887)	274,250,479
Lehman Brothers (3)	434,592,614	276,359,002	33,250,000	309,609,002	(796,322,784)	(486,713,782)	0
Mellon Financial (4)	63,387,356	7,115,917	10,708,205	17,824,122	1,212,310	19,036,432	28,833,326
Merrill Lynch	127,231,556	52,400,569	49,757,692	102,158,261	(20,192,048)	81,966,213	6,583,385
Morgan Stanley	339,906,794	24,729,360	33,053,887	57,783,247	(144,474,839)	(86,691,592)	62,513,526
State Street	136,857,334	14,441,482	11,053,079	25,494,561	(51,530,173)	(26,035,612)	48,404,149
Wells Fargo	360,778,278	138,867,516	19,113,535	157,981,051	(2,758,746)	155,222,305	114,546,238
All firms	$6,457,666,773	$1,132,496,684	$469,411,959	$1,601,908,643	-$2,013,683,157	-$411,774,514	$939,328,179

million, respectively. In other words, the CEOs of Goldman Sachs and Lehman Brothers enjoyed *realized* cash gains of $132 million and $485 million, respectively, during 2000–8 but suffered *unrealized* paper losses that exceeded these amounts. Overall, the evidence from individual net CEO payoffs is consistent with the managerial incentives hypothesis and inconsistent with the unforeseen risk hypothesis.

5.5   ROBUSTNESS CHECK: DIFFERENT SAMPLE PERIODS

Table 5.3, Panel B, notes that, as a group, these 14 CEOs experienced a cash inflow of $1,398 million from their net trades during 2002–8. In addition, these 14 CEOs received cash compensation worth $667 million during this period. Combining these two numbers, as a group, CEOs of the 14 banks experienced CEO payoffs worth $2,065 million, including costs associated with exercising options. As noted earlier, these CEOs suffered combined losses from beneficial stock holdings in 2008 of $2,013 million. Consistent with our findings for the 2000–8 period, the data for the CEOs of the 14 companies as a group are consistent with the managerial incentives hypothesis and inconsistent with the unforeseen risk hypothesis.

The sum of net trades and cash compensation for 2002–8 is greater than the value lost in 2008 (from beneficial stock holdings) for CEOs at half the 14 sample firms. Even for the CEOs of the banks with net CEO payoff losses, the realized CEO payoffs for 2002–8 are quite substantial, ranging from $35 million up to $391 million. Notice that these CEO payoff amounts were taken off the table by the CEOs of these seven banks during 2002–8, before they incurred the large 2008 losses from the drop in value of their stockholdings. Similar to our conclusion for 2000–8, we interpret this evidence as consistent with the managerial incentives hypothesis and inconsistent with the unforeseen risk hypothesis.

Table 5.3, Panel C, focuses on the period 2004–8. As a group, these 14 CEOs experienced a cash inflow of $1,132 million from their net trades. In addition, these 14 CEOs received cash compensation worth $469 million during this period. As noted earlier, these CEOs suffered combined losses from beneficial stock holdings in 2008 of $2,013 million. The net CEO payoff for the 14 CEOs as a group is negative $412 million for 2004–8. This evidence is inconsistent with the managerial incentives hypothesis and consistent with the unforeseen risk hypothesis. It is worth noting that the net CEO payoffs for the 14 CEOs as a group would be positive were it not for the large negative net CEO payoff of $486 million for Lehman Brothers (which declared bankruptcy in September 2008). Even for Lehman Brothers, the realized cash from CEO payoff during 2000–8 is $310 million – this amount was taken off the table; of course, the unrealized paper losses during this period are $796 million.

The sum of net trades and cash compensation for 2004–8 is greater than the value lost in 2008 (from beneficial stock holdings) for CEOs in half the 14 sample firms. Even for the CEOs of the seven banks with negative net CEO payoffs, the realized cash from CEO payoffs for 2004–8 ranges from $15 million to $310 million. We note that the abovementioned sums of money were taken off the table by the CEOs of these banks during 2004–8, before they incurred the large unrealized paper losses in 2008 from the drop in value of their stockholdings.

5.6   COMPARING TBTF, L-TARP, AND NO-TARP BANKS

The dollar value of the net trades of the 14 TBTF bank CEOs during 2000–8 provides an important perspective on the payoffs these executives received from working in their banks. As noted earlier, theories of optimal diversification and liquidity (e.g., see Hall and Murphy 2002) predict that risk-averse and undiversified executives would exercise options and sell stock during 2000–8 regardless of whether they believed stock prices would fall in 2008. An important question is whether the net trades of the 14 TBTF bank CEOs are normal or abnormal. We compare the net trades of the 14 TBTF bank CEOs with the net trades of the 49 L-TARP bank CEOs and the 37 No-TARP bank CEOs. Since TBTF banks are considerably larger than L-TARP and No-TARP banks, we consider the ratio of the CEO's net trades during the sample period to the CEO's holdings at the beginning of the period. We consider three sample periods: 2000–8, 2002–8, and 2004–8.

To the extent that the diversification and liquidity needs of the TBTF bank CEOs are similar to the diversification and liquidity needs of the L-TARP and No-TARP bank CEOs, the ratio of the CEO's net trades during the sample period to the CEO's holdings at the beginning of the period would be equal for these three subgroups of CEOs. If the ratio of the CEO's net trades during the sample period to the CEO's holdings at the beginning of the period are significantly greater for TBTF bank CEOs compared with No-TARP bank CEOs, this would suggest that TBTF bank CEOs sold significantly more stock during 2000–8, even after controlling for diversification and liquidity concerns.

As detailed in Table 5.4, the median ratio of the CEO's net trades during 2000–8 to the CEO's holdings in 2000 is 59.7% for the TBTF banks compared with 17.6% for the L-TARP banks and 4.0% for the No-TARP banks.[7] We find consistent results for the two other sample periods. The median ratio of the CEO's net trades during 2002–8 to the CEO's holdings in 2002 is 21.9% for the TBTF banks compared with 8.4% for the L-TARP banks and 2.6% for the No-TARP banks. The median ratio of the CEO's net trades during 2004–8 to the CEO's holdings in 2004 is 11.8% for the TBTF banks compared with 3.5% for the L-TARP banks and 0.1% for the No-TARP banks.[8] This provides strong evidence that net trades of the 14 TBTF bank CEOs during 2000–8 were abnormally high, even after controlling for diversification and liquidity needs of TBTF bank CEOs. This evidence is consistent with the managerial incentives hypothesis and inconsistent with the unforeseen risk hypothesis.

Figure 5.2 illustrates the stark difference in the median total net trades of the 14 TBTF bank CEOs compared with the 37 No-TARP bank CEOs during 2000–8, 2002–8, and 2004–8. Figure 5.2A highlights the dollar values of the net trades. To address the liquidity and diversification needs of these CEOs, we consider the ratio of the net trades to their respective stock holdings in the beginning of the period (see

Table 5.4 *CEO Trading and CEO Holdings*

This table compares the total CEO trading activity and CEO stock ownership by period and by sample. The three time periods are 2000–8, 2002–8, and 2004–8. The three samples are the 14 TBTF firms, the 49 L-TARP firms, and the 37 No-TARP firms. Net trades are calculated as all open-market sales of stock less open-market purchases and cost of exercising options.

	Total net trades, 2000–8	Total net trades, 2002–8	Total net trades, 2004–8	Ratio of trades to beginning holdings, 2000–8	Ratio of trades to beginning holdings, 2002–8	Ratio of trades to beginning holdings, 2004–8
			TBTF firms (n = 14)			
Mean	$126,528,838	$99,881,678	$80,892,620	103.4%***	52.2%***	23.4%**
Median	$66,842,520	$41,898,585	$32,602,548	59.7%***	21.9%**	11.8%**
			L-TARP firms (n = 49)			
Mean	$5,724,901	$4,893,079	$3,158,121	100.4%***	19.1%*	10.2%*
Median	$1,090,134	$878,228	$561,761	17.6%*	8.4%*	3.5%*
			No-TARP firms (n = 37)			
Mean	$11,826,280	$11,239,377	$9,107,443	43.9%	12.1%	−1.3%
Median	$1,226,977	$599,057	$32,818	4.0%	2.6%	0.1%

Statistical significant for difference of ratios: * indicates significantly different from No-TARP sample at the 10% level; ** indicates significantly different from No-TARP sample at the 5% level; *** indicates significantly different from No-TARP sample at the 1% level.

Panel (A): In Dollars

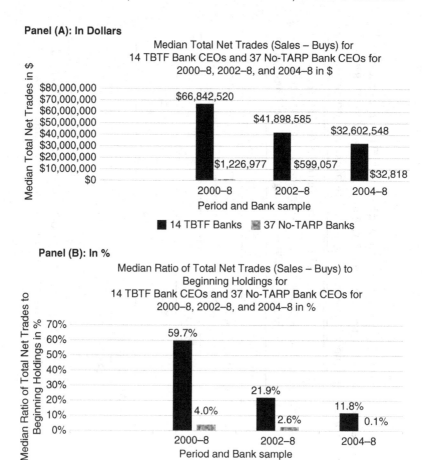

FIGURE 5.2 CEO net trades for 14 TBTF banks and 37 No-TARP banks: (A) in dollars; (B) in percent. Net trades are calculated as all open-market sales of stock less open-market purchases and cost of exercising options. TBTF bank CEOs sold significantly more of their stock holdings than No-TARP bank (smaller banks that did not receive taxpayer-funded bailout funds) CEOs in both absolute and relative senses during 2000–8, 2002–8, and 2004–8. (*Source:* Author's calculations.)

Figure 5.2B). For each of the periods 2000–8, 2002–8, and 2004–8, the median ratio of total net trades to stock holdings in the beginning of the particular period of the 37 No-TARP bank CEOs is significantly less than for the 14 TBTF bank CEOs.

5.7   ROBUSTNESS CHECK: NET TRADES OF OFFICERS AND DIRECTORS

In the preceding analysis we have focused on the trades and incentives of the CEO because the CEO is the most significant decision maker. However, other officers and directors can have a significant impact on a bank's trading/investment strategies. Table 5.5 provides data on the net trades of the officers and directors of these 14 banks. Data on the compensation and beneficial holdings are less readily available or unavailable for the officers and directors. We note the data on net trades to provide as complete a perspective as possible regarding the incentives of decision makers in these banks. Officers and directors of these 14 banks were involved in 14,687 sales during 2000–8 but only 1,671 buys during the period. Officers and directors acquired stock via option exercises in 3,454 separate transactions. Net trades, including the costs of exercising options, of officers and directors of these 14 banks sum to almost $127 billion. On the high side, net trades of officers and directors of Goldman Sachs were $32 billion, followed by AIG at $28 billion and Citigroup at $19 billion. Notice that these figures do not include the value of any cash compensation received by these officers and directors from their banks.

Figure 5.3 illustrates the annual net trades of all 14 TBTF bank CEOs and insiders, respectively. The intertemporal profile of the annual net trades is quite revealing. The years with the two largest amounts of annual net trades for the CEOs were just prior to the 2008 crash, namely, 2007 and 2005. Similarly, the year with the largest amount of annual net trades for the insiders was also just prior to the 2008 crash, namely, 2007.

5.8   SHAREHOLDER RETURNS TO TBTF, L-TARP, AND NO-TARP BANKS

Table 5.6 summarizes abnormal shareholder returns for the TBTF, L-TARP, and No-TARP banks for 2000–8, 2002–8, and 2004–8. We use the Fama-French-Carhart four-factor model to compute these

Table 5.5 *Trades by All Insiders, Including Officers and Directors, 2000–8*

This table presents the stock ownership, trading, and compensation information for the CEOs of the 14 identified firms during 2000–8. Panel A presents the trades by firm. Panel B presents the trades by year, summing all 14 firms' trades. The value of buys and value of sales represent the cumulative cash flows realized through stock acquisitions or dispositions during the period. The value of option exercises represents the cost of exercising options, calculated as the number of options exercised multiplied by the exercise price. Net trades are calculated as all open-market sales of stock less open-market purchases and cost of exercising options. The ratio of net trading to posttrade Form 4 holdings represents the ratio of stock traded to the amount of stock owned following each trade, based on the information disclosed on the Form 4 filing with the SEC

Panel A: Trades by All Insiders, 2000–8, by Firm

Company	No. of buys	No. of option exercises	No. of sales	Value of buys	Value of option exercises	Value of sales	Value of net trades (sales – buys), 2000–8	Ratio of net trading to posttrade Form 4 holdings (average across years)
AIG	213	343	356	$845,336,054	$99,348,973	$28,607,422,695	$27,662,737,668	2.6%
Bank of America	101	179	1,929	622,740,251	491,762,285	2,599,516,805	1,485,014,269	17.5%
Bank of New York	1,018	254	2,926	577,717,648	112,548,478	5,940,553,101	5,250,286,975	8.3%
Bear Stearns	57	14	267	767,736,009	27,640,980	12,272,990,704	11,477,613,715	5.7%
Citigroup	77	520	1,268	3,197,466,366	1,528,122,839	23,688,319,446	18,962,730,241	11.7%

Countrywide Financial	20	1,077	1,241	1,155,309,803	324,718,206	8,427,583,600	6,947,555,591	11.9%
Goldman Sachs	12	7	1,950	5,547,803,152	10,090,836	37,725,387,806	32,167,493,818	12.2%
JP Morgan Chase	43	135	378	523,367,697	267,793,650	4,838,519,988	4,047,358,641	9.2%
Lehman Brothers	8	96	1,166	1,375,487,324	423,175,832	4,638,292,995	2,839,629,839	21.1%
Mellon Financial	26	207	574	145,818,377	44,642,852	1,666,696,004	1,476,234,775	7.7%
Merrill Lynch	14	75	692	519,773,797	70,775,414	2,804,184,934	2,213,635,723	14.2%
Morgan Stanley	32	114	485	615,610,159	197,124,169	9,661,073,884	8,848,339,556	5.7%
State Street	6	82	808	164,101,279	58,954,559	552,267,889	329,212,051	21.6%
Wells Fargo	44	351	647	1,086,739,992	698,093,602	5,057,961,919	3,273,128,325	16.7%
All firms	**1,671**	**3,454**	**14,687**	**$17,145,007,908**	**$4,354,792,675**	**$148,480,771,771**	**$126,980,971,188**	**9.7%**

Table 5.5 (cont.)

Panel B: Trades by All Insiders, 2000–8, by Year

Year	No. of buys	No. of option exercises	No. of sales	Value of buys	Value of option exercises	Value of sales	Value of net trades (sales – buys), 2000–8	Ratio of net trading to posttrade Form 4 holdings (average across years)
2000	246	579	1,344	$4,717,183,583	$1,157,085,399	$17,019,980,683	$11,145,711,701	19.7%
2001	230	323	1,167	2,270,309,993	252,859,783	20,829,849,138	18,306,679,362	9.3%
2002	242	273	819	2,089,804,441	307,255,898	8,275,345,275	5,878,284,936	19.5%
2003	182	371	1,305	1,180,185,242	347,236,054	14,316,327,557	12,788,906,261	6.6%
2004	193	468	1,853	1,281,017,607	481,009,313	18,373,207,366	16,611,180,446	5.9%
2005	192	529	1,816	1,108,591,232	405,368,091	15,342,500,464	13,828,541,141	6.1%
2006	168	504	2,417	2,612,637,201	853,471,050	20,348,529,583	16,882,421,332	10.8%
2007	95	324	2,522	1,606,875,211	397,003,384	26,880,668,526	24,876,789,931	5.1%
2008	123	83	1,444	278,403,398	153,503,703	7,094,363,180	6,662,456,079	3.5%
All years	1,671	3,454	14,687	$17,145,007,908	$4,354,792,675	$148,480,771,771	$126,980,971,188	9.7%

Panel (a): CEO Net Trades

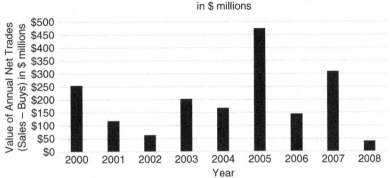

Value of Annual Net Trades (Sales – Buys) of
All 14 TBTF CEOs for the years 2000 through 2008
in $ millions

Panel (b): Insider Net Trades

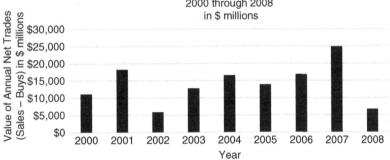

Value of Annual Net Trades (Sales – Buys) of
All TBTF Insiders (officers and directors) for the years
2000 through 2008
in $ millions

FIGURE 5.3 Value of CEO and insider net trades for 14 TBTF banks: (A)
CEO net trades; (B) insider net trades. TBTF bank CEOs and insiders sold
significantly large sums of their stock holdings in the years just prior to
the 2008 financial crash. Net trades are calculated as all open-market sales
of stock less open-market purchases and cost of exercising options.
(*Source:* Author's calculations.)

abnormal returns. Shareholders of the No-TARP banks enjoyed significantly more positive returns than TARP bank shareholders for
2000–8, 2002–8, and 2004–8. Shareholders of the No-TARP banks
also enjoyed significantly more positive returns than L-TARP bank
shareholders for these periods. This evidence, coupled with the

Table 5.6 *Fama-French-Carhart Four-Factor Abnormal Return Regressions*
This table presents the summary results from Carhart (1997) four-factor
regressions performed on each of the three samples – No-TARP, L-TARP,
and TBTF – as well as on arbitrage portfolios comparing the No-TARP
sample with each of the others. Equally weighted portfolios are formed
using daily returns for all firms within each sample. These daily portfolio
returns are then regressed in the model:

$$R_{\text{Portfolio}-t} = \alpha + \beta_1 (R_{\text{Mkt}} - R_f)_t + \beta_2 (\text{SMB})_t + \beta_3 (\text{HML})_t + \beta_4 (\text{UMD})_t + \varepsilon_t$$

where $R_{\text{Mkt}} - R_f$ is the market factor, or the excess return on the
market portfolio; SMB is the size factor, or the excess return on a
portfolio long small company stocks and short large company stocks;
HML is the value factor, or the excess return on a portfolio long high
book-to-market stocks and short low book-to-market stocks; and
UMD is the momentum factor, or the excess return on a portfolio
long recent winners and short recent losers. Each of these four factors
is obtained from Ken French's website. Therefore, α represents the
abnormal return on each of the bank portfolios after controlling for
each of these four factors. $\alpha_{\text{No-TARP}}$ is the abnormal return for the 37
No-TARP firms, $\alpha_{\text{L-TARP}}$ is the abnormal return for the 49 L-TARP
firms, and α_{TBTF} is the abnormal return for the 14 TBTF firms. Two
arbitrage portfolios are formed using the bank portfolios: $\alpha_{\text{No-TARP}} -$
$_{\text{TBTF}}$ is the abnormal return for a portfolio long the 37 No-TARP firms
and short the 14 TBTF firms, and $\alpha_{\text{No-TARP-L-TARP}}$ is the abnormal
return for a portfolio long the 37 No-TARP firms and short the 49 L-
TARP firms. Abnormal returns are provided for each of the three
portfolios over each of three time periods: all years or 2000–8, 2002–
8, and, 2004–8. Abnormal returns are provided with robust t-statistics
in parentheses.

| | | Abnormal returns: *No-TARP – TBTF* | | |
		$\alpha_{\text{No-TARP}}$	α_{TBTF}	$\alpha_{\text{No-TARP – TBTF}}$
(1)	All years, daily	0.033	−0.002	0.035
		(1.90)	(0.09)	(2.45)
(2)	2002–8, daily	0.023	−0.021	0.043

Table 5.6 *(cont.)*

		Abnormal returns: *No-TARP – TBTF*		
		$\alpha_{\text{No-TARP}}$	α_{TBTF}	$\alpha_{\text{No-TARP – TBTF}}$
		(2.20)	(0.77)	(2.64)
(3)	2004–8, daily	0.021	–0.030	0.051
		(1.91)	(0.89)	(2.66)
		Abnormal Returns: *No-TARP – L-TARP*		
		$\alpha_{\text{No-TARP}}$	$\alpha_{\text{L-TARP}}$	$\alpha_{\text{No-TARP – L-TARP}}$
(1)	All years, daily	0.033	0.005	0.028
		(1.90)	(0.24)	(2.48)
(2)	2002–8, daily	0.023	–0.001	0.023
		(2.20)	(0.04)	(1.89)
(3)	2004–, daily	0.021	–0.005	0.025
		(1.91)	(0.17)	(1.62)

evidence in Tables 5.4 and 5.5, is consistent with the notion of a positive correlation between bank CEOs retaining more of the stock they receive as incentive compensation and their shareholders' return. We urge caution in interpreting this evidence because of selection bias; specifically, banks that were performing well are unlikely to have requested or received TARP funds.[9]

5.9   RISK-TAKING BY TBTF, L-TARP, AND NO-TARP BANKS

In the model developed earlier we suggest that TBTF managers engaged in high-risk (and negative net present value) investment strategies during 2000–8. As noted earlier, the annual stock sales by TBTF bank CEOs (compared with L-TARP and No-TARP bank CEOs) and their stock return during 2000–8 provide evidence consistent with this argument. In this section we provide more direct evidence on the risk-taking characteristics of the TBTF banks.

The banking literature has used the Z-score as a measure of bank risk (e.g., see Boyd and Runkle 1993; Laeven and Levine 2009; Houston et al. 2010). The Z-score measures a bank's distance from insolvency. More specifically, the Z-score is the number of standard deviations below the mean bank profit by which the profit would have to fall before the bank's equity loses all value. A high Z-score suggests a more stable bank. The evidence in columns (1) and (2) in Table 5.7 suggests that the Z-scores of TBTF banks are significantly lower than the Z-scores of No-TARP banks and that the Z-scores of L-TARP banks are also significantly lower than the Z-scores of No-TARP banks.

More recently, Chesney, Stromberg, and Wagner (2010) have suggested that asset write-downs are a good indicator of bank risk-taking. The evidence in columns (3), (4), and (5) in Table 5.7 suggests that write-downs (as a percentage of total assets) of TBTF banks are significantly greater than the write-downs (as a percentage of total assets) of No-TARP banks, as are the write-downs of L-TARP banks relative to No-TARP banks.

Finally, Gande and Kalpathy (2011) consider whether or not a bank borrows capital from various Fed bailout programs and the amount of such capital as a measure of bank risk-taking. We find that the TBTF banks borrowed significantly more than the L-TARP and No-TARP banks in terms of both absolute dollars and as a percentage of their assets.

5.10 ROBUSTNESS CHECK: ABNORMAL TRADING ACTIVITY

What is the appropriate amount of insider trading? How much should CEOs be selling? We partially addressed these questions in Section 5.6, comparing the nominal amount of trading across the three subsamples of banks. We investigate this question further here. The primary variable in our study – net trades – compares the buys, sales, and option exercises made by CEOs at the 100 financial institutions from 2000 to 2008.

Table 5.2 shows the absolute number of net trades and the net trades as a proportion of the CEO's stock ownership for each of the 14 TBTF firms. We suggest that higher numbers of net trades are

Table 5.7 *Risk Factors, Z-Scores, and Write-Downs*

This table presents statistics on the Z-score for each subsample as of the end of 2007 in column (1). This table also presents the statistics on the cumulative firm write-downs during 2007 and 2008 for each subsample in column (3) and the ratio of cumulative write-downs during 2007 and 2008 to end-of-2007 total assets in column (4). Column (2) shows the statistical significance of the differences in Z-scores of the TBTF and L-TARP bank subsamples relative to the No-TARP bank subsample. Column (5) shows the statistical significance of the differences in the ratio of write-downs to assets of the TBTF and L-TARP bank subsamples relative to the No-TARP bank subsample.

	Z-score	Vs. No-TARP sample	Write-down ($M)	Write-down-to-assets	Vs. No-TARP sample
	(1)	(2)	(3)	(4)	(5)
			TBTF firms ($n = 14$)		
Total amount ($m)	—		$293,035.0	—	
Average	19.947	***	$22,541.2	3.760%	***
25th percentile	8.919		$6,039.0	1.748%	***
Median	19.756	*	$19,872.0	3.264%	***
75th percentile	24.446	***	$33,100.0	5.133%	***

Table 5.7 (cont.)

	Z-score (1)	Vs. No-TARP sample (2)	Write-down ($M) (3)	Write-down-to-assets (4)	Vs. No-TARP sample (5)
			L-TARP firms (n = 49)		
Total amount ($M)	—		$158,777.4	—	
Average	26.242	**	$3,240.4	5.635%	***
25th percentile	10.862	**	$158.9	1.992%	***
Median	20.972		$410.2	3.425%	***
75th percentile	39.146	***	$1,143.0	6.334%	***
			No-TARP firms (n = 37)		
Total amount ($M)	—		$64,016.2	—	
Average	31.359		$2,207.5	14.829%	
25th percentile	8.506		$44.1	0.473%	
Median	21.994		$81.2	1.444%	
75th percentile	51.420		$794.1	2.608%	

* Indicates statistically different ratios at the 10% level; ** indicates statistically different ratios at the 5% level; *** indicates statistically different ratios at the 1% level.

consistent with the managerial incentives hypothesis, that CEOs sell stock to avoid the future negative repercussions of excessive risk-taking. But CEOs may decide to sell stock for many reasons other than to cash out, such as for liquidity and diversification purposes. Table 5.4 compares the net trades for the TBTF bank CEOs with the net trades of the L-TARP and No-TARP bank CEOs. There we see that the TBTF bank CEOs sold more stock than the other CEOs, both in absolute terms and as a proportion of their stock ownership.

What this analysis possibly ignores is the heterogeneity of our three subsamples. Large TBTF banks such as Citigroup and Goldman Sachs are very different from many smaller L-TARP and No-TARP banks in terms of size, operations, structure, and markets. Analyzing differences in net trades without accounting for these differences may produce inappropriate inferences; hence, we rely on the CEO and insider trading literature to control for this heterogeneity.

We estimate a Tobit model based on Aggarwal and Semwick (1999), Jenter (2005), Rozeff and Zaman (1998), and Seyhun (1986). These authors suggest the following determinants of CEO trading (in the shares of their firms' stock): firm size, book-to-market ratio, annual stock return for the prior year, stock volatility for the current year, CEO total compensation, percent CEO equity compensation (amount of equity compensation divided by total compensation for the prior year), and CEO stock holdings (value of the CEO's beneficial stock ownership at the end of the prior year).

The results in Table 5.8 highlight that even after controlling for bank and CEO characteristics, the CEOs at the TBTF firms engaged in significantly more discretionary stock sales than the No-TARP bank CEOs. More precisely, the Tobit model implies, after controlling for bank and CEO characteristics (including bank size), that the CEOs of the TBTF banks sold stock annually on average worth $36.9 million more than the No-TARP bank CEOs.

Table 5.8 *Determinants of CEO Trading*
This table presents the results from a Tobit estimation of the determinants of CEO net trades for 2000–8. The dependent variable is *net trades*, or (stock sales – stock purchases – option exercises). *Assets* are the natural logarithm of current-year assets. *Book-to-market ratio* is the book value of equity divided by market value of equity for the current year. *Return* is the annual stock return for the prior year. *Stock volatility* is the standard deviation of daily stock returns for the current year. *CEO total compensation* is the natural logarithm of all cash and equity compensation in the prior year. *Percent CEO equity compensation* is the amount of equity compensation divided by total compensation for the prior year. *CEO stock holdings* are the natural logarithm of the dollar value of the CEO's beneficial stock ownership at the end of the prior year. *TBTF dummy* is equal to 1 if the firm is one of the 14 TBTF firms and 0 otherwise. *L-TARP dummy* is equal to 1 if the firm in one of the 49 L-TARP firms and 0 otherwise. The model includes intercepts, year dummy variables, and firm fixed effects not tabulated for conciseness.

$$\begin{aligned} \text{Net Trades}_{i,t} = {} & \text{Assets}_{i,t} + \text{Book} - \text{to} - \text{Market}_{i,t} + \text{Stock Return}_{i,t-1} \\ & + \text{Stock Volatility}_{i,t} + \text{CEO Total Compensation}_{i,t-1} \\ & + \text{Percent CEO Equity Compensation}_{i,t-1} \\ & + \text{CEO StockHoldings}_{i,t-1} + \text{TBTF Dummy}_i \\ & + \text{L} - \text{TARP Dummy}_i \end{aligned}$$

	Dependent variable: Net Trades$_t$
Assets (log)$_t$	−1.232*** (0.003)
Book-to-Market$_t$	−4.154*** (0.002)
Return$_{t-1}$	−0.179 (0.904)
Stock Volatility$_t$	58.793* (0.086)
CEO Total Compensation$_{t-1}$	2.170*** (0.001)
CEO Percent Equity Compensation$_{t-1}$	9.649*** (0.000)
CEO Equity Holdings (log)$_{t-1}$	1.384*** (0.000)
TBTF Dummy	**4.198** (0.019)
L-Tarp Dummy	1.547 (0.117)
Number of observations	883
Year controls	Yes
Firm fixed effects	Yes

Coefficients are presented with *p*-values in parentheses. Statistical significance is denoted by *for 10%, **for 5%, and ***for 1%.

5.11   RELATED PAPERS

Fahlenbrach and Stulz (2011) studied the performance of 98 US banks over July 2007–December 2008 and found no evidence that banks with higher CEO option pay performed worse and no evidence that those with higher CEO equity ownership performed better during the crisis using both stock and accounting measures of performance. They measured CEOs' alignment with shareholder interests by how sensitive the CEOs' stock and option portfolios were to changes in the banks' stock value. The findings were the same for banks that received government assistance under the TARP and those that did not. They further reported that bank CEOs suffered substantial losses on their equity holdings and stock sales during the crisis, in support of their view that bank executives were acting in share-holders' interest regarding precrisis risk-taking.[10] In contrast, and as detailed earlier, we find that the precrisis level of risk of TBTF banks was much higher than that of the No-TARP banks and that executives of the TBTF banks sold much more of their common-stock holdings precrisis (2000–7) than executives of the No-TARP banks. Because those bank executives were able to realize a substan-tial amount on their equity by sales in the precrisis period compared with the large losses the executives experienced on their equity stakes during the crisis (2008), we suggest that compensation incen-tives led to excessive risk-taking (in value-reducing investment and trading strategies).[11]

Balachandran, Kogut, and Harnal (2010) studied management risk-taking incentives in financial firms during the crisis. They docu-mented that financial firms whose executives had a higher proportion of equity compensation had higher risk, measured by the probability of default, during the crisis. They concluded that "managers were over-incentivized to take on excessive risk." Bhattacharyya and Purnanandam (2011) found that banks whose CEOs' compensation had higher sensitivity to short-term earnings experienced higher mortgage default rates in the crisis and interpreted their findings as consistent with bank CEOs assuming excessive risk to boost short-term earnings.

Cziraki (2015) focused on the insider trading of CEOs and independent directors for a sample of 100 banks during 1996–2009. He documented that insider trading prior to the crisis (mid-2006 through mid-2007) is correlated with the performance of these banks during the crisis period (July 2007–December 2008). Specifically, banks whose insiders sold more stock prior to the crisis performed worse during the crisis. Furthermore, this relation is stronger for banks with a greater exposure to the residential real estate market. He concluded "that bank executives understood the exposures of their bank to housing prices and reduced their stockholdings during 2006." Note that Cziraki's evidence and conclusions are consistent with ours, noted earlier: to wit, bank executives were able to realize a substantial amount on their stock holdings (received as part of their incentive compensation) by sales in the precrisis period (2000–7) compared with the large losses the executives experienced on their equity stakes during the crisis (2008), and bank executive compensation incentives led to excessive risk-taking (in value-reducing investment and trading strategies). We also note that our and Cziraki's evidence and conclusions are at odds with those of Fahlenbrach and Stulz, who did not consider the *years prior to* July 2007 when bank executives sold substantial amounts of their stock holdings (received as part of their incentive compensation) – possibly in anticipation of significant future declines in their banks' share prices as the excessively risky investment and trading strategies soured.

Rather than study executive compensation incentives, Acharya et al. (2013) investigated bank holding company performance and nonexecutive compensation. They found that firms whose nonexecutives' precrisis compensation was sensitive only to increases in revenue took higher (excessive) risk and consequently performed worse during the financial crisis.[12] As they interpreted the data, "[T]he more sensitive non-executive compensation policies to short-term bank performance, the higher the incentives of middle-level managers to increase the volume of bank activities at the expense of the quality of the acquired positions," and this risk-taking in the crisis resulted in significant declines in firm value. Their findings are consistent with anecdotal instances of lower-level employees' trading activities producing staggering losses, such as JP Morgan's "London whale" in 2012 or Barings Bank's Nick Leeson in the early 1990s.

5.12 SUMMARY OF EVIDENCE ON BANK EXECUTIVE COMPENSATION AND RISK-TAKING

We studied the executive compensation structure in the largest 14 US financial institutions during 2000-8 and compared it with that of CEOs of 37 US banks that neither sought nor received TARP funds. We focused on the CEOs' buys and sells of their banks' stock, purchases of stock via option exercise, and their salaries and bonuses during 2000-8. We considered the capital losses these CEOs incurred due to the dramatic share price declines in 2008. We compared the shareholder returns for these 14 TBTF banks and the 37 No-TARP banks. We considered three measures of risk-taking by these banks: the bank's Z-score, the bank's asset write-downs, and whether or not a bank borrows capital from various Fed bailout programs and the amount of such capital. Finally, we implemented a battery of robustness checks including construction of a Tobit model of expected CEO trading based on the extant literature on insider and CEO trading, and we estimated abnormal CEO trading based on that Tobit model.

We found that TBTF bank CEOs were able to realize a significantly greater amount on their common-stock sales in the precrisis period (2000-7) compared with the large losses the executives experienced on their equity stake during the crisis (2008). Additionally, stock sales by TBTF bank CEOs was significantly greater than stock sales by No-TARP bank CEOs in the precrisis period in both absolute and relative (compared with their beginning-of-period holdings) terms. Finally, several different bank risk-taking measures suggested that TBTF banks were significantly riskier than No-TARP banks. Our results are mostly consistent with the argument that incentives generated by executive compensation programs are positively correlated with excessive risk-taking by banks. Also, our results are not consistent with the argument that the poor performance of the TBTF banks during the crisis was the result of unforeseen risk.

6   Executive Compensation Reform

This chapter introduces our proposal to refashion bank incentive compensation to motivate bank managers to focus on creating and sustaining long-term shareholder value, and to reduce the possibility that executives will undertake excessively risky and value-destroying trading or operating strategies. We then compare our proposal to the approach taken by legislatures and bank regulators, to recent proposals by six US federal agencies and another by the UK Prime Minister's office, and to the class of proposals advocating debt-based rather than equity-based compensation.

6.1   CRITERIA FOR EVALUATING EXECUTIVE COMPENSATION POLICIES

We suggest three criteria for evaluating executive compensation reform policies[1]:

1. Simplicity,
2. Transparency, and
3. Focus on creating and sustaining long-term shareholder value.

A simple and transparent incentive compensation structure is desirable for at least three reasons. First, the financial sector is particularly fast-moving, rendering it difficult to predict what risks may emerge as products and markets develop and how individuals respond to regulatory and contractual incentives can alter risk in unanticipated ways that can evolve in complicated ways. Moreover, in today's context of large and interconnected financial institutions and complex financial instruments, banks must grapple with unknown and unknowable risks.[2] As a consequence, the more complicated and opaque incentive package is, the more difficult it will be to determine how individuals will respond and what risks will or will not be incurred. Second, because shareholders are now required to vote on CEO compensation packages, a simple incentive structure is easier for them to understand and evaluate, reducing the need to rely on third-party vendors of proxy voting advice, the value of which has been the subject of considerable controversy.[3,4] Third, simplicity and transparency in incentive compensation packages mitigate public skepticism toward high levels of executive pay in conjunction with poor performance, particularly when a firm's failure implicates the public fisc. Finally, the focus on creating and sustaining long-term shareholder value would channel management's attention to the longer-term profitability of an investment or trading strategy. Business and legal scholars posit that managers should act in the best interests of long-term shareholders – what better way to do this than to tie management incentive compensation to long-term share price!

6.2   THE RESTRICTED EQUITY PROPOSAL

We propose that the incentive compensation of bank executives should consist only of restricted equity (restricted stock and restricted stock option) – restricted in the sense that the individual cannot sell the shares or exercise the options for one to three years after his or her last day in office. We refer to this as the *restricted equity proposal.* Many current compensation contracts require the forfeiture of restricted shares when an executive leaves the firm. Quite to the contrary, we are suggesting that restricted shares (under our restricted equity proposal) *not* be forfeited when the executive departs. In fact, we are advocating that, in general, restricted shares *only vest* after the executive leaves the bank.

If bank CEOs are offered incentive compensation contracts consistent with the restricted equity proposal, then they would have more high-powered incentives not to invest in the high-risk but unprofitable (over the long term) projects and trading strategies.[5] These CEOs would be required to hold these shares and options not only for the duration of their employment at the bank but also for one to three years subsequent to their retirement or resignation. If the trading strategy resulted in an unexpected positive cash flow in a certain year prior to the CEO's retirement or resignation, the bank's share price would go up, the CEO's net worth would go up on paper, but the CEO would not be able to liquidate his or her stockholdings. The CEO would have to make an assessment of the likelihood of the large negative cash flow outcome during the years he or she continued to be employed at the bank plus one to three additional years. After making such an assessment, a CEO would presumably be less likely to authorize or encourage the high-risk but unprofitable (over the long term) projects and trading strategies in the first place. The long-term feature of the restricted equity proposal's compensation package would operate to curb optimistic estimates of a project's long-term profitability by using high-powered financial incentives to prod the executive to attend to, and hence estimate more assiduously, all of a project's cash flows rather than solely those in the near term. If a bank does not engage in the long-term unprofitable investment project or trading strategy, then this would, of course, also serve the interests of its long-term shareholders.

Under the restricted equity proposal, all incentive compensation would be driven by total shareholder return. Specifically, we are recommending that none of the manager executive compensation be directly related to accounting-based measures of performance, such as return on capital, return on equity, and earnings per share. Accounting-based measures of performance tend to mostly focus on short-term performance. As we saw in Chapter 5, a focus on short-term performance by managers of "too big to fail" (TBTF) banks led to a serious misalignment of interest between bank managers and long-term shareholders. Our focus on total shareholder return is consistent with a recent survey of Fortune 500 directors conducted by the Rock Center for Corporate Governance at Stanford University.[6] The survey found that 51% of Fortune 500 directors consider total shareholder return to be the best measure of company performance compared with accounting-based measures such as return on capital and earnings per share.

We have suggested that the time frame extend to one to three years after retirement, but we would leave the specific horizon to the board compensation committee, to which the proposal is addressed.[7] The rationale for this extended time frame is to maintain incentives for an executive in an "end game" situation, that is, an individual making decisions when he or she is reaching retirement. At the shorter end of our proposal, management's discretionary authority to manage earnings under current US accounting conventions unravels within a one- to two-year period, while at the longer end we think three years is a reasonable period in which at least the intermediate-term results of executives' decisions will be realized.

How long would the restricted equity vesting period last in practice? Studies report that the median tenure for bank CEOs is between five and seven years.[8] Hence, on average, a CEO can expect to wait six to ten years before being allowed to sell shares or exercise options.[9] In the non–public corporation setting, it is quite common for top executives to wait for six to ten years before receiving a substantial portion of their compensation for work performed earlier. For instance, the general partners of private equity partnerships typically receive their compensation in two parts, the more substantial of which, carried interest (usually 20% of the lifetime profits generated by the partnership), is realized toward the end of the life of the partnerships, usually seven to ten years.[10] The widespread use of such a deferred compensation structure in a real-world setting where manager-owner conflicts of interest are thought to be better managed suggests that our proposal could substantially improve bank managers' incentives despite well-known differences between the private equity and public company operating environments. A further benefit of the proposal's vesting period is that because a CEO would be exposed to the impact of decisions made by his or her successor, the executive will focus more attentively on succession planning.[11,12]

How long would the vesting period last in the event of a change in control? We suggest that the same process be followed regarding the acceleration (or the lack thereof) of the vesting period for unvested stock and unvested stock options as is the case currently for the particular company. This would ensure that under the restricted equity proposal there is no additional incentive or disincentive for the CEO to seek out or accept a takeover or merger bid.

6.3   CAVEATS TO THE RESTRICTED EQUITY PROPOSAL

We note three important caveats. First, if executives are required to hold restricted shares and options, they would most likely be underdiversified.[13] Second, if executives are required to hold restricted shares and options postretirement, they may be concerned about a lack of liquidity. Third, the proposal could lead to early management departures as executives seek to convert illiquid shares and options into more liquid assets (after the one- to three-year waiting period).

The deliberate underdiversification brought about by being subject to a restricted equity plan – more of the individual's wealth will be tied to the firm because he or she cannot liquidate accumulated incentive equity payments – would lower the risk-adjusted expected return for the executive. One means of bringing an executive's risk-adjusted expected return back up to the previous level would be to increase the expected return by granting additional restricted shares and options to the executive. We would therefore expect that the amount of equity awarded under the restricted equity proposal will be *higher* than that awarded under a short-term incentive plan.

Executives might be expected to seek to reduce the underdiversification effect by entering into swap contracts that transform their restricted positions into liquid investments. To ensure that the incentive effects of restricted stock and options are not undone by self-help efforts at diversification, executives participating in such compensation plans should be prohibited from engaging in transactions, such as equity swaps or borrowing arrangements, that hedge the firm-specific risk from their having to hold restricted stock and options (where not already restricted by law).[14]

Of course, derivative transactions based on other securities, such as a financial industry stock index, could be used to undo the executives' interest in the restricted shares. To address this possibility, approval of the compensation committee or board of directors should be required for other (non-firm-specific) derivative transactions such as put options on a broader basket of securities. In addition, to ensure that underdiversification does not result in managers taking on a suboptimal level of risk compared to the risk preferences of shareholders (behavior that may be of particular concern as an aging executive nears retirement and may wish to protect the value of accrued shares), the incentive plan can be fine-tuned to provide a higher proportion in restricted options than restricted shares to increase the individual's incentive to take risk.

Concerns regarding lack of liquidity and early departure are also valid. To address these concerns, we recommended that managers be allowed to liquidate annually a modest fraction of their awarded incentive restricted shares and options of between 5% and 10%. The requirement that they must retain the great bulk of the shares several years until after retirement or departure will provide a sufficient incentive to advance long-term shareholder interests. We further propose, to mitigate liquidity and early departure concerns, that the annual corporate tax deduction for non-incentive-based compensation for individuals whose incentive compensation consists solely of a restricted equity plan be raised to $2 million.[15] Permitting 5% to 10% of each year's incentive compensation to vest and be sold will mitigate an early departure concern, particularly for lower-level managers whose bonuses may not be as large as and whose employment horizons would likely be longer than those of CEOs. We are also skeptical that the restricted equity plan will induce an onslaught of early departures by younger executives seeking to lock-in stock gains: executives who develop a reputation for early departures from firms are likely to damage their future career opportunities.

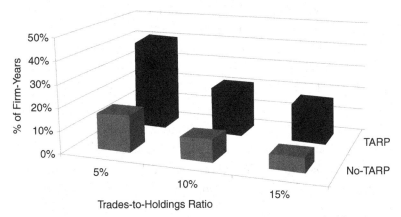

CEO Net Trades-to-Beginning Holdings
% of firm-years with Trades-to-Holdings ratio greater than:

FIGURE 6.1 Ratio of bank CEOs' net trades to beginning holdings 2000–8.
The figure shows the distribution of the percentage of firm years, over the
time period 2000–8, within two samples of bank CEOs, those of 14 firms
that received TARP funds (TARP banks, also denoted in the text as TBTF
banks) and those of 37 banks that were not TARP recipients (No-TARP
banks, banks that did not need taxpayer-funded bailout funds), when the
ratio of the CEOs' net trades, calculated as all open-market sales of stock
less open-market purchases and cost of exercising options, to the CEOs'
stock holdings, including beneficial ownership and vested stock and
exercisable options, at the beginning of the year, *exceeded* 5%, 10%, or
15%. The figure highlights the fact that it is rare for CEOs of banks that
did not need taxpayer-funded bailout funds to liquidate more than 10% of
their holdings in any given year. (*Source:* Author's calculations.)

We are also sensitive to potential tax liabilities that the restricted
equity proposal might generate for an executive. To the extent an
individual incurs a tax liability from receiving restricted shares and
options that is greater than the amount permitted to be liquidated in
the current year, then under our proposal that individual would be
allowed to sell enough additional shares (and/or exercise enough additional options) to pay the additional taxes.

Figure 6.1 provides an empirical perspective on the recommendation concerning the appropriate percentage of annual liquidations.

It shows the percentage of firm-years during 2000–8 in which US bank CEOs sold more than 5%, 10%, or 15% of the beginning holdings in any particular year during 2000–8. TARP recipient bank CEOs sold more than 5% of beginning holdings in 41% of the firm-years compared to 16% of firm-years for the CEOs of non-TARP recipients. They also sold more than 15% of beginning holdings in 17% of the firm-years compared to 6% of firm-years for the non-TARP recipient firm CEOs. These data provide the empirical rationale for allowing bank CEOs to liquidate 5% to 10% of their stock and option holdings in a particular year. More specifically, the experience of non-TARP recipient bank CEOs suggests that it is rare for CEOs (whose banks did not need bailout funds) to liquidate more than 10% of their holdings in any given year.

Given these data, the more limited equity shares that we would permit to be annually liquidated may seem low compared with the amounts that bank executives have been able to realize in the past (i.e., in the precrisis years). However, this is not necessarily the case when a longer time frame is considered. The proposal only limits the annual *cash* payoffs the executives can realize. The present value of all salary and stock compensation can be higher than bank managers have received historically because the amount of restricted stock that can be awarded to a bank manager is essentially unlimited per our proposal. Of course, the higher value would only be realized were the managers to invest in projects that lead to value creation that persists in the long term. In addition, concern over the proposal's impact on liquidity needs or early departures, when contrasting it with the bank CEOs' past stock sales, can stand a bit of perspective. Consider as a reference point the fact that the adjusted gross income (AGI) of the top 0.1% in 2004 had a threshold of $1.4 million,[16] while in 2011 the AGI cutoff for the top 0.1% was $1.7 million.[17] Accordingly, permitting executives a cash salary of $2 million and the ability to liquidate 5% to 10% of annual incentive compensation is far from financially punitive.

The restricted equity proposal will no doubt encourage managers to seek a considerably higher proportion of fixed cash salaries to compensate for the restricted ability to realize the value of equity incentive awards. But we posit that the higher deductible cash base ($2 million), along with the modest amount of realizable equity gains, should both mitigate such efforts by management and decrease the probability that the members of compensation committees will perceive a need to succumb to such efforts. Indeed, there is evidence that bank directors are not potted plants when it comes to executive compensation, because they adjust executives' incentive compensation in response to the level of prior risk-taking, although the feedback loop was not present at a subset of the very largest institutions.[18]

There are other potential concerns with our restricted equity proposal. For example, some have suggested that our proposal would disincentivize the banks' use of various derivative contracts for corporate business purposes. If these derivative contracts are value-increasing investment strategies, then these strategies should not be discouraged – nor does our proposal discourages such value-increasing strategies. However, if these derivative contracts are value-decreasing investment strategies, then these strategies should be discouraged – our restricted equity proposal discourages such value-decreasing strategies by negatively affecting the stock and stock option holdings of bank managers. Recall that our restricted equity proposal requires bank managers to hold their shares and options for one to three years after their last day in office; hence they have to carefully evaluate the long-term value impact of a particular derivative contract, and in so doing, they will serve the interests of long-term shareholders.

Another concern: How would the restricted equity proposal address stock market downturns that are not the fault of CEOs and occur after they leave office? In an efficient market, stock market downturns are unpredictable. To be fair, it is possible that a stock market downturn could occur immediately after a manager leaves office. To address this concern, we suggested earlier that managers be allowed to sell 5% to 10% of their shares and options every year. Additionally, to compensate managers for the additional risk of the long holding period, we have suggested that their stock and stock option incentive packages be larger (than the current situation, where they are not required to hold the shares and options for such long periods).

6.4   RESTRICTED EQUITY PROPOSAL AND NET CEO PAYOFF

One way to evaluate the effectiveness of the restricted equity proposal is to analyze the impact on the net CEO payoffs to the CEOs of the TBTF banks *if* the restricted equity proposal had been adopted by these banks (rather, their corporate boards) prior to 2000. In Table 6.1, Panel A, no adjustment has been made to the cash compensation of the TBTF bank CEOs, but we consider scenarios where their annual stock sales are limited to 5%, 10%, and 15%, respectively, of the amount of stock they owned at the start of that year. Without any cash compensation restriction or annual stock sales restriction, the mean net CEO payoff for the TBTF bank CEOs during 2000–8 was $46.3 million (the median was $19.5 million); with a 5% sales restriction, the mean net CEO payoff for the TBTF bank CEOs during 2000–8 would have been a *loss* of $114.1 million (the median a *loss* of $11.1 million). Also, with a 10% sales restriction, the mean net CEO payoff for the TBTF bank CEOs during 2000–8 would have been a *loss* of $85.2 million (the median a *loss* of $1.0 million). Hence an annual stock sale restriction of about 5% would have imposed a negative compensation impact (negative net CEO payoff) on the TBTF bank CEOs – *this is the disciplining effect of the restricted equity proposal and, correspondingly, would have served to discourage the TBTF bank CEOs from engaging in high-risk but negative net present value (NPV) projects during 2000–8.* This disciplining effect is much stronger when we restrict cash compensation to $2 million annually (and paying the remainder of the cash compensation in stock) (see Table 6.1, Panel B).

Table 6.1 *Restricted Equity Proposal's Impact on Net CEO Payoff*

Panel A: No Adjustment to Cash Compensation

	Value of stock holdings, beginning of 2000	Total net trades, 2000–8 (A)	Total cash compensation, 2000–8 (B)	CEO payoff, 2000–8 (A) + (B)	Estimated value lost, 2008 (C)	Net CEO payoff, 2000–8 (A) + (B) + (C)
TBTF firms (n = 14): no limit on cash compensation or stock sales						
Mean values	$494,177,483	$126,528,838	$63,659,807	$190,188,646	($143,834,511)	$46,354,134
Median values	$166,266,190	$66,842,520	$65,645,943	$144,938,011	($78,475,455)	$19,490,420
TBTF firms: no limit on cash compensation, 5% limit on stock sales						
Mean values	$494,177,483	$74,388,500	$63,659,807	$138,048,308	($252,191,109)	($114,142,802)
Median values	$166,266,190	$43,950,140	$65,645,943	$127,101,247	($142,463,456)	($11,082,266)
TBTF firms: no limit on cash compensation; 10% limit on stock sales						
Mean values	$494,177,483	$91,236,910	$63,659,807	$154,896,717	($240,128,970)	($85,232,253)
Median values	$166,266,190	$52,585,347	$65,645,943	$134,258,269	($134,639,108)	($1,003,982)
TBTF firms: no limit on cash compensation, 15% limit on stock sales						
Mean values	$494,177,483	$115,188,624	$63,659,807	$178,848,431	($226,036,842)	($47,188,411)
Median values	$166,266,190	$64,050,260	$65,645,943	$141,392,724	($129,640,367)	$11,908,780

Note: Different (5%, 10%, 15%) limits on stock sales. Net trades are calculated as all open-market sales of stock less open-market purchases and cost of exercising options.

Panel B: Annual Compensation Limited to $2 Million (Remaining Cash Compensation Assumed as Paid in Stock)

	Value of stock holdings, beginning of 2000	Total net trades, 2000–8 (A)	Total cash compensation, 2000–8 (B)	CEO payoff, 2000–8 (A) + (B)	Estimated value lost, 2008 (C)	Net CEO payoff, 2000–8 (A) + (B) + (C)
TBTF firms (n = 14): no limit on cash compensation or stock sales						
Mean values	$494,177,483	$126,528,838	$63,659,807	$190,188,646	($143,834,511)	$46,354,134
Median values	$166,266,190	$66,842,520	$65,645,943	$144,938,011	($78,475,455)	$19,490,420
TBTF firms: 5% limit on stock sales and annual cash compensation limit of $2 million						
Mean values	$494,177,483	$77,169,748	$14,916,148	$92,085,896	($271,361,890)	($179,275,994)
Median values	$166,266,190	$48,961,305	$14,586,768	$64,826,910	($150,349,823)	($99,085,632)
TBTF firms: 10% limit on stock sales and annual cash compensation limit of $2 million						
Mean values	$494,177,483	$96,361,808	$14,916,148	$111,277,956	($255,361,804)	($144,083,848)
Median values	$166,266,190	$55,316,891	$14,586,768	$71,036,125	($139,025,867)	($20,036,816)
TBTF firms: 15% limit on stock sales and annual cash compensation limit of $2 million						
Mean values	$494,177,483	$117,028,234	$14,916,148	$131,944,382	($230,025,197)	($98,080,815)
Median values	$166,266,190	$66,163,971	$14,586,768	$82,694,813	($132,158,964)	$6,254,813

Note: Different (5%, 10%, 15%) limits on stock sales. Net trades are calculated as all open-market sales of stock less open-market purchases and cost of exercising options.

Figure 6.2A illustrates the median net CEO payoffs for the TBTF bank CEOs during 2000–8 with no restriction on cash compensation and scenarios where annual stock sales are limited to 5%, 10%, and 15%, respectively, of the amount of stock owned by the CEOs at the start of that year. Figure 6.2B illustrates the median net CEO payoffs for the TBTF bank CEOs during 2000–8 with $2 million annual restriction on cash compensation (and paying the remainder of the cash compensation in stock) and scenarios where their annual stock sales are limited to 5%, 10%, and 15%, respectively, of the amount of stock the CEOs owned at the start of that year. These figures highlight the empirical fact that if, per our restricted equity proposal, the TBTF bank CEOs' stock sales were limited to about 5% of the amount they owned in the beginning of that year, this would have imposed a negative compensation impact (negative net CEO payoff) when considering the entire 2000–8 period. The negative compensation impact would have discouraged the TBTF bank CEOs from investing in high-risk but value-destroying investment projects and trading strategies.

6.5 WHO WILL IMPLEMENT THE RESTRICTED EQUITY PROPOSAL?

Given the amount of government regulation already directed at banks' incentive compensation plans, which may well have perverse effects, we are not advocating adopting our proposal solely as an additional regulation, although in our judgment its adoption would be much more efficacious than existing regulations. Rather, our proposal is directed at bank compensation committees, who, we urge, should voluntarily adopt a restricted equity plan as the preferred mechanism for aligning management's incentives with long-term shareholder wealth creation and to mitigate the taking of excessive risk. In implementing the proposal, we think that corporate boards should be the principal decision makers regarding:

(A)

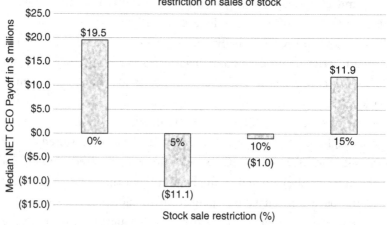

(B)

FIGURE 6.2 (A) Impact of stock sales restrictions on net CEO payoff. This panel highlights that if, per our restricted equity proposal, the TBTF bank CEOs' stock sales were limited to about 5% of the amount they owned at the beginning of that year, this would have imposed a negative compensation impact (negative net CEO payoff) when considering the entire 2000–8 period. The negative compensation impact would have

1. The *mix* of restricted stock and restricted stock options a manager is awarded.
2. The *amount* of restricted stock and restricted stock options the manager is awarded.
3. The maximum percentage of holdings a manager can liquidate annually.
4. The number of years after retirement/resignation for the stock and options to vest.

6.6   COMPARISON WITH REGULATORY INITIATIVES INCLUDING CLAWBACKS

Regulatory initiatives regarding bankers' incentive compensation have emphasized the use of equity (as opposed to cash) bonuses, deferral, and clawbacks to achieve compensation that does not encourage untoward risk-taking. These are features of worldwide regulation because the approach – reducing incentives for excessive risk-taking – was incorporated into the Basel Committee's supervisory principles at the direction of the G-20 and all nations in which globally important banks are located.[19] The G-20 incentive compensation principles did not mandate any particular design or structure, but by requiring that incentive compensation be adjusted for risk, symmetric with risk outcomes, and sensitive to the time horizon of risks, they were universally interpreted to require deferred equity compensation and clawbacks.

CAPTION FOR FIGURE 6.2 (cont.)

discouraged the TBTF bank CEOs from investing in high-risk but value-destroying investment projects and trading strategies. (B) Impact of stock sales and salary restrictions on net CEO payoff. This panel highlight that if, per our restricted equity proposal, the TBTF bank CEOs' stock sales were limited to about 5% of the amount they owned in the beginning of that year and a $2 million restriction on cash compensation (with the remainder of the cash compensation paid in stock), this would have imposed a significant negative compensation impact (negative net CEO payoff) when considering the entire 2000–8 period. The negative compensation impact would have discouraged the TBTF bank CEOs from investing in high-risk but value-destroying investment projects and trading strategies. (*Source:* Author's calculations.)

The G-20 incentive compensation principles were subsequently clarified and operationalized into implementation standards.[20] The standards suggest that a "substantial portion of incentive compensation be variable," of which "a substantial proportion, such as more than 50%" should be equity based and of which "a substantial proportion ... such as 40 to 60%" should be deferred for at least three years. Deferred equity compensation is, of course, at the heart of our proposal. As this guidance makes clear, though, regulators have not gone so far as to require banks to adopt all equity-based incentive compensation or long-term vesting periods that extend beyond retirement or resignation, as we recommend. Hence, in our judgment, bank compensation committees should not settle for mere compliance with the suggested standards because they fall well short of adequately guarding against excessive risk-taking, nor should banking regulators shrink from further scrutinizing bank activities when incentive compensation packages merely meet the implementation standards.

The implementation standards address the *symmetric risk* principle by requiring that a substantial proportion of the variable equity compensation be subject to a share retention policy, with the unvested component of that deferred compensation to be subject to clawback on "negative contributions" (i.e., poor realized performance) of the firm and business line.[21] Congress codified clawbacks for all firms in the 2002 Sarbanes-Oxley Act, with further elaboration in the Dodd-Frank Act, laying out as a specific trigger an accounting restatement.[22] Dodd-Frank, for instance, mandates Securities and Exchange Commission (SEC) rulemaking to require issuers with accounting restatements to recover from any executive officer incentive compensation amounts erroneously paid in excess of what they would have received had the accounting statements been correct within a three-year window prior to the restatement. On July 1, 2015, the SEC proposed a new rule implementing provisions of Dodd-Frank that require listed companies to adopt policies to claw back incentive-based compensation from their executives in the event of an accounting restatement that has been paid in the three years prior to the restatement.[23] Recently, the *Wall Street Journal* (March 24, 2016, p. C1) reported that "Wall Street bonuses are about to get locked up for even longer ... regulators plan to require banks to hold back much of an executive's bonus beyond the three years already adopted by many firms." Besides the problems with clawbacks (detailed next), bonuses have an additional problem, namely, TBTF bank managers' compensation derived from sale of their banks' stock is usually twice as large, or larger, than their compensation from salary and bonus (see Table 5.3, Panels A, B, and C).

Clawback provisions such as those in Dodd-Frank are not, in our judgment, as effective an incentive mechanism as the restricted equity proposal. They are inherently difficult to compute (e.g., it is unclear how to calculate the Dodd-Frank clawback measure when the award was not based on an accounting target) and entail litigation costs of uncertain dimension at present.[24] Further, specific triggers for clawbacks are blunt instruments: excessive risk-taking causing firm losses need not produce a restatement (the decline in value of large financial institutions during the financial crisis of 2008 was not accompanied by, or in response to, accounting restatements), nor might a three-year (or five-year) horizon be enough time for a flawed investment or trading strategy to negatively affect accounting earnings.[25]

By contrast, the restricted equity proposal has an inherent clawback feature that renders unnecessary intricate mechanisms requiring repayments of bonuses on income from transactions whose value proved illusory. Because executives are compensated in equity that is not received until years after it is earned – one to three years after they leave the firm – they cannot capture short-lived share price gains from transactions whose value is not long-lasting. The compensation will be dissipated as the value of the firms' shares decline on realization of the project's or investment strategy's losses. In other words, executives will receive less in value than the originally granted incentive stock compensation if the stock price drops thereafter. This automatic clawback is, accordingly, simpler to administer than the specified regulatory clawbacks, avoiding definitional, and consequently litigation, pitfalls.

The European Union has gone further than the G-20 and Basel-endorsed approach and capped banks' incentive pay to no more than the individual's fixed salary. In our judgment, a proposal could not be more wrong-headed than that legislation if the objective is to incentivize bank executives to maximize firm value and reduce excessive risk. It is, of course, quite possible that the motivation of members of the European Parliament in adopting the cap was to punish bank employees and express moral outrage at their outsized pay packages and not to affect banks' risk-taking incentives. In our judgment, if that was the motivation, then the solution is misplaced because it undermines the fashioning of an effective compensation system for banks. Concerns about income inequality are best addressed via a national debate on whether the concern should be about income inequality per se or the relation among income equality, economic growth, and the economic well-being of citizens.

There is a well-developed and widely accepted economics literature on the fashioning of incentives to achieve consonance between managers' actions and shareholders' interest through the use of stock and option compensation.[26] The less the executive receives in incentive compensation, the less he or she will be motivated to act so as to maximize share value. The core problem of excessive risk-taking is not one of compensation *levels* but of compensation *structure*. Moreover, the likely result of any restriction capping one component of compensation is to increase another component. Since the original package proportions would have reflected a package maximizing manager utility, the new package will require a compensating adjustment that costs the bank more than before.[27] In short, such a restriction will make pay even less sensitive to performance than it was before the crisis, which is the precise opposite of what is desirable in an incentive compensation plan.

6.7 COMPARISON WITH DEBT-BASED COMPENSATION
PROPOSALS

As noted earlier, a number of recent reform proposals have advocated compensating bank managers with some of the bank's debt securities rather than (or in addition to) equity-based incentive pay.[28] Although specifics of the proposed debt or debt-like compensation differ, the rationale is the same: to address the moral hazard of debt. Shareholders, in a levered firm, have an incentive to take on very high-risk projects even if these high-risk projects do not increase the company's long-term value. The reason is, given limited liability, that the shareholders obtain the entire upside but do not have to pay creditors in full on the downside.[29] Deposit insurance only exacerbates the moral hazard problem because the government stands behind the deposit, and it reduces creditors' incentives to monitor managers' risk-taking or otherwise seek contractual protections against risk-taking. Of course, this moral hazard problem resulting in a threat to the fisc is universally recognized: banks are for this very reason subject to extensive supervision, regulation, and examination.

All the debt-based proposals are, in our judgment, inferior to our restricted stock proposal, particularly given the earlier-noted desirable criteria that compensation plans be simple to understand and implement, transparent to monitor, and aligned with long-term firm value. First, reform proposals advocating a package of equity and debt or debt-like securities are far more complex and opaque than the restricted equity proposal. For example, most senior securities of financial institutions are either not publicly traded or trade very infrequently; the absence of market prices renders it difficult to value debt-based compensation packages. In addition, given that banks' capital structures are changing over time, executives' portfolios will require frequent rebalancing to maintain proportionate holdings, which will require a complicated, and therefore costly, administration.[30]

Second, government bailouts of banks, particularly in the 2008 global financial crisis, have by and large focused on bailing out creditors, not shareholders. Given that experience, providing a portion of bank executives' compensation in debt would not lead the executives to take a socially optimal level of lower risk because they could quite plausibly conclude that they need not expect to lose the value of debt securities on the downside, while they will still expect to obtain the upside on the equity portion. If the executives' debt is written so as to not be able to participate in a government bailout, then those securities would be of lesser value than those sold to investors, whose prices and terms incorporate the reasonable expectation of a bailout should the institution fail, rendering market prices, such as exist for the debt, inapposite for valuing executives' compensation. Yet this is the linchpin of such proposals, in which price signals of the riskiness of the debt, such as proportionate values of debt and equity securities, determine executives' compensation.

Third, although in theory a manager holding a mix of debt and equity securities might not take on inappropriate risk, it might well be otherwise. The gain on an equity position from following a high-risk strategy might well exceed the loss on the position attributable to senior securities in the executives' portfolios. Moreover, if the value of the equity position is quite low compared with the senior securities in a compensation package, a manager would still have an incentive to take on risky projects, given the upside made possible by the equity position.[31] Furthermore, the incentive to undertake riskier projects would be greater than the incentive to take on such projects created by our restricted equity proposal because with restricted stock the upside cannot be realized until years after the manager is no longer with the firm. Indeed, as discussed earlier, incentive compensation paid in the form of restricted stock is more likely to decrease than increase managers' risk-taking because it increases the underdiversification of executive portfolios, in addition to the long-term holding period for the stock.

The concern over moral hazard in relation to bank risk-taking induced by deposit insurance that motivates the proposals to use debt for bank executives' incentive compensation is, of course, as we have noted, well recognized, and we do not wish to dismiss its seriousness.

But we think that it is daunting to determine, no less effectively implement, an optimal incentive compensation structure combining debt and equity. It would in fact be extraordinarily difficult to determine how the incentives would work, that is, how managers would react, to such compensation.[32] Moreover, the problem becomes more acute if the manager's loyalty is divided across firm stakeholders, as would be the case in these complicated multisecurity structured compensation packages. If we move out of the realm of decisions regarding a specific investment, such as selling a particular structured product, to higher-level firm decision issues, the manager may not make decisions to maximize firm value because the conflicts of interest across the classes of securities might make it difficult, if not impossible, to determine the appropriate course to follow.[33]

Finally, the empirical research on which some debt-based compensation advocates offer in support of their proposals – that firms whose executives receive higher deferred compensation and pension benefits, which are considered to be debt-like because they are unsecured future claims, are less risky – when evaluated more closely, we believe, cuts against the position.[34] That research also finds that as the level of deferred compensation and pension benefits rises, total enterprise value falls (i.e., increases in debt values are swamped by decreases in equity value). The compensation package must mirror exactly the firm's total security package, which, as we have already discussed, is practically impossible to implement.

There is a further problem with debt-based incentive compensation from a social welfare point of view: it is not desirable from society's perspective to run banks in debtholders' rather than shareholders' interest because banks that seek to minimize risk-taking might be induced to restrict their lending and lend only to the safest borrowers, a business strategy that is not conducive to economic growth. As elaborated later in this book, we think instead that the moral hazard of debt problem is best addressed directly by raising bank equity capital requirements. By revising the capital structure to make the probability of insolvency less probable, the restricted equity proposal would operate in the range in which bank managers' incentives, aligned with long-term share price value maximization, will also be aligned with long-term firm value maximization. Indeed, in most circumstances, banks operate far from insolvency, in which equity rather than debt-based compensation provides superior incentives for firm value maximization.

6.8 NONFINANCIAL COMPANIES AND THE RESTRICTED EQUITY PROPOSAL

While our focus here is on banks, the incentives generated by the aforementioned compensation structure would be relevant for maximizing long-term shareholder value in other industries. For example, consider the cases of Enron, WorldCom, and Qwest, whose senior executives have been convicted of criminal violation of insider trading laws.[35,36] Senior executives in those companies made misleading public statements regarding the earnings of their respective companies. Those misleading statements led to a temporary rise in the share prices of the companies. The executives liquidated significant amounts of their equity positions during the period while their companies' share prices were temporarily inflated. If these executives' incentive compensation had consisted of only restricted stock and restricted stock options that they could not liquidate for one to three years after their last day in office, they would not have had the financial incentive to make the abovementioned misleading statements. Hence corporate board compensation committees in companies in nonfinancial industries should also give the restricted equity executive incentive compensation structure serious consideration.

6.9 RECENT DEVELOPMENTS: EXECUTIVE INCENTIVE COMPENSATION

6.9.1 April 21, 2016, "Incentive-Based Compensation Arrangements"

Section 956 of the Dodd-Frank Act requires six US agencies (Federal Reserve System, Federal Deposit Insurance Corporation, Federal

Housing Finance Agency, Office of the Comptroller of the Currency, National Credit Union Administration, and the SEC) to jointly propose regulation to prohibit incentive-based compensation that would encourage "excessive" risk-taking by banks. On April 21, 2016, these six agencies proposed new regulations entitled "Incentive-Based Compensation Arrangements."[37] These new regulations took a tiered approach: more stringent regulations for banks with assets more than $250 billion, somewhat less stringent regulations for banks with assets between $50 billion and $250 billion, and even less stringent regulations for banks with assets in the $1 billion to $50 billion range. Given our focus on TBTF banks, the following discussion pertains to new regulations for banks with assets of more than $250 billion. These April 2016 regulations cover bonuses; specifically, *they do not cover compensation derived from the sale of stock.*[38] Besides senior bank executives, the new April 2016 regulations cover "significant risk-takers in the bank," defined as employees with a third of their compensation based on incentive compensation and among the top 5% of salary earners in the bank or those who can commit 0.5% or more of the net worth or bank assets. The April 2016 regulations require deferral of at least 60% of the incentive compensation for a period of at least four years and forfeiture of all unvested deferred incentive-based compensation. The deferral and forfeiture can be triggered by poor financial or nonfinancial performance due to "inappropriate" risk-taking, among other events. The April 2016 regulations also require clawback provisions that allow a bank to recover incentive-based compensation from a manager for a period of seven years following the incentive-compensation vesting date. The clawback can be triggered by "(i) misconduct that resulted in significant financial or reputational harm to the bank; (ii) fraud; or (iii) intentional misrepresentation of information used to determine the manager's incentive-based compensation."

We support the essence of the April 2016 "Incentive-Based Compensation Arrangements" proposed by the six agencies. These agencies have done an impressive amount of analysis and used the theoretical and empirical financial economics literature to motivate their proposed regulations. The deferral, forfeiture, and clawback provisions are focused on discouraging "inappropriate" risk-taking by banks. A critical question is: What is *inappropriate* risk-taking by banks? From a financial viewpoint, the risk of a project or trading strategy would be inappropriate if the NPV of the project or trading strategy is negative. However, the measurement of such risk (and associated cash flows) is subject to both manager biases and estimation errors, as we discussed in Chapter 3. Enforcing deferral, forfeiture, and clawback provisions can lead to very large potential losses on managers (see Table 5.3, Panels A, B, and C). Given the potential losses of tens or hundreds of millions of dollars, affected managers are likely to *litigate* the occurrence of a particular trigger event or the measurement of the "inappropriate" risk. Given the inherent uncertain outcome of any litigation, the disciplining effect of the April 2016 regulations on bank manager inappropriate risk-taking behavior would be muted.

The restricted equity proposal has an inherent clawback (and deferral and forfeiture) feature that renders unnecessary intricate mechanisms requiring repayments (forfeiture) of bonuses on income from transactions whose value proved illusory. Because executives are compensated in equity that is not received until years after it is earned – one to three years after they leave the firm – they cannot capture short-lived share price gains from transactions whose value is not long-lasting. The compensation will be dissipated as the value of the firm's shares decline on the realization of the project's or investment strategy's losses. In other words, executives will receive less in value than the originally granted incentive stock compensation if the stock price drops thereafter. Hence this automatic clawback inherent in the restricted equity proposal is simpler to administer than the specified regulatory clawbacks, avoiding definitional, and consequently litigation, pitfalls.

We note a second concern with the April 2016 regulations that cover bonuses but do not cover compensation derived from the sale of stock. TBTF bank managers' compensation derived from the sale of their banks' stock is usually *twice* as large, or greater, than their compensation from salary and bonus (see Table 5.3, Panels A, B, and C). Hence, even if the April 2016 regulations are successful in discouraging some inappropriate risk-taking by banks, the adverse incentives from compensation derived from the sale of stock remains a potent problem. Our restricted equity proposal would address this problem as well.

6.9.2 Brexit and Prime Minister May's Executive Compensation Initiative

On June 23, 2016, the United Kingdom voted to leave the European Union – the Brexit vote. Subsequent to the vote, the United Kingdom elected a new prime minister. Prime Minister May has noted that reforming executive incentive compensation would be one of her government's priorities. On July 21, 2016, Prime Minister May's proposed making annual shareholder votes on executive compensation *binding*.[39]

In 2002, the United Kingdom was the first country to require an annual *nonbinding* shareholder vote on executive pay in publicly listed UK companies; this became popularly known as "say on pay." Proponents of "say on pay" suggest that it increases the accountability of directors to shareholders regarding executive compensation. Furthermore, proponents argued that "say on pay" would better align executive compensation with corporate transparency and performance. Ferri and Maber (2013) have conducted an extensive empirical analysis of the impact of the 2002 UK "say on pay" requirement. They do not find any differences in the level of CEO pay or changes in the growth of CEO pay before and after the 2002 UK requirement (see table IX in Ferri and Maber 2013). However, they do find a moderating effect on the level of CEO pay for companies that experienced poor prior performance.

Ferri and Maber (2013) also conclude that "the regulation's announcement triggered a positive stock price reaction at firms with weak penalties for poor performance." However, a more careful review of their own evidence, which they report in their Appendix Table I, does not support the positive market reaction conclusion. For example, in their Appendix Table I, Panel B, they consider four events in 2002 that increased the probability of enactment of the regulation and should lead to positive stock returns. The raw returns for companies with excess CEO pay are significantly positive for only two of these four events, significantly negative for one of these four events, and statistically insignificant for the fourth event. On the basis of this evidence, it would be difficult to argue that the stock market responded positively to the 2002 UK "say on pay" requirement.

The United States adopted a "say on pay" mandate in 2011. Cai and Walkling (2011) find that the US "say on pay" mandate "creates value for companies with inefficient compensation, but can destroy value for others." They conclude: "The market reacts negatively to labor sponsored proposal announcements and positively when these proposals are defeated."

Summarizing the extant evidence on the impact of "say on pay" requirements in the United States and the United Kingdom on company value and performance – there is some evidence that "say on pay" can benefit company value in certain situations and can be harmful to company value in other situations. There is no evidence that "say on pay" can benefit company value in all situations.[40] Given the evidence, making annual shareholder votes on executive compensation binding would be inconsistent with enhancing company value and performance.

Despite the obvious attractiveness of "say on pay" (on the surface, allowing shareholders a voice on management compensation appears to be a sensible proposition), why is the evidence not consistently supportive of "say on pay"? The answer lies in understanding what counts as *pay* in "say on pay" regulations and in the aforementioned studies. Related to this is the question – How should shareholders and public policymakers think about an optimal "pay" package for managers? "Say on pay" regulations (and the aforementioned studies) mostly include the following items as pay: annual salary, annual bonus, annual stock grants, and annual stock option grants. An important component of management compensation is managers' compensation derived from sale of their companies' stock that they have received previously. The evidence in Table 5.3 (Panels A, B, and C) documents that managers' compensation derived from the sale of their banks' stock is usually *twice* as large, or larger, than their compensation from salary and bonus. Hence, even if the "say on pay" regulations are successful in discouraging nonoptimal pay practices (including annual salary, annual bonus, annual stock grants, and annual stock option grants), the adverse incentives from compensation derived from the sale of stock remain a potent problem. This was the problem that led to the financial distress of the big banks in the United States, the United Kingdom, and Europe in 2008 and of Enron, Worldcom, Qwest, and others in 2002.

Instead of focusing on "say on pay" regulations, we believe that public policymakers (as well as corporate board members and institutional investors) should focus their efforts on an "optimal" executive compensation policy. We suggest the following three criteria for evaluating executive compensation reform policies:

1. Simplicity,
2. Transparency, and
3. Focus on creating and sustaining long-term shareholder value.

As we argued earlier, a simple and transparent incentive compensation structure is desirable because "say on pay" requires shareholders to vote on CEO compensation packages; hence a simple incentive structure is easier for them to understand and evaluate, reducing the need to rely on third-party vendors of proxy voting advice, the value of which has been the subject of considerable controversy.[41] Second, simplicity and transparency in incentive compensation packages mitigate public skepticism toward high levels of executive pay in conjunction with poor performance. Finally, the focus on creating and sustaining long-term shareholder value would channel management's attention to the longer-term profitability of an investment strategy (including investment in human capital, i.e., corporate employees). Business and legal scholars posit that managers should act in the best interest of long-term shareholders – what better way to do this than to tie management incentive compensation to long-term share price!? The restricted equity proposal (the incentive compensation of executives should consist only of restricted equity – restricted in the sense that the individual cannot sell the shares or exercise the options for one to three years after his or her last day in office) – developed earlier is our suggestion for the most important component of an optimal paypolicy in "say on pay" regulations.

7   Director Compensation Policy

Director compensation typically consists of a cash component (called the *retainer*), smaller cash amounts paid for attendance at board and committee meetings, and incentive compensation in the form of stock and stock option grants that vest over a period of time of a few years. While the theoretical and empirical literature on executive compensation is extensive, the literature on director compensation is relatively modest. We think that it is plausible to assume that incentives operate similarly in both employment positions. If, for example, directors can liquidate their vested stock and options and a director feels the need to liquidate the position in the near future, then the director may focus on short-term performance that may be to the detriment of long-term shareholder value and the public fisc. It would therefore be prudent for bank director incentive compensation to be structured along the lines of the *restricted equity proposal* that we advanced for bank executives in Chapter 6.

7.1   DIRECTOR COMPENSATION: PRELUDE

The early twentieth century witnessed not only the phenomenal growth of the US economy but also the growth of those corporate entities whose activities comprised that economy. Corporations were no longer local ventures, owned, controlled, and managed by a handful of local entrepreneurs, but instead had become national in size and scope. Concomitant with the rise of the large-scale corporation came the development of the professional management class, whose skills were needed to run such far-flung enterprises. And as the capitalization required to maintain such entities grew, so did the number of individuals required to contribute the funds to create such capital. Thus we saw the rise of the large-scale public corporation – owned not by a few but literally by thousands of investors located throughout the nation and indeed the globe. And with this growth in the size and ownership levels of the modern corporation, individual shareholdings in these ventures became proportionally smaller and smaller, with no shareholder or shareholding group owning enough stock to dominate the entity. Consequently, the professional managers moved in to fill this control vacuum. Through control of the proxy process, incumbent management nominated its own candidates for board membership. The board of directors, theoretically composed of the representatives of various shareholding groups, instead was comprised of individuals selected by management. The directors' connection with the enterprise generally resulted from a prior relationship with management, not the stockholding owners, and they often had little or no shareholding stake in the company.

Adolf Berle and Gardiner Means, in their path-breaking book, *The Modern Corporation and Private Property*, described this phenomenon of the domination of the large public corporation by professional management as the separation of ownership and control. The firm's nominal owners, the shareholders, in such companies exercised virtually no control over either day-to-day operations or long-term policy. Instead, control was vested in the professional managers who typically owned only a very small portion of the firm's shares.

One consequence of this phenomenon identified by Berle and Means was the filling of board seats with individuals selected not from the shareholding ranks but chosen instead because of some prior relationship with management. Boards were now comprised either of the managers themselves (the *inside directors*) or associates of the managers not otherwise employed by or affiliated with the enterprise (the *outside* or *nonmanagement directors*). This new breed of outside director often had little or no shareholding interest in the enterprise and, as such, no longer represented their own personal financial stakes or those of the other shareholders in rendering board service. However, as the shareholders' legal fiduciaries, the outside directors were still expected to expend independent time and effort in their roles, and consequently, it began to be recognized that they must now be compensated directly for their activities.

The consequences of this shift in the composition of the board were to exacerbate the manager-shareholder conflict of interest inherent in the corporate form. Without the direct economic incentive of substantial stock ownership, directors, given a natural loyalty to their appointing party, and the substantial reputation enhancement and monetary compensation board service came to entail had little incentive other than their legal fiduciary duties to engage in active managerial oversight. It may also be argued that the large compensation received for board service may have actually acted as a disincentive for active management monitoring, given management control over the director appointment and retention process.

Since the identification of this phenomenon, both legal and finance theorists have struggled to formulate effective solutions. Numerous legal reforms have been proposed, often involving such acts as the creation of the professional *independent director*,[1] the development of strengthened board fiduciary duties,[2] or the stimulation of effective institutional shareholder activism.[3] All it seems have proven ineffective because the passive board still flourishes. Shareholders, mindful of disasters at Archer-Daniels-Midland, W.R. Grace, Morrison Knudsen, and more recently, Enron, WorldCom, and Qwest are keenly aware of this problem.[4] Yet the solution may be simple and obvious. Traditionally, directors, as large shareholders, had a powerful personal incentive to exercise effective oversight. It was the equity ownership that created an effective incentive. To recreate this powerful monitoring incentive, directors must become substantial shareholders once again. This is the theoretical underpinning behind the argument for equity-based compensation for corporate directors. The idea is to reunite ownership and control through meaningful director stock ownership, leading to better management monitoring resulting in superior company performance.[5]

7.2   DIRECTOR OWNERSHIP AND COMPANY PERFORMANCE

In a recent study, we focused on director stock ownership and director stock ownership requirements for the Standard & Poor's (S&P) 500 companies during 2003 and 2005.[6] Directors in an increasing number of S&P 500 companies are mandating a stock requirement on themselves. In 2003, about 35% of S&P 500 companies had director stock ownership requirements. In 2005, about 62% of S&P 500 companies had director stock ownership requirements – typically directors were required to own stock worth about 4.1 times the cash retainer; this is detailed in Table 7.1.[7] Tables 7.1 and 7.2 highlight the diversity in director stock ownership requirements across the S&P 500 companies – they also highlight that one director ownership policy is unlikely to "fit all" or be optimal for all companies. Additionally, and more interestingly, Table 7.3 documents that *companies in which directors owned more stock performed better in future years.*

In another recent study we focused on the relation between director stock ownership and company performance for the largest 1,500 US companies during 1998 and 2012.[8] Consistent with the findings of the study noted earlier, we also found that *companies in which directors owned more stock performed better in future years;* these results are illustrated in Figure 7.1.

7.3   DIRECTOR OWNERSHIP AND THE FIRING OF UNDERPERFORMING CEOS

The primary responsibility of the corporate board of directors is to engage, monitor, and, when necessary, replace company management. The central criticism of many modern public company boards has been their failure to engage in the kind of active management oversight that results in more effective corporate performance. It has been suggested that substantial equity ownership by outside directors creates a personally based incentive to actively monitor. An integral part of the monitoring process is the replacement of the CEO when circumstances

Table 7.1 *Director Stock Ownership Requirements for S&P 500 Firms during 2003 and 2005*

This table provides a summary of stock ownership requirements for the S&P 500 firms that disclosed a policy during the years 2003 and 2005. *Multiple of retainer requirement* is defined as a policy requiring directors to hold a multiple of x times their annual retainer. *Multiple of cash retainer requirement* is a policy requiring directors to hold a multiple of x times their annual cash retainer. *Share requirement* is given in thousands of shares and indicates a policy requiring directors to own a fixed number of shares. *Dollar value of holdings requirement* indicates a policy requiring directors to hold a fixed dollar value of shares in the firm. *Multiple of shares received as compensation* requires directors to hold a multiple of shares that they receive as compensation. *Multiple of total director compensation* requires directors to hold a multiple of their total annual compensation. *Other policy* relates to options holdings, caps on holding requirements, and requirements that govern accumulated holdings (over multiple years). The sum of the "Number of firms" column, indicating the number of firms with each type of policy, is greater than the total number of firms with ownership policies due to cases in which there exist multiple policies for a single firm.

	2003			2005		
	Number of firms	Mean req.	Median req.	Number of firms	Mean req.	Median req.
Multiple of retainer requirement	75	3.57	3	127	3.66	3
Multiple of cash retainer requirement	14	4	5	50	4.08	5
Share ownership requirement (000 shares)	50	5.46	5	83	7.13	5
Dollar value of holdings requirement ($000)	15	$131	$100	33	$200	$200
Multiple of shares received as compensation	9	1.89	1	14	2.29	1
Multiple of total director compensation	3	1	1	4	1	1
Other policy	30			17		

Table 7.2 *Examples of Ten S&P 500 Firms with Director Ownership Guidelines (2005)*

Company	Guideline	Time horizon	Notes
3M	2× annual retainer	Within 3 years	
Abbott Labs	5,000 shares	Within 5 years	Includes restricted units
ADC Telecommunications	"Directors are encouraged to own stock of the Company to align more closely their interest with those of the shareholders in general"		Does not fall under ownership requirement definition used in this chapter because ownership is "encouraged" (not required)
Adobe Systems	5,000 shares	Within 2 years: Requirement is "25% of net shares acquired from Adobe for 2 years unless, following the sale of such shares, the total shares exceeds 5,000"	
AES Corp	10,000 units		Includes options, stock, or restricted units Dollar value calculated is based on stock ownership

Table 7.2 (cont.)

Company	Guideline	Time horizon	Notes
Aetna	Value equal to $400,000	Met within 5 years of appointment	
Affiliated Computer	Class A stocks with value equal to a minimum of 3× annual retainer	Met within 3 years for all directors; new directors within 5 years	
Agilent Technologies	Value of 3× annual cash retainer		
Alberto Culver	At least $100,000 in common stock		
Alcoa	At least 10,000 shares		

Table 7.3 *Firm Performance and Director Dollar Value of Holdings*

This table presents results of OLS regressions in which the dependent variables are firm performance measures. ROA is year-ahead return on assets, defined as earnings before interest, depreciation, and taxes divided by total assets. Q is defined as equity market capitalization plus book value of assets minus book value of common equity and divided by book value of assets. Explanatory variables are *Median Director Holdings*, the natural log dollar value of director equity holdings; *Sales*, defined as natural log of total revenue in millions of dollars; *Leverage*, defined as the ratio of total debt to the book value of assets; *Retainer*, the annual cash retainer, as reported in ExecuComp; *CEO Pay Slice*, defined as the ratio of CEO pay to the pay of the firm's top five executives; *G-Index* (see Gompers, Ishii, and Metrick 2003); *R&D*, the reported research and development expenditures divided by sales; and *Industry ROA*, defined as the median earnings before interest, depreciation, and taxes divided by total assets for all COMPUSTAT firms in the industry (2-digit SIC code), which is used as a control in the ROA regression only. *Year_2005* is a dummy variable equal to 1 for the 2005 data. Industry fixed effects based on the Fama-French 49 industries and an intercept are also included in the regression but are not reported.

	Dependent variable: ROA_{t+1}		Dependent variable: Q_{t+1}	
	Coefficient	t-Statistic	Coefficient	t-Statistic
Dollar Median Director Holdings$_t$	0.005***	2.68	0.135***	5.04
Sales$_t$	-0.089*	-1.77	-3.561***	-4.83
Leverage$_t$	-0.062***	-3.05	-1.858***	-6.44
Retainer$_t$	0.012**	1.98	0.045	0.50
CEO Pay Slice$_t$	0.020	1.17	0.011	0.04
G-Index$_t$	0.000	0.44	-0.046***	-2.99

Table 7.3 (cont.)

	Dependent variable: ROA_{t+1}		Dependent variable: Q_{t+1}	
	Coefficient	t-Statistic	Coefficient	t-Statistic
$R\&D_t$	−0.190***	−6.06	−0.821*	−1.77
Year_2005	0.010*	1.89	−0.102	−1.36
No. of observations	798		808	
Adjusted R^2	0.386		0.386	

* Indicates statistical significance at the 10% level; ** indicates significance at the 5% level; and *** indicates significance at the 1% level.

All Years: 1998–2012	All Firms	Q1 - Low	Q2	Q3	Q4 - High
Director Ownership	$1,296,013	$203,803	$721,361	$1,729,170	$4,628,386
ROA: t+1 to t+2	12.71%	10.42%	12.11%	13.74%	14.60%
Adjusted ROA: t+1 to t+2	0.06%	−0.90%	−0.24%	0.34%	0.83%

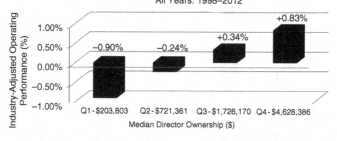

1998–2002	All Firms	Q1 - Low	Q2	Q3	Q4 - High
Director Ownership	$678,278	$125,003	$429,966	$1,134,173	$4,867,461
ROA: t+1 to t+2	12.41%	10.05%	12.47%	13.33%	13.80%
Adjusted ROA: t+1 to t+2	0.10%	−1.01%	−0.03%	0.43%	0.62%

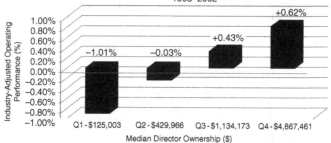

FIGURE 7.1 Relationship between dollar board ownership by quartiles and industry-adjusted return on assets for the subsequent two years for the 1,500 largest US companies. Companies perform better as their directors own more stock in them. Performance is measured as industry-adjusted return on assets over the subsequent two years. Director ownership is measured in dollars (number of shares × share price) of the median director. Directors are rank-ordered by their stock ownership in the company from high to low; the middle director in this rank-ordering is designated as the *median director*. (*Source:* Author's calculations.)

2003–5	All Firms	Q1 - Low	Q2	Q3	Q4 - High
Director Ownership	$1,063,340	$280,438	$753,348	$1,582,483	$3,979,773
ROA: t+1 to t+2	12.72%	10.35%	12.10%	13.61%	14.89%
Adjusted ROA: t+1 to t+2	0.05%	−0.90%	−0.40%	0.27%	1.07%

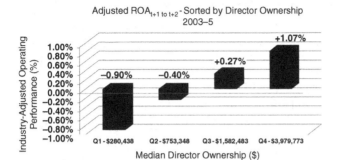

2006–8	All Firms	Q1 - Low	Q2	Q3	Q4 - High
Director Ownership	$1,252,203	$312,000	$853,755	$1,694,417	$4,012,531
ROA: t+1 to t+2	13.34%	10.36%	13.18%	14.21%	15.72%
Adjusted ROA: t+1 to t+2	0.04%	−1.10%	−0.10%	0.24%	1.00%

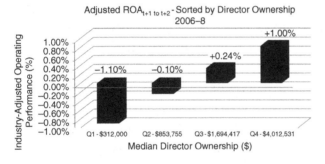

2009–12	All Firms	Q1 - Low	Q2	Q3	Q4 - High
Director Ownership	$2,139,007	$426,576	$1,042,136	$2,042,035	$6,723,000
ROA: t+1 to t+2	12.61%	10.11%	12.44%	14.11%	14.80%
Adjusted ROA: t+1 to t+2	0.05%	−0.96%	−0.07%	0.12%	1.02%

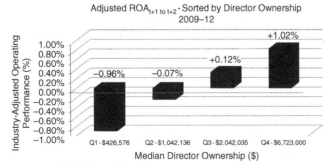

FIGURE 7.1 (cont.)

warrant. An active, non-management-obligated board will presumably make the necessary change sooner rather than later because a poorly performing management team creates more harm to the overall enterprise the longer it is in place. However, a management-dominated board, because of its loyalty to the company executives, will take much longer to replace a poorly performing management team because of strong loyalty ties. Consequently, it may be argued that companies in which the CEO is replaced expeditiously in times of poor performance may have more active and effective monitoring boards than those in which ineffective CEOs remain in office for longer periods of time. An examination, therefore, of the equity-holding positions of the outside directors of the companies where CEO succession occurs more expeditiously and those where it does not should provide some evidence of the effect of equity ownership on management monitoring by outside directors.

In a recent study, we focused on about 2,000 CEO changes during 1998–2012 for the 1,500 largest US companies.[9] The study examined company press releases and media articles to determine whether the CEO departure was disciplinary or not. CEO turnover was classified as *nondisciplinary* if the CEO died, if the CEO was older than 63, if the change was the result of an announced transition plan, or if the CEO stayed on as chairman of the board for more than a year. CEO turnover was classified as *disciplinary* if the CEO resigned to pursue other interests, if the CEO was terminated, or if no specific reason was given for removal. The study documents (see Figure 7.2) that *directors who own more stock are more likely to discipline or fire the CEO when the stock price performance of their company has been subpar in the previous two years.*

Table 7.4 documents the director ownership and CEO stock sales in the "too big to fail" (TBTF) banks and the No-TARP banks. Ironically, while the No-TARP banks are much smaller than the TBTF banks, the median value of director ownership in the No-TARP banks is greater than for the TBTF banks ($2.0 million to $1.6 million). However, as detailed in Chapter 5, the median value

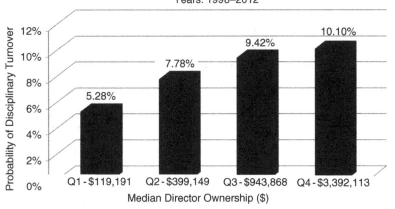

FIGURE 7.2 Probability of disciplinary CEO turnover among the worst-performing largest 1,500 US companies during 1998–2012, sorted by director ownership quartiles (Q1 through Q4). Director ownership is measured in dollars (number of shares × share price) of the median director. Directors are rank-ordered by their stock ownership in the company, from high to low; the middle director in this rank-ordering is designated as the *median director*. Corporate boards in which the median director owns more stock are more likely to discipline/fire their CEO if the share price performance of the company has been particularly poor during the past two years. (*Source:* Author's calculations.)

of CEO NET trades (= stock sales – stock purchases – option exercises) is much greater for the TBTF bank CEOs ($66.8 million) than for the No-TARP bank CEOs ($1.2 million). This is consistent with the argument that director ownership serves as a disciplining corporate governance mechanism that discourages CEO stock sales.

7.4   DIRECTOR COMPENSATION POLICY PROPOSAL

We propose that director compensation for banks *and* nonfinancial companies should be structured along the lines of the restricted equity proposal. Our proposal is based on the empirical findings discussed earlier, specifically

Table 7.4 *Bank CEO Net Trades and Bank Director Ownership during 2000–8*

TBTF refers to the 14 too-big-to-fail financial institutions, including Bank of America, Bank of New York Mellon, Citigroup, Goldman Sachs, JP Morgan Chase, Morgan Stanley, State Street, Wells Fargo, Merrill Lynch, Bear Stearns, Lehman Brothers, and AIG. No-TARP sample includes 37 lending institutions that did not receive TARP funds.

CEO Net Trades = Stock Sales – Stock Purchases – Option Exercises

	TBTF firms ($n = 14$)	No-TARP firms ($n = 37$)
Sample period: All years, 2000–8		
Median value of CEO net trades	$66,842,520	$1,226,977
Median value of director ownership	$1,557,749	$2,039,645

- Companies in which directors own more stock performed better in the future years.
- Directors who own more stock are more likely to discipline or fire the CEO when the stock price performance of their company has been subpar in the previous two years.

We propose that all compensation (including incentive compensation) of corporate directors should consist only of restricted equity (restricted stock and restricted stock options) – restricted in the sense that the director cannot sell the shares or exercise the options for one to three years after his or her last board meeting. With regard to cash compensation – we are recommending that corporate directors not be paid any retainer fees or other cash compensation.[10]

We note three caveats to our proposal for director compensation policy; these are similar to the caveats we noted in Chapter 6 for executive compensation policy. First, if directors are required to hold restricted shares and options, they would most likely be underdiversified. Second, if directors are required to hold restricted shares and options after retirement, they may be concerned with lack of liquidity. Third, the proposal could lead to early director departures as directors seek to convert illiquid shares and options into more liquid assets (after the one- to three-year waiting period).

The deliberate underdiversification brought about by being subject to a restricted equity plan – more of the individual's wealth will be tied to the firm because he or she cannot liquidate accumulated incentive equity payments – would lower the risk-adjusted expected return for the director. One means of bringing a director's risk-adjusted expected return back up to the previous level would be to increase the expected return by granting additional restricted shares and options to the director. We would therefore expect that the amount of equity and options awarded under the restricted equity proposal will be *higher* than that awarded under a short-term incentive plan.

Concerns regarding lack of liquidity and early departure are also valid. To address these concerns, we recommended (consistent with our earlier recommendation for executives) that directors be allowed to liquidate annually a modest fraction of their awarded incentive restricted shares and options of between 5% and 10%. The requirement that they must retain the great bulk of the shares for several years until after their last board meeting will provide a sufficient incentive to advance shareholder long-term interests.

We are also sensitive to potential tax liabilities that the restricted equity proposal might generate for a director. To the extent that a director incurs tax liability from receiving restricted shares and options that is greater than the amount permitted to be liquidated in the current year, under our proposed that individual would be allowed to sell enough additional shares (and/or exercise enough additional options) to pay the additional taxes.

7.5 WHO WILL IMPLEMENT THE RESTRICTED EQUITY PROPOSAL FOR CORPORATE DIRECTORS?

Our proposal is directed at corporate board compensation committees, which, we urge, should voluntarily adopt a restricted equity plan as the preferred mechanism for aligning their incentives with that of long-term shareholders. In implementing the proposal, we think that corporate boards should be the principal decision makers regarding

1. The *mix* of restricted stock and restricted stock options a director is awarded,
2. The *amount* of restricted stock and restricted stock options the director is awarded,
3. The maximum percentage of holdings that the director can liquidate annually, and
4. Number of years for the stock and options to vest subsequent to the director's last board meeting.

We recommend that board compensation committees use the restricted equity plan as a *starting point* for their discussion on board compensation. However, as Tables 7.1 and 7.2 highlight, one size does not fit all. Corporate boards need to use their understanding of the unique set of opportunities and challenges of their companies to design a director compensation plan that would serve the interests of long-term shareholders.

7.6 MIDLEVEL MANAGERS

The restricted equity incentive compensation proposal is appropriate for only the senior-most executives and directors in a company. The restricted equity incentive compensation proposal is *not* appropriate for midlevel managers and even less appropriate for rank-and-file employees; the underdiversification problem would be a particularly serious problem for rank-and-file employees. Once the incentives of senior executives are aligned with those of long-term shareholders, the senior executives should be entrusted with the task of constructing incentive programs for midlevel managers.

8   Are Large Banks Riskier?

[T]he risk of failure of "large, interconnected firms" must be reduced, whether by reducing their size, curtailing their interconnections, or limiting their activities.

> – Paul Volcker, former Chairman of the Federal Reserve in statement to
> the Senate Banking Committee on May 9, 2012

An often heard statement by many policymakers and financial market experts over the past couple of years has been that if a financial firm is too big to fail, then it is too big. I couldn't agree more.

> – Thomas Hoenig, member of the Board of the FDIC and former President
> and CEO of the Federal Reserve Bank of Kansas City, in speech to
> US Chamber of Commerce on March 24, 2010

But giant banks, operating on the belief that they are backed by government, turn these otherwise manageable episodes into catastrophes. Is there a better alternative? Yes, reducing the size and complexity of the largest banks.

> – Richard Fisher, President and CEO of the Federal Reserve Bank of Dallas

The [Dodd-Frank] law hasn't ended the problem of banks so big that their collapse would endanger the financial system and economy, forcing the government to rescue them in a crisis ... policy makers must give serious consideration to a range of options, including, breaking up large banks into smaller, less connected, less important entities.

> – Neel Kashkari, President of the Federal Reserve Bank of Minneapolis
> (*The Wall Street Journal*, February 16, 2016)

Are large banks riskier? Some argue that governments have to bail out a large failing financial institution because its failure may present a threat to the proper functioning of the financial intermediation process and cause severe disruption to the economy.[1] When firms are perceived to be "too big to fail" (TBTF), they have a propensity to assume excessive risks to profit in the short term. Indeed, TBTF policy has been blamed by many as one of the main factors causing distortion in financial firms' risk-taking incentives (for example, see Boyd, Jagannathan, and Kwak 2009).

In turn, researchers and policymakers have proposed an array of regulations. Limiting the size of financial institutions is a frequent suggestion.[2] However, many concerns are associated with this proposed reform to limit bank size. First, it is difficult to determine the correct size threshold. Second, this simple size metric will miss many small firms that perform critical payment processing and pose significant systemic risk, even if the first issue can be solved (see Stern and Feldman 2009). In addition, opponents of such a proposal often cite the literature on scale economies; they are concerned that such restraint could weaken the global competitiveness of US financial firms and cause loss of market share. Further, Dermine and Schoenmaker (2010) argue that capping the size is not the best tool, based on the finding that countries with relatively small banks also faced large bailout costs; in addition, they caution that capping the size can have unintended effects, such as lack of credit risk diversification.

Is size the problem? We draw on our recent work (Bhagat, Bolton, and Lu 2015) to shed light on the issue by studying the size effect on the risk-taking of US-based financial institutions, including commercial banks, investment banks, and life insurance companies. Using data on the size and risk-taking of financial institutions from 2002 to 2012, we investigated whether cross-sectional variation in the size of firms is related to risk-taking. Our measures of risk-taking were comprehensive. They included two model-based measures (namely, the Z-score and Merton's distance to default [Merton DD]), a market-based measure (volatility of stock returns), and an accounting-based measure (write-downs). We focused primarily on Z-scores and Merton DD; the other risk measures served as robustness checks.

If size does affect risk-taking as measured by Z-score, then an interesting question is, How does size affect the components of the Z-score? Focusing on the components of the Z-score – namely, leverage, return on assets, and volatility of earnings – allows policymakers to target the risk-taking problem of financial institutions more directly.

We established the following findings: first, firm size is positively correlated with risk-taking, even when controlling for observable firm characteristics such as market-to-book ratio and corporate governance structure. The relationship between bank size and risk is plagued by endogeneity concerns. Banks are more likely to pursue riskier activities (even if they have a negative net present value[NPV]) as they get bigger because of TBTF regulatory bias and the increasing likelihood of a government bailout if things go bad; however, it is also possible that risky banks strive to grow in size to obtain TBTF status (e.g., see Brewer and Jagtiani 2009; and Molyneux, Schaeck, and Zhou 2010). It is unclear whether large banks undertake riskier activities or an omitted variable affects both risk and size. To account for this, we adopted an instrumental variables approach. We considered three instruments for bank size: the bank's number of employees; the bank's net plant, property, and equipment (PP&E); and an indicator variable for whether a firm is incorporated in Delaware. We used a battery of robustness tests to verify the validity and strength of our instruments.

Our second finding was that the decomposition of Z-score reveals that firm size has a consistent and significant negative impact on the equity-capital-to-total-assets ratio; we did not find a consistent relation between firm size and return on assets or earnings volatility. These findings suggest that financial firms engage in excessive risk-taking mainly through increased leverage. However, they also suggest that economies of scale do not exist for banks. Regressions with volatility of stock return as the dependent variable indicated that size-related diversification may not exist in the financial sector because size is positively associated with return volatility.

Third, we found that our earlier developed corporate governance measure (Bhagat and Bolton 2008), calculated as median director dollar stockholding, is negatively associated with risk-taking. This has important policy implications: to wit, policymakers interested in discouraging banks from engaging in excessive risk should focus on bank director compensation and stock ownership.

Fourth, we found that investment banks, but not insurance companies, engage in more risk-taking than commercial banks. Finally, we documented that the positive relation between bank size and risk was present in the precrisis period (2002–6) and the crisis period (2007–9) but not in the postcrisis period (2010–12). Perhaps the intense scrutiny put on bank risk-taking by the bank regulators, senior policymakers, and the media in the postcrisis period may have curbed the appetite and ability of large banks to engage in high-risk investments.

Our analysis is critical from a public policy perspective because the risk-taking behavior of financial institutions affects financial and economic fragility, as well as economic growth (see Bernanke 1983; Calomiris and Mason 1997, 2003a, 2003b; and Keely 1990). Our findings have important policy implications that are particularly relevant today as the calls for tougher restrictions and reinforcement of corporate governance on the financial sector accelerate. First, they suggest that instead of just limiting firm size, it may be more effective for regulators to strengthen and enhance regulations on equity capital requirements for all financial institutions. This suggestion regarding increased bank equity capital requirements is consistent with the recent recommendations of Admati and Hellwig (2013), Bhagat and Bolton (2014), and Fama (2010). Also, in recent op-eds, the *Wall Street Journal* has recommended significantly higher equity capital requirements for banks. Second, our finding on corporate governance indicates that median director dollar stockholding can be used as an effective internal corporate risk control mechanism.

8.1 BACKGROUND

While there is a substantial literature that examines the risk-taking behavior of financial institutions (see Saunders, Strock, and Travlos 1990; Demsetz and Strahan 1997; Stiroh 2006; Laeven and Levine 2009; Houston et al. 2010; and Demirguc-Kunt and Huizinga 2011), to our knowledge, we are the first to focus exclusively on the relation between size and risk-taking of financial institutions. While the study by Boyd and Runkle (1993) is the closest to this study, there are significant differences. First, the scope of their study is limited by focusing on only large bank holding companies (BHCs), while our sample included commercial banks, investment banks, and insurance companies, which have a larger variation in size. We argued that since the recent financial crisis was not caused by BHCs alone, excluding non-BHCs will not provide a complete picture about risk-taking in the financial industry. Second, Boyd and Runkle's (1993) analysis is univariate between size and risk. We considered covariates that, in theory, might affect bank risk-taking. Another paper that is close to ours is that of Demsetz and Strahan (1997), who focused on BHC diversification and size. They concluded that BHC size-related diversification does not translate into reductions in risk because size was uncorrelated or positively correlated with stock return variance in many years of their sample period. In their regression analysis, however, they found that firm size had a significant effect in reducing firm-specific risk for their sample period (1980–93).

The recent financial crisis has generated tremendous interest in the study of risk-taking of financial institutions. Laeven and Levine (2009) considered a sample of the largest 270 banks in 48 countries. They found a significant positive relation between the cash flow rights of the largest shareholder of the bank and bank risk measured as Z-score. They also documented a positive relation between bank size and bank risk. Beltratti and Stulz (2012) exploited variation in the cross section of performance of 164 large banks (defined as banks with total assets greater than $50 billion) across the world during the period of financial turmoil (2007–8). They found that smaller banks with concentrated ownership and more noninterest income are associated with higher idiosyncratic risk. Consistent with our results, they documented a negative relation between bank size and Z-score. However, their relation was statistically not significant – possibly due to the limited cross-sectional variation in their bank size measure because they only considered banks with more than $50 billion in assets. Berger and Bouwman (2013) considered a comprehensive sample of US banks during 1984–2010 and documented a positive relation between bank size and bank credit risk (defined as the bank's Basel I risk-weighted assets divided by total assets). Based on a US sample of financial institutions, Cheng, Hong, and Scheinkman (2010) investigated whether compensation structure contributes to excessive risk-taking. They found that risk-taking, measured as firm beta and return volatility, is correlated with short-term pay such as options and bonuses. Bolton, Mehran, and Shapiro (2010) proposed addressing the excessive risk-taking by tying executive compensation to both stock and debt prices. Baker and McArthur (2009) estimated that the gap in funding costs between small and TBTF firms averaged 0.29 percentage points in the period 2000–7 and that this gap widened to an average of 0.78 percentage points in 2008–9. Rime (2005) found that the TBTF status had a significant positive impact on bank issuer ratings. Lastly, using an international sample of banks, Demirguc-Kunt and Huizinga (2011) found that systemically large banks achieved lower profitability and without a clear impact on risk. Their results suggest that it is not in the bank shareholders' interests but that it is in managers' interests (via higher pay and status) for a bank to become large relative to its national economy.

The role of corporate governance in coping with risk is not obvious. Standard theory on corporate governance predicts that firms with better governance increase firm value by adopting projects with positive NPV. However, this does not preclude the possibility of the firm investing in projects with risky cash flows. Therefore, it might be in the interest of shareholders to take on risky projects as long as they are value-enhancing. In addition, option theory (Black and Scholes 1973; Merton 1974) suggests that, all else being equal, the value of an option increases with volatility of the underlying asset.[3] Since a company's shareholders are essentially holding a call option with the total value of the company as the underlying asset and the face value of debt as the exercise price, it follows that the more volatile the company's cash flow is, the more valuable is the call option. Thus the value of common stock increases with the volatility of the company's cash flow. Based on these arguments, we might expect a positive association between effective corporate governance and risk-taking.

This relation, however, can go in the opposite direction. As Rajan (2006) and Diamond and Rajan (2009) point out, the compensation structure is different in the finance industry in that the performance of CEOs is evaluated based in part on the earnings the CEOs generate relative to their peers. With this pressure, executives have incentives to take excessive risk to profit in the short run even if the projects are not truly value-maximizing; this is identical to the situation discussed in Chapter 3. As noted in Diamond and Rajan (2009), "[E]ven if managers recognize that this type of strategy is not truly value-creating, a desire to pump up their stock prices and their personal reputations may nevertheless make it the most attractive option for them" (p. 607). If this argument is correct, we would expect financial institutions with better governance to set incentives and controls to avoid taking risks that do not benefit shareholders. Thus we should see a negative relation between effective corporate governance and risk-taking. Because of these two countervailing arguments, the impact of corporate governance on risk-taking in the financial industry remains an empirical question. To the extent there is a negative relation between good corporate governance and bank risk, this would be an important tool for policymakers to focus on.

8.2 SAMPLE AND VARIABLE CONSTRUCTION

Our main sources of data were Compustat, the Center for Research in Security Prices (CRSP), RiskMetrics, and Bloomberg, supplemented by hand-collected data from companies' Securities and Exchange Commission (SEC) filings on EDGAR. We defined the financial industry as all financial institutions consisting of commercial banks, investment banks, and life insurance companies, as classified by their four-digit Standard Industrial Classification (SIC). Specifically, firms with the four-digit SIC codes of 6020, 6211, and 6311 are identified as commercial banks, investment banks, and life insurance companies, respectively; this classification is similar to that of Cheng, Hong, and Scheinkman (2010). We used this narrower classification on the grounds that it greatly reduced unobservable heterogeneity among firms within each category; thus it alleviated omitted variable bias and enhanced comparability.

The starting point for the sample selection was Compustat, where we collected annual accounting data on all US commercial banks, investment banks, and life insurance companies. Our sample spanned the period 2002–12. Following Boyd and Runkle (1993) and John, Litov, and Yeung (2008), we required that firms have at least five consecutive years of data on key accounting variables over the period to be included in the sample. This process yielded an initial sample of 702 unique financial institutions or an unbalanced panel of 6,277 firm-year observations comprising 599 commercial banks, 60 investment banks, and 43 life insurance companies. In our sample, insurance companies included such firms as AIG, Prudential Financial, and Lincoln National Corp, while investment banks included such firms as Bear Stearns, Lehman Brothers, and Goldman Sachs.

We used a stratified sampling process to avoid selection bias when dealing with governance and CEO ownership data. The governance data were available through RiskMetrics, and the CEO ownership data were available through RiskMetrics and Compustat's Execucomp. However, RiskMetrics only provides data for Standard and Poor's (S&P) 1500 companies, which include around 10% of financial firms; Execucomp covers slightly more but still not nearly all of our sample financial institutions. Because of this, we took a random sample of 250 commercial banks (from the full sample of 599 commercial banks) plus all of the 60 investment banks and 43 life insurance companies from those available in Compustat. From this sample, we hand-collected data on governance and ownership from company proxy statements for firms that were not covered by RiskMetrics and Execucomp. The advantage of this stratified sampling process is that it avoids the problem of selection bias on observables (specifically, firm size) because firms in the S&P 1500 are, by definition, relatively large, whereas the Compustat database that we began with includes financial institutions of all sizes.

8.2.1 Risk-Taking

One of our two primary measures for firm risk-taking was the Z-score, which equals the average return on assets (ROA) plus the equity-capital-to-total-assets ratio (EAR), divided by the standard deviation of asset returns [σ(ROA)]:

$$Z\text{-score} = \frac{(\text{ROA} + \text{EAR})}{\sigma(\text{ROA})}$$

Following Laeven and Levine (2009) and Houston et al. (2010), we calculated EAR as total assets minus total liabilities divided by total assets. The Z-score has been widely used in the recent literature as a measure of bank risk. The Z-score measures the distance from insolvency. A higher value of Z-score indicates less risk-taking. Since the Z-score is highly skewed, we followed Laeven and Levine (2009) and Houston et al. (2010) and used the natural logarithm of the Z-score as the risk measure. In calculating Z-score, annual values of ROA and EAR are used, and σ(ROA) is the standard deviation of annual ROA calculated over the preceding five-year period for each firm-year observation. For more on Z-score as a measure of risk-taking, see Boyd and Runkle (1993); Boyd, De Nicolo, and Jalal (2006); or Beltratti and Stulz (2010).

Our second measure of risk-taking was Merton distance to default (Merton DD), with a high value indicating less risk-taking. Merton DD has been used in the literature to forecast bankruptcy. Merton DD builds on Merton (1974), who modeled firm equity as a call option on the underlying value of the firm with an exercise price equal to the face value of the firm's liabilities.[4] Similar to Z-score as a measure of risk-taking, the Merton DD measure also attempts to gauge the probability that a firm will go bankrupt over the forecasting horizon. Unlike Z-score, which is based solely on accounting information, the Merton DD measure is based on market and accounting data. We followed the iterative procedure described in Bharath and Shumway (2008) to calculate the value of the monthly distance to default for each firm in our sample and then aggregated them into yearly DD by taking a simple average of the monthly DD value. For more on Merton DD as a measure of risk-taking, see Duffie, Saita, and Wang (2007) and Bharath and Shumway (2008).

While Merton DD has been used as a measure of risk-taking in general, there is a growing literature that successfully employs Merton-like models, or, more generally, structural credit risk models, in quantifying bank risk. There are a number of examples of this approach in the recent literature. Anginer and Demirguc-Kunt (2014) apply the Merton (1974) contingent claim model to measure default risk and credit risk codependence for a sample of banks in over 65 countries. Calice et al. (2012) use the Merton model in examining the relationship between the volatility in the credit default swap markets and valuation of the assets of 16 large, complex financial institutions. Chen et al. (2014) incorporate Merton's idea to construct a lattice-based multiperiod structural credit risk model to analyze default risk. Lastly, Jessen and Lando (2014) demonstrate the robustness of Merton DD (as a measure of default risk) to model misspecifications.

As a robustness check, we considered additional risk-taking measures, including standard deviation of stock returns and accounting write-downs.[5] The standard deviation of stock returns indicates the market's perception about firms' risk-taking, and accounting write-downs reflect ex-post realization of a firm's tail risk. For equity volatility, we used the standard deviation of daily stock returns within each sample year. For write-downs for each firm, we followed Vyas (2011) and defined write-downs as the net credit losses recognized by financial institutions through accounting treatments, which include fair-value adjustments, impairment charges, loan loss provisions, and charge-offs during 2007–8.

8.2.2   Firm Size

The potential candidates for measuring firm size include accounting-based measures such as total assets and total revenue and market based measures such as market capitalization. Following the existing literature, we focused primarily on total assets and used total revenue as a robustness check. We considered bank size as a continuous variable. We considered a binary dummy variable for TBTF banks. However, correctly identifying the size threshold when a financial institution becomes too big to fail was not obvious, especially over our entire sample period that includes an expansion and a recession. More important, as we showed later in the paper, although we did observe a positive association between firm size and risk-taking, this relation was driven not only by size per se but also by the unusually high leverage of the larger banks. This suggests that regulations designed to rein in the risk-taking of financial firms should focus more on equity capital requirements than on bank size alone.

8.2.3   Corporate Governance

We employed a new measure of corporate governance, the median director dollar stockholding, developed in our earlier work (Bhagat and Bolton 2008). This variable was motivated by the idea that directors, as economic agents, will be more likely to fulfill their monitoring and advising duties when they have "skin in the game" (i.e., holding a substantial amount of common stock of the companies where they serve on the board). This is consistent with the industry practice that many firms either require or encourage directors to own certain numbers of shares in the company (e.g., nonemployee directors at Nike are required to own Nike stock valued at five times their annual cash retainer – which was around $100,000 in 2013 – or more while they are on the Nike board[6]). Therefore, the functioning of corporate boards will be affected by directors' stock ownership. This variable could potentially be a measure of overall good governance because it is the corporate boards that ultimately make, or at least approve, all important corporate decisions that ultimately affect firm performance. The most significant advantage of this governance measure over other commonly used governance measures such as the G-index (Gompers, Ishii, and Metrick 2003) comes from its simplicity, and thus it is less susceptible to measurement errors. Constructing governance indices inevitably involves measuring and summing up a multitude of governance attributes such as governance processes, compensation structure, and charter provisions – and thereby ascribing weights to the various governance factors in the index. If the weights assigned to each of these attributes are not consistent with those used by informed market participants, then incorrect inferences would be drawn regarding the relationship between governance and performance.

In our earlier work (Bhagat and Bolton 2008), we considered the dollar value of stock ownership of the median director as the measure of stock ownership of (nonemployee) board members. Our focus on the median director's ownership, instead of the average ownership, was motivated by the political economy literature on the median voter (see Shleifer and Murphy 2004; Milavonic 2004). Also, directors, as economic agents, are more likely to focus on the impact on the dollar value of their holdings in the company rather than on the percentage ownership. As mentioned earlier, RiskMetrics provides limited data on financial firms (177 of 702 firms), so we supplemented its data by hand collecting director ownership information from proxy statements.[7]

8.2.4 CEO Ownership

Risk-averse managers are inclined to take on less than optimal firm risk in order to protect their firm-specific human capital because their employment income is usually tied to changes in firm value. This is an agency problem, in essence, as described in Jensen and Meckling (1976), Amihud and Lev (1981), and Smith and Stulz (1985). However, stock ownership by managers may be used to induce them to act in a manner that is consistent with the interest of shareholders. Thus we expect to see a positive relation between CEO ownership and risk-

taking. Researchers have documented the impact of ownership structure on firm risk-taking. For instance, in analyzing nonfinancial firms,
Agrawal and Mandelker (1987) found a positive relation between stock
holdings of managers and the changes in firm variance, while John,
Litov, and Yeung (2008) found that managers enjoying large private
benefits of control select suboptimally conservative investment
strategies. Saunders, Strock, and Travlos (1990) found that stockholder-
controlled banks exhibit higher risk-taking behavior than manager-
controlled banks. Demsetz, Saidenberg, and Strahan (1997) documented
that the significant relationship between ownership structure and
risk-taking exists only at low-franchise-value banks. Laeven and
Levine (2009) found that bank risk is generally higher in banks that
have controlling shareholders. We used CEO ownership percentage as
our measure for bank ownership structure. Like the governance variable, we hand collected CEO ownership data from company proxy
statements in addition to the data provided by RiskMetrics and
Execucomp for firms that were not covered by those two sources.

8.2.5 Market-to-Book Ratio and Age

Market-to-book value ratio has been identified as an important risk
factor in the asset pricing literature. For instance, Fama and French
(1992) point out that firms with high ratios of book-to-market value
(or low market-to-book) are more likely to be in financial distress.
We computed this variable by dividing the market value of equity by
the book value of equity for each firm and year.

In the banking literature, market-to-book-value ratio has often
been used as a proxy for bank charter value (see Demsetz, Saidenberg,
and Strahan 1997; Goyal 2005). A charter has value because of barriers
to entry into the industry, and usually it is defined as the discounted
stream of future profits that a bank is expected to earn from its access
to protected markets. Since loss of charter imposes substantial costs,
it is argued that charter value can incentivize banks to adopt prudent
decision making (see Keeley 1990; Carletti and Hartmann 2003).
Empirical models of bank risk have focused on this disciplinary role

of charter value. Based on a sample of 367 bank holding companies from 1991 to 1995, Demsetz, Saidenberg, and Strahan (1997) found that charter value is negatively associated with bank risk-taking. Galloway, Lee, and Roden (1997) also found that banks with low charter value assumed significantly more risk.

Finally, we used firm age to control for firm experience, and we expected that more experienced firms would be better at handling risk than less experienced firms.

8.2.6 Financial Institution– and Financial Crisis–Specific Variables

We included three indicator variables to capture the unique characteristics of both different types of financial institutions and the unique characteristics of our 2002–12 time period. We used an *investment bank* indicator if the firm was an investment bank to capture how a nondepository institution might differ from a commercial bank. We used an *insurance company* indicator if the firm was an insurance company to capture the restrictions imposed by insurance regulations. And we used a *financial crisis* indicator if the observation occurred during 2007–9 to capture the uniqueness of this three-year period.

8.2.7 Summary Statistics

Table 8.1 presents the summary statistics for all key variables. The variable definitions and the data sources are described in Appendix B, Table B.4. The Z-score had a mean of 46.4 and a standard deviation of 49.7. This fairly high standard deviation and the wide range in Z-scores suggested a considerable cross-sectional variation in the level of firm risk. Consistent with Laeven and Levine (2009) and Houston et al. (2010), our Z-score measure was right-skewed, and we used the log Z-score in our analysis, which was more normally distributed. Our sample statistics of the *probability of default* (Merton) were consistent with reported sample statistics in Bharath and Shumway (2008). Table 8.2 presents the correlation

Table 8.1 *Summary Statistics*

This table reports summary statistics of the main variables for US financial institutions during the period 2002–12. *Z-score* is firm's return on assets plus the capital asset ratio divided by the standard deviation of return on assets. *Merton distance-to-default* is the Merton-KMV distance-to-default measure of credit risk. *Naive distance-to-default* is the distance-to-default measure from Bharath and Shumway (2008). *Probability-of-default (Merton)* is the estimated probability of default using the *Merton distance-to-default* variable and a cumulative normal distribution. σ(RET) is the standard deviation of daily stock returns for each firm-year. *Total assets* is the book value of total assets in millions. *ROA* is the return on assets, or net income divided by total assets. *EAR* is the equity-capital-to-assets ratio, or total equity divided by total assets. σ(ROA) is the volatility of the firm's return on assets (net income divided by total assets) calculated over the previous five years. *Tier 1 capital ratio* is the ratio of tier 1 capital to assets. *Director ownership* is the median dollar value of stock owned by the members of the board of directors, in thousands of dollars. *CEO ownership* is percentage of stock owned by the CEO in each firm-year. *Firm age* is the calculated based on when the firm first appears in the CRSP monthly stock returns database. Mean and median values are given, along with the standard deviations of each variable.

	Number of observations	Mean	Median	Standard deviation
Z-score	7,095	46.36	32.98	49.73
Merton distance-to-default	4,756	4.46	3.59	3.81
Naive distance-to-default	4,756	3.72	3.86	4.41
Probability-of-default (Merton)(%)	4,756	10.98	0.01	26.47
σ(RET)	5,599	0.48	0.35	0.31
Total assets	7,095	33,605	1,572	174,486
Total revenue	7,095	3,531	101	13,268
ROA (%)	7,095	1.07	0.79	3.07
EAR (%)	7,095	13.81	10.57	14.05
σ(ROA) (%)	7,095	1.15	0.37	1.95
Tier 1 capital ratio (%)	5,344	11.94	11.18	3.59
Market-to-book	7,002	1.08	1.00	0.29
Director ownership ($000)	1,622	1,759	841	3,317
CEO ownership (%)	2,205	2.30	1.01	3.56
Firm age	7,095	16.61	13.00	10.44

Table 8.2 *Correlation Coefficients for the Main Regression Variables*

	Z-score	Merton distance-to-default	Naive distance-to-default	Probability-of-default (Merton)	σ(RET)	Total assets	Total revenue	ROA	EAR	σ(ROA)	Tier 1 capital ratio	Market-to-book	Director ownership ($000)	CEO ownership (%)	Firm age
Z-score	—	0.500	0.554	-0.320	0.567	0.061	0.050	-0.256	0.005	0.553	0.107	0.012	-0.214	0.033	0.064
Merton distance-to-default	0.542	—	0.873	-0.914	0.680	-0.044	-0.034	-0.485	-0.329	0.087	0.241	-0.334	-0.081	-0.083	-0.053
Naive distance-to-default	0.424	0.950	—	-0.806	0.773	-0.051	-0.046	-0.583	-0.334	0.080	0.223	-0.326	-0.070	-0.086	-0.042
Probability-of-default (Merton)	-0.260	-0.945	-0.844	—	-0.768	0.042	0.037	0.629	0.382	-0.059	-0.197	0.174	0.083	0.058	0.050
σ(RET)	0.554	0.702	0.703	-0.371	—	-0.112	-0.087	-0.378	-0.137	0.211	0.036	-0.150	-0.057	-0.019	-0.052
Total assets	0.071	-0.051	-0.060	0.066	-0.113	—	0.772	0.004	-0.033	-0.031	0.241	-0.052	0.087	-0.247	0.599
Total revenue	0.054	-0.054	-0.043	0.029	-0.092	0.789	—	0.004	-0.027	-0.034	0.187	-0.056	0.094	-0.252	0.526
ROA	-0.220	-0.507	-0.502	0.620	-0.384	0.004	0.004	—	0.618	0.188	-0.016	0.796	0.139	0.160	0.075
EAR	0.006	-0.377	-0.389	0.373	-0.126	-0.028	-0.022	0.721	—	0.523	-0.084	0.566	0.001	0.077	0.053
σ(ROA)	0.538	0.082	0.066	-0.076	0.247	-0.030	-0.035	0.190	0.499	—	0.038	0.356	-0.104	0.047	0.014
Tier 1 capital ratio	0.087	0.270	0.317	-0.367	0.033	0.280	0.229	-0.016	-0.096	0.043	—	0.011	0.246	-0.005	0.110

Market-to-book	0.015	−0.302	−0.227	0.247	−0.140	−0.048	−0.059	0.768	0.560	0.397	0.010	—	0.210	0.156	0.054
Director ownership ($000)	−0.211	−0.092	−0.092	0.078	−0.047	0.081	0.069	0.139	0.001	−0.123	0.207	0.210	—	0.098	−0.070
CEO ownership (%)	0.038	−0.079	−0.098	0.116	−0.019	−0.254	−0.194	0.154	0.091	0.053	−0.005	0.191	0.112	—	−0.105
Firm age	0.057	−0.061	−0.067	0.035	−0.053	0.592	0.639	0.071	0.051	0.015	0.103	0.048	−0.067	−0.112	—

Note: Pearson correlation coefficients are below the diagonal, and Spearman nonparametric correlation coefficients are above the diagonal. The sample consists of US financial institutions during the period 2002–12. All variables are as defined in Table 8.1 and Appendix B, Table B.4.

among the key variables. As expected, all three risk measures (Z-score, Merton DD, and equity volatility) are highly correlated.

8.3 BANK SIZE AND BANK RISK

Our primary measures of risk-taking (*bank risk*) were Z-score and Merton DD, with a higher Z-score and a higher Merton DD associated with less risk-taking. We began by examining whether larger size is associated with greater risk. For brevity, we used the label "size" in referring to the natural logarithm of size in the remainder of the chapter; in our primary analyses, we measured size by the firm's total assets.

Our baseline model was as follows:

$$\text{Bank Risk}_i = \alpha + \beta_1 \text{Total Assets}_i + \beta_2 \text{Market-to-Book}_i$$
$$+ \beta_3 \text{Director Ownership}_i + \beta_4 \text{CEO Ownership}_i$$
$$+ \beta_5 \text{Firm Age}_i + \beta_6 \text{Investment Bank}_i$$
$$+ \beta_7 \text{Insurance Company}_i$$
$$+ \beta_8 \text{Financial Crisis dummy}_i + \varepsilon_i \qquad (8.1)$$

Table 8.3, Panel A, presents the results of the regression analysis with log Z-score as the dependent variable. Table 8.3, Panel B, presents the results of the regression analysis with Merton DD as the dependent variable. They are estimated using robust regressions to minimize the influence of outliers in the data. To control for unobserved differences among individual banks, we also used the fixed-effects (FE) estimator. Size enters negatively and is significant at conventional levels in most models: larger firms are riskier.

The governance variable enters positively and is significant at the 1% level in most regressions, meaning that better governance, as measured by median director dollar stockholding, is associated with less risk-taking. This result provides evidence that the conjecture based on Diamond and Rajan (2009) is correct.[8] Investment banks are significantly riskier than commercial banks; coefficients on the investment bank dummy are negative and significant at the 1% level.

Table 8.3 *Firm Size (Total Assets) and Risk-Taking*

This table presents the regression results analyzing Equation (8.1) on the relationship between firm size and risk-taking. Robust regressions are estimated. In Panel A, the dependent variable is natural logarithm of Z-score; in Panel B, the dependent variable is the natural logarithm of Merton DD. The sample consists of US financial institutions during the period 2002–12. The measure of firm size is the natural log of total assets. Robust regressions estimation is used in models (1) and (2), and fixed-effects (FE) estimation is used in model (3). Z-score is defined in Appendix B, Table B.4; Merton DD is as described in Appendix B, Table B.4. *Market-to-book* is the market-to-book ratio. *Director ownership* is the dollar value of the median director stock ownership in natural logarithm form. *CEO ownership* is the percent of stock owned by the CEO. *Firm age* is the age of the firm in each year. *Investment bank* is an indicator variable equal to 1 if the firm is an investment bank and 0 otherwise. *Insurance company* is an indicator variable equal to 1 if the firm is an insurance company and 0 otherwise. *Crisis period dummy* is an indicator variable equal to 1 if the observation occurs during 2007–9 and 0 otherwise. Coefficients are provided with standard errors below in parentheses.

Panel A: Z-Score as a Measure of Risk-Taking, Assets as a Measure of Size

	Dependent variable: ln(Z-score)		
	Robust (1)	Robust (2)	FE (3)
Assets (ln)	**-0.027* (-0.018)**	**-0.033* (-0.017)**	**-0.613*** (-0.211)**
Market-to-book	0.112* (-0.066)	0.118* (-0.07)	0.248 (-0.216)
Director ownership (ln)	**0.158*** (-0.052)**	**0.187*** (-0.056)**	**0.213*** (-0.057)**
CEO ownership	-1.918*** (-0.617)	-1.986** (-0.816)	-1.044 (-0.873)

Table 8.3 (cont.)

	Dependent variable: ln(Z-score)		
	Robust (1)	Robust (2)	FE (3)
Firm age	0.025** (-0.01)	0.028** (-0.01)	—
Investment bank	—	-0.144*** (-0.033)	—
Insurance company	—	0.088 (-0.143)	—
Crisis period dummy	-1.025** (-0.437)	-1.588*** (-0.04)	-0.833*** (-0.111)
Constant	2.758*** (-0.378)	2.869*** (-0.391)	7.631*** (-1.813)
Year controls	Yes	Yes	Yes
Sample period	2002–12	2002–12	2002–12
No. of observations	1,427	1,427	1,427
R^2	0.267	0.298	0.291

Panel B: Merton Distance to Default as a Measure of Risk-Taking, Assets as a Measure of Size

	Dependent variable: ln(Merton DD)		
	Robust (1)	Robust (2)	FE (3)
Assets (ln)	-0.079** (-0.035)	-0.081** (-0.036)	-0.277*** (-0.078)
Market-to-book	0.341* (-0.18)	0.355* (-0.19)	0.156 (-0.114)

Director ownership (ln)	**0.103***** (-0.025)	**0.101***** (-0.021)	**0.020*** (-0.013)
CEO ownership	-1.106* (-0.573)	-1.007 (-0.661)	-0.243 (-0.855)
Firm age	0.055** (-0.027)	0.059** (-0.024)	—
Investment bank	—	-1.758*** (-0.151)	—
Insurance company	—	0.994 (-0.826)	—
Crisis period dummy	-1.252** (-0.501)	-1.296*** (-0.486)	-0.576*** (-0.168)
Constant	1.448*** (-0.2)	1.401*** (-0.207)	4.008*** (-0.089)
Year controls	Yes	Yes	Yes
Sample period	2002–12	2002–12	2002–12
No. of observations	1,219	1,219	1,219
R^2	0.367	0.578	0.477

Note: The boldface type highlights the relation between bank risk and size (*Assets*) and bank risk and governance (*Director Ownership*).

*, **, and *** indicate significance at the 10%, 5%, and 1% levels, respectively.

Also, as expected, the crisis period dummy variable indicates that bank risk was high during 2007–9. CEO ownership has a positive correlation with bank risk but enters insignificantly in the fixed-effects model. As expected, the sign of firm age is positive.

To summarize our results so far: bank size is positively correlated with risk-taking. Better governance is associated with reduced risk-taking.

8.3.1 Endogeneity of Firm Size

Empirical corporate finance research is plagued by the problem of endogeneity, and this research is no exception. Specifically, we are concerned about the joint determination of risk-taking and firm size. Previous research indicated that banks are willing to pay a large premium to make acquisitions that will make them sufficiently large and TBTF (Brewer and Jagtiani 2009). Therefore, although firms are more likely to pursue risk-taking activities when they become larger, it is also likely that high-risk firms have the incentive to increase their sizes to achieve TBTF status. To address this issue, we used the identification strategy of instrumental variables (IVs). In particular, we used three different instrumental variables: whether or not the firm is incorporated in Delaware, the natural logarithm of the number of employees at the firm, and the natural logarithm of the net plant, property, and equipment.

We made use of variation in whether or not a firm incorporated in Delaware as an instrument for firm size because when a company decides to go public, the decision where to incorporate, while not random, should be exogenous to the unobservable factors that affect firms' risk-taking as induced by the moral hazard of TBTF. The validity of an instrument critically hinges on this exclusion restriction. Empirical legal and financial studies have investigated extensively why a firm would choose Delaware as its domicile. For example, Daines (2001) found that there is a wealth effect associated with Delaware incorporation due to the fact that Delaware corporate law encourages takeover bids and facilitates the sale of public firms by reducing the cost of acquiring a Delaware firm. Conceptually, this wealth effect should have nothing to do with a firm's risk-taking. Bebchuck and Cohen (2003) indicated that favorable antitakeover protections are important for a state to attract out-of-state incorporation. Romano (1985) argued that Delaware's large store of legal precedent reduces transaction costs and uncertainty about legal liability. Lastly, Fisch (2000) noted the peculiar role of the Delaware judiciary in corporate lawmaking, arguing that Delaware lawmaking offers Delaware corporations a variety of benefits, including flexibility, responsiveness, insulation from undue political influence, and transparency. While these factors affect a firm's domicile decision, all of them appear centered around the legal environment of Delaware. In addition, other researchers have argued that a firm's choice of domicile is unimportant and trivial (Black 1990). This literature suggests that our instrumental variable – dummy for Delaware incorporation – does not belong to the structural equation; we thus expect that it is a valid instrument.

The other two instrument variables – number of employees at the firm and net plant, property, and equipment – are likely correlated with bank size. However, given the recent banking literature (e.g., Berger and Bouwman 2013; Laeven and Levine 2009; Vallascas and Keasey 2012), it is not obvious why these two variables would be systematically related to a bank's risk-taking.

While the three instrument variables have ex ante theoretical plausibility, we conducted a battery of specification tests to validate the strength and relevance of these instrument variables. We considered Hausman's endogeneity test and the following instrument strength and validity tests: Stock and Yogo (2005) weak instrument test, Hahn and Hausman (2002) instrument validity test, Hansen (1982) and Sargan (1988) overidentification test, and Anderson-Rubin (1949) joint significance test.

The two-stage least squares IV approach involves estimating the following second-stage structural model using the predicted values from the first-stage instrumental variables equation:

$$\text{Bank Risk}_i = \alpha + \beta_1 \text{Total Assets}_i + \beta_2 \text{Market-to-Book}_i$$
$$+\beta_3 \text{Director Ownership}_i + \beta_4 \text{CEO Ownership}_i$$
$$+\beta_5 \text{Firm Age}_i + \beta_6 \text{Investment Bank}_i$$
$$+\beta_7 \text{Insurance Company}_i + \beta_8 \text{Financial}$$
$$\text{Crisis dummy}_i + \varepsilon_i \qquad (8.2)$$

First-stage instrumental variables model:

$$\text{Total Assets}_i = \alpha + \beta_1 \text{Delaware}_i + \beta_2 \text{Employees}_i + \beta_3 \text{PP \& E}_i$$
$$+\beta_4 \text{Director Ownership}_i + \beta_5 \text{CEO Ownership}_i$$
$$+\beta_6 \text{Firm Age}_i + \beta_7 \text{Investment Bank}_i$$
$$+\beta_8 \text{Insurance Company}_i + \beta_9 \text{Financial}$$
$$\text{Crisis dummy}_i + \varepsilon_i \qquad (8.3)$$

where Delaware_i is a dummy variable that equals 1 if firm i is Delaware incorporated, Employees_i is the natural logarithm of employees at the firm, and $\text{PP\&E}_i$ is the natural logarithm of net plant, property, and equipment at the firm; the rest of the variables are defined as in Equation (8.1).

Identification of the IV model requires a strong correlation between the instruments (Delaware dummy, Employees, and PP&E) and firm size. Results from the first-stage regression on size [ln(Assets)] are presented in Table 8.4, Panel A. We performed a weak instrument test, as proposed by Stock and Yogo (2005); if the F-statistic from the first-stage regression exceeds the critical value (using 5% bias), the instrument is deemed to be valid. The critical value is 16.38, which is less than the F-statistic; hence we concluded that the instruments are not weak.

Results from IV estimates for risk-taking, as measured by Z-score and Merton DD, are reported in Table 8.4, Panel B. After controlling for the endogeneity between firm size and risk, we find that larger firms are associated with greater risk-taking, as measured by Z-score and Merton DD; specifically, a 1% increase in total assets

Table 8.4 *Two-Stage Least-Square (2SLS) IV Regression of Firm Size on Risk-Taking*

This table presents the two-stage least-squares (2SLS) regression analysis estimating Equations (8.2) and (8.3) on the relationship between firm size and risk-taking. The sample consists of US financial institutions during the period 2002–12. All variables are as defined in Table 8.1 and Appendix B. In Panel A, the first-stage estimation of Equation (8.3) is presented using the first-stage instruments to obtain the predicted value of firm size using *Total assets*. In the estimation of the first-stage Equation (8.3), three different instrumental variables for firm size are considered: *Delaware*, an indicator variable equal to 1 if the firm is incorporated in Delaware and 0 otherwise, *Number of employees*, the natural logarithm of the total number of employees at the institution in each year, and *PP&E*, the natural logarithm of net plant, property, and equipment at the institution in each year. Model (4) includes all three instrumental variables. In Panels B and C the estimation of the structural Equation (8.2) is presented using the predicted values of size from the first stage to estimate the relationship between firm size and risk-taking. Robust regressions (Robust) and fixed-effects (FE) estimation are used. The natural logarithm of *Total assets* is the measure of size based on the first-stage analysis in Panel A. In Panel B, the dependent variables are *Z-score* and *Merton DD*; in Panel C, the dependent variables are the standard deviation of daily stock returns in each year, the natural logarithm of the cumulative accounting write-downs during 2007–8, and the ratio of cumulative accounting write-downs to total assets; and the dependent variables are *Naive distance to default* and *Probability of default (Merton)*. *Market-to-book* is the market-to-book value for the year. *Director ownership* is the dollar value of the median director stock ownership in natural logarithm form. *CEO ownership* is the percentage of stock owned by the CEO. *Firm age* is the age of the firm in each year. *Investment bank* is an indicator variable equal to 1 if the firm is an investment bank and 0 otherwise. *Insurance company* is an indicator variable equal to 1 if the firm is an insurance company and 0 otherwise. *Financial crisis dummy* is an indicator variable equal to 1 if the observation occurs during 2007–9 and 0 otherwise. In Panel A, the partial F-statistic on the instrument is provided along with the relevant critical value from the Stock and Yogo (2005) weak instruments test using 5% relative bias tolerance. Appendix B presents and explains more thorough tests of endogeneity. Coefficients are provided with standard errors below in parentheses.

Panel A: First-Stage Regression, Predicting Firm Size Using Total Assets

	Dependent variable: ln(Assets)			
	(1)	(2)	(3)	(4)
Delaware	1.418***	—	—	1.055***
	(0.284)	—	—	(0.020)
Number of employees	—	1.026***	—	1.001***
	—	(0.014)	—	(0.017)
PP&E	—	—	2.367***	2.349***
	—	—	(0.028)	(0.026)
Market-to-book	-0.277*	-0.258	-0.269*	-0.255*
	(0.154)	(0.219)	(0.151)	(0.014)
Director ownership (ln)	0.481***	0.479***	0.466***	0.477***
	(0.102)	(0.094)	(0.087)	(0.091)
CEO ownership	-2.553**	-2.310**	-2.448**	-2.471**
	(1.094)	(0.938)	(1.020)	(1.031)
Firm age	0.071***	0.066***	0.072***	0.074***
	(0.007)	(0.007)	(0.008)	(0.008)
Investment bank	1.561***	1.546***	1.618***	1.627***
	(0.043)	(0.040)	(0.044)	(0.043)
Insurance company	1.857***	1.951***	2.003***	1.918***
	(0.055)	(0.051)	(0.056)	(0.054)
Crisis period dummy	1.387*	1.366*	1.391*	1.388*
	(0.077)	(0.074)	(0.074)	(0.072)
Constant	-3.279***	-3.010***	-3.155***	-3.338***
	(0.081)	(0.089)	(0.087)	(0.084)
Year controls	Yes	Yes	Yes	Yes
Sample period	2002–12	2002–12	2002–12	2002–12
No. of observations	1,483	1,483	1,483	1,483
R^2	0.682	0.863	0.857	0.893
First-stage F-statistic	19.34	18.76	20.07	34.61
Stock and Yogo (2005) weak instrument test critical value	16.38	16.38	16.38	22.30
Instruments strong?	Yes	Yes	Yes	Yes

Panel B: Second-Stage Regression, Predicting Risk-Taking, Assets as a Measure of Size

	ln (Z-score) Robust (1)	ln (Z-score) FE (2)	ln(Merton DD) Robust (3)	ln(Merton DD) FE (4)
Assets (ln)	−0.025***	−0.042*	−0.055**	−0.072**
	(0.008)	(0.026)	(0.024)	(0.036)
Market-to-book	0.153*	0.217	0.595*	0.448*
	(0.086)	(1.035)	(0.366)	(0.261)
Director ownership (ln)	0.078***	0.279***	0.158**	0.187*
	(0.015)	(0.092)	(0.071)	(0.118)
CEO ownership	−1.001	−1.307	−1.769	−1.639
	(0.955)	(1.128)	(1.800)	(1.299)
Firm age	0.012*	—	0.054**	—
	(0.006)	—	(0.021)	—
Investment bank	−0.082***	—	−0.066***	—
	(0.014)	—	(0.061)	—
Insurance company	0.088	—	0.311	—
	(0.076)	—	(0.901)	—
Crisis period dummy	−1.366***	−0.701***	−1.854***	−2.244***
	(0.351)	(0.069)	(0.218)	(0.315)
Constant	3.681***	5.873***	6.251***	9.021***
	(0.269)	(1.066)	(0.856)	(1.344)
Year controls	Yes	Yes	Yes	Yes
Sample period	2002–12	2002–12	2002–12	2002–12
No. of observations	1,421	1,421	1,202	1,202
R^2	0.354	0.328	0.618	0.663

Panel C: Second-Stage Regression, Alternate Measure of Risk-Taking, Assets as a Measure of Size

	Dependent Variable	
	Probability of default (Merton) Robust (3)	Probability of default (Merton) FE (4)
Assets (ln)	0.015**	0.024***
	(0.007)	(0.007)

Table 8.4 (*cont.*)

	Dependent Variable	
	Probability of default (Merton) Robust (3)	Probability of default (Merton) FE (4)
Market-to-book	−0.043**	−0.049
	(0.020)	(0.047)
Director ownership (ln)	**−0.031***	**−0.025***
	(0.009)	(0.013)
CEO ownership	0.096*	0.167
	(0.052)	(0.130)
Firm age	−0.007***	—
	(0.002)	—
Investment bank	−0.013***	—
	(0.004)	—
Insurance company	−0.029	—
	(0.055)	—
Crisis period dummy	0.306***	0.298***
	(0.042)	(0.051)
Constant	−0.302***	−0.573***
	(0.051)	(0.103)
Year controls	Yes	Yes
Sample period	2002–12	2002–12
No. of observations	1,202	1,202
R^2	0.237	0.327

Note: A 1% increase in total assets increases probability of default by 2.4% (in fixed-effects estimation). Well-governed financial institutions, as measured by director ownership, are correlated with less risk-taking. A 1% increase in director ownership is associated with a 2.5% decrease in probability of default (in fixed-effects estimation). The boldface type highlights the relation between bank risk and size (*Assets*) and bank risk and governance (*Director Ownership*).

*, **, and *** indicate significance at the 10%, 5%, and 1% levels, respectively.

decreases Z-score by 0.042% (column 2) and decreases Merton DD by 0.072% (column 4). Well-governed financial institutions, as measured by director ownership, are correlated with less risk-taking. The size of the coefficient on director ownership is also economically consequential. A 1% increase in director ownership is associated with a 0.279% (column 2) increase in Z-score and a 0.187% (column 4) increase in Merton DD. Investment banks and the crisis period (2007–9) are associated with greater risk-taking.

Results from IV estimates for risk-taking, as measured by probability of default, are, perhaps, more intuitive to interpret and are reported in Table 8.4, Panel C. After controlling for the endogeneity between firm size and risk, we find that larger firms are associated with greater risk-taking, as measured by probability of default; specifically, a 1% increase in total assets increases probability of default by 2.4% (in FE estimation). Well-governed financial institutions, as measured by director ownership, are correlated with less risk-taking. The size of the coefficient on director ownership is also economically consequential. A 1% increase in director ownership is associated with a 2.5% decrease in probability of default (in FE estimation).

8.5 FINANCIAL CRISIS TIME PERIOD EFFECTS

The 2002–12 time period is unique in that it contains data before, during, and after the largest financial crisis in recent history. As such, it is possible that different subperiods within our sample may have different relationships between bank size and risk-taking. For example, the intense scrutiny put on bank risk-taking by the bank regulators, senior policymakers, and the media in the postcrisis period may have curbed the appetite and ability of large banks to engage in high-risk investments. To address this, we considered three subperiods: the precrisis period of 2002–6, the crisis period of 2007–9, and the postcrisis period of 2010–12. We estimate Equation (8.2) using 2SLS during each of these periods, with both Z-score and Merton DD as our measures of risk-taking. The results are presented in Table 8.5. The strong relationships we observed earlier between firm size and risk-taking are

Table 8.5 *Size and Risk-Taking across Financial Crisis Periods*

This table shows the relationship between firm size and risk-taking before, during, and after the 2007–9 financial crisis. The sample consists of US financial institutions during the period 2002–12. All variables are as defined in Table 8.1 and Appendix B. The 2SLS results from estimating Equation (8.3) are presented; the first-stage regression includes all three instrumental variables. Panel A presents the results using *Z-score* as the dependent variable measure of risk-taking; Panel B presents the results using *Merton DD* as the dependent variable measure of risk-taking; panels A and B present the results using *Total Assets* as the measure of firm size. Model (1) considers only the observations from 2002 to 2006, Model (2) considers only the observations during 2007–9, and Model (3) considers only the observations during 2010–12. The predicted value of firm size obtained in the first-stage regression is the measure of firm size. *Market-to -book* is the market-to-book value for the year. *Director ownership* is the natural logarithm of the dollar value of median director stock ownership. *CEO ownership* is the percentage of stock owned by the CEO. *Firm age* is the age of the firm in each year. *Investment bank* is an indicator variable equal to 1 if the firm is an investment bank and 0 otherwise. *Insurance company* is an indicator variable equal to 1 if the firm is an insurance company and 0 otherwise. Robust regressions estimation is used in the second-stage regressions. Coefficients are provided with standard errors below in parentheses.

Panel A: Size and Risk-Taking across Financial Crisis Periods, Second-Stage Regression Predicting Risk-Taking, Z-Score as Measure of Risk-Taking, Assets as a Measure of Size

	Dependent Variable: *ln (Z-score)*		
	Precrisis 2002–6 (1)	Crisis 2007–9 (2)	Postcrisis 2010–12 (3)
Assets (ln)	−0.021** (0.009)	−0.035* (0.021)	−0.012 (0.016)
Market-to-book	0.156* (0.087)	0.166* (0.094)	0.143 (0.186)
Director ownership (ln)	0.059***	0.093***	0.085*

Table 8.5 (cont.)

	Dependent Variable: *ln (Z-score)*		
	Precrisis 2002–6 (1)	Crisis 2007–9 (2)	Postcrisis 2010–12 (3)
	(0.011)	(0.014)	(0.055)
CEO ownership	−1.055	−1.036	−0.641*
	(0.863)	(0.710)	(0.397)
Firm age	0.019*	0.010*	0.004
	(0.011)	(0.006)	(0.008)
Investment bank	−0.097***	−0.080**	−0.054
	(0.018)	(0.034)	(0.049)
Insurance company	0.054	0.087	0.099*
	(0.061)	(0.073)	(0.061)
Constant	2.369***	3.774***	4.427***
	(0.355)	(0.366)	(0.856)
Year controls	Yes	Yes	Yes
Sample period	2002–6	2007–9	2010–12
No. of observations	625	409	387
R^2	0.511	0.298	0.183

Panel B: Size and Risk-Taking across Financial Crisis Periods, Second-Stage Regression Predicting Risk-Taking, Merton DD as a Measure of Risk-Taking, and Assets as a Measure of Size

	Dependent variable: ln(Merton DD)		
	Precrisis, 2002–6 (1)	Crisis, 2007–9 (2)	Postcrisis, 2010–12 (3)
Assets (ln)	**−0.068*****	**−0.077*****	**−0.029***
	(0.012)	(0.019)	(0.180)
Market-to-book	0.663*	0.563*	0.488
	(0.385)	(0.311)	(0.401)
Director ownership (ln)	**0.144***	**0.169****	**0.153****
	(0.092)	(0.081)	(0.073)

Table 8.5 (cont.)

	Dependent variable: ln(Merton DD)		
	Precrisis, 2002–6 (1)	Crisis, 2007–9 (2)	Postcrisis, 2010–12 (3)
CEO ownership	−1.257*	−1.965	−2.066
	(0.696)	(1.660)	(1.364)
Firm age	0.043**	0.061*	0.064*
	(0.019)	(0.381)	(0.388)
Investment bank	−0.063***	−0.074**	−0.055***
	(0.013)	(0.034)	(0.019)
Insurance company	0.363	0.300	0.245
	(0.436)	(0.499)	(0.277)
Constant	5.239**	7.144***	7.003***
	(2.193)	(1.364)	(1.554)
Year controls	Yes	Yes	Yes
Sample period	2002–6	2007–9	2010–12
No. of observations	536	344	322
R^2	0.628	0.476	0.287

Note: The boldface type highlights the relation between bank risk and size (Assets) and bank risk and governance (Director Ownership).
*, **, and *** indicate significance at the 10%, 5%, and 1% levels, respectively.

most pronounced in the precrisis and crisis periods for both measures of risk-taking. In the postcrisis period, there is no consistent significant relation between bank size and risk-taking; this is consistent with the argument that the intense public scrutiny put on bank risk-taking in the postcrisis period may have curbed the appetite and ability of large banks to engage in high-risk investments.

8.6 DECOMPOSITION OF Z-SCORE

The Z-score has three components: ROA, EAR, and σ(ROA). A higher level of return on assets (ROA) and higher equity-to-capital-assets ratios (EAR) translate into higher Z-scores, while a larger standard deviation of ROA translates into lower Z-scores. Thus when we find a positive relation between size and risk-taking, it may be attributable to a lower ROA, a lower EAR, and/or a higher standard deviation. Therefore, it is possible that size may not necessarily increase the risk of assets, but rather the drop in Z-score may instead be attributed to a decline in the average bank capital ratio or ROA. To further explore how the various components of Z-score are correlated with size, we ran regressions treating each of these Z-score components as a separate dependent variable. The empirical results are reported in Table 8.6.

We see that an increase in size is associated with a decrease in equity-capital-to-assets ratio at the 1% significance level. As for the economic effect, on average, a 1% increase in size translates into a 0.012% to 0.054% reduction in equity-capital-to-assets ratio. We did not find a consistent significant relation between size and ROA or earnings volatility. These results indicate that the lower Z-score for large banks is driven primarily by a reduction in capital assets ratio. This is consistent with some of the conclusions drawn by the aforementioned studies that used structural credit risk models to analyze financial institution risk. For instance, Calice et al. (2012), Flannery (2014), and Chen et al. (2014) found, within the context of Merton-like models, that the financial system was undercapitalized and required massive capital infusions to stabilize it during the crisis. Specifically, on the basis of simulation results, Calice et al. (2012) documented that even under favorable asset volatility scenarios, there was a substantial need for capital injections for a sample of 16 large, complex financial institutions from around the world. Applying a lattice-based multiperiod credit risk model to the case of Lehman Brothers, Chen et al. (2014) showed that there was a substantial increase in default probability during the first few months of 2008, and in a hypothetical exercise, they also showed that Lehman would have needed an equity capital infusion of $15 billion to reduce the probability of default below 5% given the market conditions of March 2008. Flannery (2014) documented substantial market value of the government guarantees against bank insolvency – on the

Table 8.6 *Decomposition of Z-Score*

This table presents the 2SLS results from estimating equation (8.1) using the components of Z-score as the dependent variables. The sample consists of US financial institutions during the period 2002–12. All three instruments are used to predict *Assets* in the first-stage. Panel A presents the results using robust regressions estimation in the second-stage structural regression. Panel B presents the results using fixed-effects estimation in the second-stage structural regression. In Model (1), the dependent variable is EAR, or equity-capital-to-assets ratio, measured as the ratio of total equity to total assets. In Model (2), the dependent variable is ROA, or return on assets, measured as net income divided by total assets. In Model (3), the dependent variable is the standard deviation of annual ROA. *Assets (ln)* is the predicted value of total assets for the firm-year. *Market-to-book* is the market-to-book value ratio. *Director ownership* is the natural logarithm of the dollar value of median director stock ownership. *CEO ownership* is the percentage of stock owned by the CEO. *Firm age* is the age of the firm. *Investment bank* is an indicator variable equal to 1 if the firm is an investment bank and 0 otherwise. *Insurance company* is an indicator variable equal to 1 if the firm is an insurance company and 0 otherwise. Coefficients are provided followed by standard errors in parentheses.

Panel A: Robust Regressions in Second-Stage Regression

	EAR (1)	ROA (2)	σ(ROA) (3)
Assets (ln), predicted	**-0.012*****	**0.002**	**-0.005*****
	(0.002)	(0.002)	(0.000)
Market-to-book	0.044**	0.024*	0.009*
	(0.021)	(0.015)	(0.005)
Director ownership (ln)	**0.023****	**0.148*****	**-0.003*****
	(0.011)	(0.023)	(0.000)
CEO ownership	-0.445*	0.087*	-0.008*
	(0.271)	(0.050)	(0.004)
Firm age	-0.766*	-0.002	0.015
	(0.408)	(0.041)	(0.056)
Investment bank	-1.244*	-0.694	1.334**
	(0.689)	(0.601)	(0.490)
Insurance company	0.033	0.048	0.431
	(0.478)	(0.079)	(0.407)

Table 8.6 *(cont.)*

	EAR (1)	ROA (2)	σ(ROA) (3)
Constant	1.329**	−0.108**	0.058**
	(0.526)	(0.042)	(0.025)
Year controls	Yes	Yes	Yes
Sample period	2002–12	2002–12	2002–12
No. of observations	1,421	1,421	1,421
R^2	0.623	0.745	0.316

Panel B: Fixed Effects in Second-Stage Regression

	EAR (1)	ROA (2)	σ(ROA) (3)
Assets (ln), predicted	**−0.054***	**−0.024***	**−0.005***
	(0.015)	(0.005)	(0.003)
Market-to-book	0.034	0.077*	0.000
	(0.084)	(0.040)	(0.015)
Director ownership (ln)	**0.055***	**0.099***	**−0.002***
	(0.034)	(0.015)	(0.000)
CEO ownership	−0.331	0.144**	−0.115*
	(0.752)	(0.054)	(0.607)
Firm age	−0.441	0.344	0.881
	(0.369)	(0.869)	(0.977)
Investment bank	−1.880*	−1.075	−0.446
	(1.035)	(0.866)	(0.894)
Insurance company	0.077*	0.166	0.330
	(0.046)	(0.244)	(0.476)
Constant	1.004***	0.344***	0.099***
	(0.301)	(0.092)	(0.016)
Year controls	Yes	Yes	Yes
Sample period	2002–12	2002–12	2002–12
No. of observations	1,421	1,421	1,421
R^2	0.194	0.366	0.201

Note: The boldface type highlights the relation between bank risk and size (*Assets*) and bank risk and governance (*Director Ownership*).

*, **, and *** indicate significance at the 10%, 5%, and 1% levels, respectively.

order of 30% of bank capitalization for the largest 25 US bank holding companies during 2007–11.

Corporate governance (director ownership) is positively associated with ROA and negatively associated with earnings volatility. These results suggest that better governance enhances firm performance (ROA), consistent with Bhagat and Bolton (2008), who note a significant and positive relationship between director ownership and contemporaneous and next year's ROA. The risk-reducing mechanism of corporate governance appears to work its way through an increase in ROA and a reduction in earnings volatility.

8.7   SUMMARY

In this chapter we detailed our analysis of the effect of size on the risk-taking of US-based financial institutions. Using data on the size and risk-taking of financial institutions from 2002 to 2012, we investigated whether cross-sectional variation in the size of banks is related to risk-taking. Our measures of risk-taking are comprehensive. They include two model-based measures (namely, the Z-score, and Merton's DD), a market-based measure (volatility of stock returns), and an accounting-based measure (write-downs). We documented four important facts. First, bank size is positively correlated with risk-taking, even when controlling for endogeneity between size and risk-taking. Our second finding was that the decomposition of Z-score reveals that bank size has a consistent and significant negative impact on the bank equity-capital-to-total-assets ratio; we did not find a consistent relation between bank size and ROA or earnings volatility. *These findings suggest that banks engage in excessive risk-taking mainly through increased leverage.* They also suggest that economies of scale do not exist for banks. Regressions with volatility of stock return as the dependent variable indicate that size-related diversification benefits may not exist in the financial sector because size is positively associated with return volatility. Third, we found that our recently developed corporate governance measure, calculated as median director dollar stockholding, is negatively associated with risk-taking. This has important policy implications, to wit: policymakers interested in discouraging banks from engaging in excessive risk should focus on bank director compensation and stock ownership. Finally, we documented that the positive relation between bank size and risk was present in the precrisis period (2002–6) and the crisis period (2007–9) but not in the postcrisis period (2010–12). Perhaps the intense scrutiny put on bank risk-taking by the bank regulators, senior policymakers, and the media in the postcrisis period may have curbed the appetite and ability of large banks to engage in high-risk investments.

9 Bank Capital Structure and Executive Compensation

We advocate meaningful higher and simpler capital requirements to bank capital structure reform that, coupled with the *restricted equity proposal*, should incentivize bank executives not to take on projects of excessive risk that diminish shareholder value. We think that the evidence is compelling that not only precrisis but also postcrisis regulatory capital requirements were and are too low.

The strongest form of bank capital is common equity, which can absorb losses without disrupting the bank's ongoing business activities. There are three ways that bank capital can affect bank risk. First, with more bank capital, bank owners and managers will have more "skin" in the game and hence will focus more carefully on risk management (borrower screening and ongoing monitoring) and avoid excessive risk-taking that arises as a consequence of limited liability and taxpayer-funded bailouts. This is the essence of the argument we made in Chapters 3, 4, 5 and 6 and the arguments in the extant literature, notably, Holmstrom and Tirole (1997); Allen, Carletti, and Marquez (2011); and Mehran and Thakor (2011). Second, greater bank capital discourages risk-shifting in a bank, leading to safer bank investment and trading strategies (Smith and Warner 1979; Calomiris and Kahn 1991; Acharya, Mehran, and Thakor 2011). Finally, greater bank capital increases the bank's ability to absorb negative earnings shocks and survive (Repullo 2004).

9.1 SIMPLIFYING BANK CAPITAL REQUIREMENTS AND BANK TRANSPARENCY

Similar to our recommendation for executive compensation reform, we suggest three criteria for evaluating bank capital reform programs:

154

1. Simplicity,
2. Transparency, and
3. Focus on creating and sustaining long-term shareholder value without any expectation of taxpayer-funded bailouts.

Large international banks' capital requirements have been globally harmonized under the Basel Accords since 1988. Basel capital calculations take into account an asset's risk; that is, banks are required to hold more capital for riskier assets, such as corporate loans, than they are required to hold for what are considered safer assets, such as government debt. The initial accord has been revised several times, with each succeeding revision resulting in more complex calculations of risk layered on top of existing provisions. Under Basel I, regulators established standardized risk weights for broad categories of assets. Banks were then required to hold a minimum of 8% capital against those assets.[1] The standardized approach was emended under Basel II for the largest banks to apply a methodology by which regulators enlist banks' own more sophisticated internal risk management models to determine their risk-based capital requirements ("internal ratings based" [IRB]).[2]

We recommend pegging bank capital to the ratio of *tangible common equity to total assets* (i.e., to total assets independent of risk) rather than the risk-weighted capital approach that is at the core of Basel.[3,4] In this we endorse the position advocated by two experienced bank regulators, Thomas Hoenig, Vice Chairman of the FDIC, and Andrew Haldane, Executive Director, Financial Stability of the Bank of England. They have both called for abandoning Basel III's complicated risk-weighted approach in favor of leverage ratios.[5] Similarly, we contend that Basel III's approach to capital needs to be recalibrated to emphasize the *leverage ratio* (ratio of tangible common equity to total assets) over the risk-weighted minimum, which would require a ratio far higher than its present 3%, which has been set as a backstop to the risk-weighted ratio rather than the mainstay of capital requirements.

Hoenig's and Haldane's emphasis on the leverage ratio over risk-weighted capital measurements is, in part, a reaction to Basel III's daunting complexity and obscurity.[6] As Haldane has remarked, Basel III's multiple requirements and definitions of capital and risk-weight computations are so exceedingly complicated that they now reach over 600 pages compared with Basel I's 30-page text, and for a large bank to comply, it now requires several million calculations, as opposed to Basel I's single figures.[7] These data suggest that it is, at present, all but impossible for any individual – investor, regulator, or bank executive – to get a good handle on the risk that such institutions are bearing.

Moreover, in our judgment, as the complexity of the risk-weight calculation has increased with each regulatory permutation, it magnifies what is a behavioral constant in the financial regulatory landscape: banks will game regulatory requirements to minimize the capital they must hold. It is axiomatic that the more complicated the system, the more leeway banks will have to engage in such activity, termed *regulatory arbitrage*, reconfiguring their portfolios to achieve the maximum risk with the minimum amount of capital. In turn, the more room banks have to engage in such activity, the more difficult it becomes for regulators and investors to evaluate bank capital and monitor compliance.[8]

The far simpler capital measure presented by a leverage ratio would cabin banks' ability to engage in complex manipulation across risk weights and assets to minimize the amount of equity in their capital structure. Importantly and relatedly, although it does not prevent gaming by increasing the risk of assets held, a leverage-ratio requirement is easier for regulators and investors to monitor compliance with, as well as to evaluate banks' relative risk, because it will increase the comparability of banks' risk and performance compared with the IRB approach. This would have a beneficial feedback effect on bank managers' incentives to take risks because better-informed investors and regulators better convey their preferences regarding risk.

Demirguc-Kunt, Detragiache, and Merrouche (2013) analyzed whether better-capitalized banks performed better (in terms of stock returns) during the 2007–8 crisis. They considered a sample of 381 banks in 12 countries. In the financial crisis, they found a positive relation between capital and stock returns. Additionally, this positive relation was stronger when capital was measured by leverage ratios and not Basel risk-weighted capital, suggesting that the stock market did not view Basel risk adjustments as informative. Finally, they documented that the positive relation between capital and stock returns was mostly driven by higher-quality capital, such as common stock.

9.2 RESTRICTED-EQUITY-MORE-EQUITY-CAPITAL PROPOSAL

Following the global financial crisis, the Basel accord was further amended, first (Basel 2.5), to increase the capital requirements for securitized and off-balance-sheet assets at the core of the global crisis that had had preferential treatment and, second (Basel III), to add a further capital conservation buffer equal to 2.5% of risk-weighted assets to the existing 8% minimum capital requirement (which is not expected to impose a new minimum because a breach imposes a restriction on paying out dividends and bonuses rather than corrective regulatory action), along with a 3% leverage ratio and requirements to hold a specified amount of liquid assets.[9] A leverage ratio calculates the amount of capital in proportion to total assets independent of risk. Although new to international regulation, US banking regulators had long imposed a 4% leverage ratio on domestic banks in addition to the Basel risk-weighted minimum capital requirement.[10]

The postcrisis refinements to Basel II also expanded the assets against which capital must be held, increased the risk weights allocated to specific assets, and restricted the definition of bank capital such that even without the additional capital buffer (which has a long phase-in period) and despite retaining the Basel II capital minimum, banks would have to hold more capital than previously if they were not to alter the composition of their portfolios in response. The final piece of Basel III is an agreement by the Basel Committee that the largest, globally systemically important banks (G-SIBs) should be subject to enhanced capital requirements. G-SIBs will be classified into different "buckets" according to the institution's systemic importance, with the surcharge of additional risk-weighted capital ranging from 1% to 2.5% (because no banks will be placed into the highest bucket, calling for 3.5%).[11] As with the capital conservation buffer, if a G-SIB's capital falls below the required surcharge, it will be penalized by restrictions on payouts to shareholders and employees, along with development of a remediation plan to increase its capital, rather than be subjected to more stringent corrective action, as could occur on a breach of minimum capital requirements.[12]

Although the increase in capital requirements is a move in the right direction, to our mind, the Basel III level is still too low to be consistent with our third criterion for evaluating bank capital reform programs, that is, focus on creating and sustaining long-term shareholder value without any expectation of taxpayer-funded bailouts. We come to this understanding by reference, as a benchmark, to the level of capital held by banks before the crisis and the level that markets required of banks before governments stepped in to insure depositors. Consider precrisis capital levels: a comprehensive study of leverage across banks and countries indicates that at the start of the financial crisis, US banks' average capital was approximately 10% to 12% (i.e., around 90% of their capital structure consisted of debt securities).[13] At a debt level of 90%, a market shock adversely affecting asset value of slightly over 2% could push a firm below the minimum capital requirement, subjecting it to corrective regulatory action, and such firms' executives therefore would be operating in what is analogous to the insolvency zone for nonfinancial firms, in which managers' incentives and shareholders' interest align in taking extraordinarily high-risk gambles on firm value due to limited liability.

Moreover, although from the perspective of capital regulation precrisis banks might have appeared to be well capitalized, because they were operating above the regulatory minimum threshold, the financial crisis demonstrated that this assumption was mistaken.[14] Yet Basel III will raise the amount of required equity only to 4.5% (the minimum Tier 1 equity capital requirement). Such a requirement would hardly appear to be sufficient to withstand a repeat of the recent near-catastrophic collapse of short-term financing markets and the banking sector, in which the shock to asset values was as large as the amount of bank's capital (i.e., some large banks' equity declined from 10% to near zero).[15]

Consider also historical capital levels. Prior to the introduction of deposit insurance, US banks routinely held capital over 10%.[16,17] This level would appear to have been market driven because it exceeded (indeed was unrelated to) the amount required by regulation at the time. For instance, some states during this period required banks to hold a capital to deposit ratio of 10%, and national banks were subject to a similar requirement as of 1914.[18] UK banks similarly had much higher capital, with leverage into the 1960s equal to half the rate of recent decades.[19] The higher level of capital held in the pre–deposit insurance world suggests that it is the level at which creditors expected bank management's risk-taking to be controlled. In our judgment, this is probative evidence that Basel requirements are too low, for it suggests that creditors are willing to invest in banks with today's lower level of equity because of the modern phenomenon of government bailouts, in which all creditors, not just insured depositors, are covered.[20] We should note that a number of commentators have similarly advocated capital requirements significantly higher than 10%.[21]

Our bank capital proposal has two components:

- Bank capital should be calibrated to the ratio of *tangible common equity to total assets* (i.e., to total assets independent of risk), *not* the risk-weighted capital approach that is at the core of Basel. Tangible common equity includes common stock plus retained earnings (both via the income statement and unrealized value changes on cash flow hedges).
- Bank capital should be *at least 20%* of total assets.

We refer to our bank capital proposal as *restricted-equity-more-equity-capital proposal* to highlight the complementary nature of our bank capital proposal and the restricted equity proposal (which is at the core of our proposal to reform bank manager and director incentive compensation, as discussed in Chapters 6 and 7).

Some might consider bank capital of 20% to be excessive, too much, or too costly. We note two responses. First, the economic costs on a bank's shareholders of having 20% or greater bank capital are never carefully reasoned or stated. In Chapter 10, we discuss flaws in the arguments that banks should be financed mostly with debt. Second, the "costs" of 20% bank capital should be considered in the context of the economic and social costs that are imposed on the country by thinly capitalized banks undertaking high-risk (but value-destroying) projects. Recall that the financial crisis that started in 2007 has cost the economy a shortfall of $2.2 trillion and, more important, 4.4 million fewer jobs in the United States (see Hall 2014).

9.3   REGULATORY HYBRID SECURITIES (GONE-CONCERN CAPITAL): COCO BONDS AND TLACS

Earlier we noted that the strongest form of bank capital is common equity that can absorb losses without disrupting the bank's ongoing business activities; hence common equity can be thought of as *going-concern capital*. Recently, other forms of capital, referred to as *regulatory hybrid securities*, which can absorb losses after conversion to equity, have been proposed. We can think of these regulatory hybrid securities as *gone-concern capital* because they convert to equity only when the existing amount of common stock is insufficient to cover losses. The gone-concern capital comes in various flavors, such as contingent convertible bonds and total-loss-absorbing-capacity securities; these are discussed next.

French et al. (2010) in *The Squam Lake Report* proposed a thoughtful solution to the current thin equity capitalization of large banks: "The government should promote a long term debt instrument that converts to equity under specific conditions. Banks would issue

FIGURE 9.1 Balance sheet of a large bank. This figure presents stylized depictions of a large bank's capital structure under three scenarios: the current situation, the regulatory hybrid security proposal, and the restricted-equity-more-equity-capital proposal.

these bonds before a crisis, and if triggered, the automatic conversion of debt into equity would transform an undercapitalized or insolvent bank into a well-capitalized bank at no cost to taxpayers." These *contingent convertible bonds* are popularly known as *CoCos*. Subsequent to the financial crisis of 2008, European banks have issued CoCos worth about $450 billion (see Avdjiev et al. 2015). In the United States, banks issued a somewhat different security – senior debt whose face value could be reduced in the event of imminent bank failure; these securities are called *total-loss-absorbing-capacity securities* (TLACs).

Figure 9.1 provides a stylized depiction of a large bank's capital structure under three scenarios: the current situation, the regulatory hybrid security proposal, and the restricted-equity-more-equity-capital proposal noted earlier.

A potential advantage of the regulatory hybrid security proposal is that it requires less equity capital upfront. However, several authors have raised concerns about the incentive and legal problems the triggering mechanism would generate (which would lead to the conversion of the hybrid capital to equity) (e.g., see Flannery 2014; Duffie 2010; McDonald 2010). The recent experience of Deutsche Bank, UniCredit SpA, Barclays Plc, and Royal Bank of Scotland suggests that the security-design concerns raised about CoCos are quite real.[22] The illiquidity of bond markets raises concerns about the effectiveness of TLACs.[23] In a recent speech, Tom Hoenig, Vice Chairman of the FDIC, noted his skepticism with TLACs.[24]

Taylor and Kapur (2015) suggested a thoughtful and innovative reform to the bankruptcy process; they refer to it as "Chapter 14."[25] In essence, a specialized panel of bankruptcy judges would recapitalize the financially troubled big bank by requiring the bank's long-term unsecured debt holders to bear the losses such that the new bank would not be in bankruptcy. If the bank's long-term unsecured debt holders agree to bear the losses, the process appears to be viable. However, given the large dollar figures involved (e.g., the long-term unsecured debt holders would have to agree to losses over tens of billions of dollars), litigation is a real possibility. Prior agreements can make such litigation difficult but not impossible. The very threat of such litigation would cause uncertainty in the minds of investors, leading to potential disruption in the bank's financial market transactions.

As noted earlier, a potential advantage of the regulatory hybrid security proposal and the Chapter 14 proposal is that they require less equity capital upfront. If the banks had significantly more equity capital upfront, this would preclude the need for the regulatory hybrid security or Chapter 14 bankruptcy reform. A question that arises is, *Why are banks not capitalized with significantly more equity capital than the current norm?*

Chapter 10 discusses the flaws in the current received wisdom that large banks should be mostly financed with debt; in other words, we question the potential advantage of the regulatory hybrid security and Chapter 14 proposals' requirement of less equity capital *upfront*. Besides providing the correct incentives to managers to create and sustain long-term shareholder value, the restricted-equity-more-equity-capital proposal has the advantage of being simple and transparent. Capital market participants, especially bondholders, will value simplicity and transparency in a bank's capital structure – in light of their recent experience with large banks.

9.4 BANK CEO STOCK TRADING AND BANK CAPITAL

In Chapters 6 and 7, we showed that misaligned bank CEO incentive compensation and misaligned bank CEO incentives led to abnormally large bank CEO stock sales during 2000–8, and the CEO stock sales (more precisely, CEO net trades, which are stock sales minus stock purchases minus option exercise price) were related to the excessive risk-taking behavior of the "too big to fail" (TBTF) banks. In this section we investigate the relation between CEO net trades and bank capital.

As noted earlier, large TBTF banks like Citigroup and Goldman Sachs are very different from many smaller L-TARP and No-TARP banks in terms of size, operations, structure, and markets. Analyzing differences in CEO net trades without accounting for these differences may produce inappropriate inferences; hence we rely on the CEO and insider trading literature to control for this heterogeneity.

We estimate a Tobit model based on Aggarwal and Semwick (1999), Jenter (2005), Rozeff and Zaman (1998), and Seyhun (1986). This literature suggests the following determinants of CEO trading (in the shares of their firm's stock): firm size, book-to-market ratio, annual stock return for the prior year, stock volatility for the current year, CEO total compensation, percent CEO equity compensation (amount of equity compensation divided by total compensation for the prior year), and CEO stock holdings (value of the CEO's beneficial stock ownership at the end of the prior year).

The results in Table 9.1 indicate that even after controlling for bank and CEO characteristics, banks that have more equity in their capital structure are associated with smaller CEO stock sales during 2000–8. The Tobit model estimate implies that bank CEOs at the 25th percentile of bank capital-to-assets ratio sold $54.9 million more of their bank stock than CEOs at the 75th percentile of bank capital-to-assets ratio.

9.5   MANAGER INCENTIVES AND RISK-SHIFTING

There is a consensus in corporate finance that with risky debt outstanding, managers acting in the interest of shareholders have an incentive to invest in high-risk projects even if they are value-decreasing (negative net present value [NPV]) (e.g., see Smith and Warner 1979). Consistent with this argument, several authors have argued that bank

Table 9.1 *CEO Trading and Bank Capital*

This table presents the results from a Tobit estimation of the determinants of CEO *Net trades* for 2000–8. The dependent variable is *Net trades*, or (stock sales – stock purchases – option exercises). *Assets* are the natural logarithm of current year assets. *Book-to-market* ratio is the book value of equity divided by market value of equity for the current year. *Return* is the annual stock return for the prior year. *Stock volatility* is the standard deviation of daily stock returns for the current year. *CEO total compensation* is the natural logarithm of all cash and equity compensation in the prior year. *Percent CEO equity compensation* is the amount of equity compensation divided by total compensation for the prior year. *CEO stock holdings* are the natural logarithm of the dollar value of the CEO's beneficial stock ownership at the end of the prior year. *Capital-to-assets* is the book value of stockholders' equity divided by total assets in the current year. *TBTF dummy* is equal to 1 if the firm is one of the 14 TBTF firms and 0 otherwise. *L-TARP dummy* is equal to 1 if the firm in one of the 49 later-TARP firms and 0 otherwise. The model includes intercepts, year dummy variables, and firm fixed effects, not tabulated for conciseness. Coefficients are presented with *p*-values in parentheses.

	Dependent variable: Net Trades$_t$
Assets (log)$_t$	−1.344***(0.001)
Book-to-Market$_t$	−3.404***(0.007)
Return$_{t-1}$	−0.365(0.805)
Stock Volatility$_t$	36.806(0.289)
CEO Total Compensation$_{t-1}$	2.004***(0.003)
CEO% Equity Compensation$_{t-1}$	10.152***(0.000)
CEO Equity Holdings (log)$_{t-1}$	1.325***(0.000)
Capital-to-Assets$_t$	**−43.147***(0.006)**
TBTF dummy	**4.247**(0.016)**
L-Tarp dummy	1.673*(0.088)
No. of observations	883
Year controls	Yes
Firm fixed effects	Yes

Statistical significance is denoted by *for 10%, **for 5%, and ***for 1%, respectively. The boldface type highlights the relation between CEO trading and bank equity (*Capital-to-Assets*) and CEO trading in too-big-to-fail banks (TBTF dummy).

CEO compensation should be restructured so as to maximize the value of bank equity *and* debt. For example, Bolton, Mehran, and Shapiro (2010) (BMS) suggested that bank managers' compensation should be tied to the bank's default probability, as reflected in its credit default spread (CDS).

Conceptually, we are supportive of the BMS suggestion and think that it has considerable merit. However, we note two concerns with this recommendation. First, the aforementioned shareholder-bondholder conflict of interest becomes relevant when the bank has risky debt outstanding. If a bank's debt is relatively "safe," the relevance of this recommendation is less critical. However, if the bank debt is quite risky, the recommendation is quite relevant. At what point does a bank's debt transition from being relatively safe to quite risky? Second, and related to the first point, Bhagat and Romano (2009, 2010) emphasized that executive compensation structures should be transparent and simple; the transparency and simplicity criteria would enhance investor confidence in the company's compensation and governance structure. Tying managers' compensation to the bank's CDS would make managers' compensation both less transparent and less simple. Furthermore, managers will have an incentive to misrepresent financial/accounting numbers (which may be partially under their control) that outside analysts use to compute the CDS.

9.6   RECENT DEVELOPMENTS: BANK EQUITY CAPITAL

On June 2, 2016, two Federal Reserve Board governors signaled that big banks will be required to hold more equity.[26] We applaud the efforts of these Federal Reserve Board governors. We hope that the Federal Reserve requires bank capital to be calibrated to the ratio of tangible common equity to total assets (i.e., to total assets independent of risk) not the risk-weighted capital and require the denominator to include balance-sheet assets and off-balance-sheet assets (of structured investment vehicles). This latter requirement would dampen the concerns with the shadow banking system discussed in Chapter 10. Second, and more important, bank capital should be at least 20% of total assets –

for reasons noted in our bank capital proposal (restricted-equity,-more-equity-capital proposal) discussed in Section 9.2.

On June 23, 2016, US House Financial Services Committee Chairman Jeb Hensarling released a discussion draft of the Financial CHOICE (Creating Hope and Opportunity for Investors, Consumers and Entrepreneurs) Act.[27] The Financial CHOICE Act allows banks that have a leverage ratio of at least 10% to elect exemption from Basel III capital and liquidity standards and the Dodd-Frank Act Section 165 heightened prudential standards. The denominator of this leverage ratio would include total balance-sheet and off-balance-sheet assets; importantly, these total assets would be independent of risk. We applaud this proposal of the Financial CHOICE Act. As discussed in Section 9.1, the simple capital measure presented by the aforementioned leverage ratio (where the total assets in the denominator are independent of risk) would restrict banks' ability to engage in complex manipulation across risk weights and assets to minimize the equity in their capital structure. Importantly and relatedly, although it does not prevent gaming by increasing the risk of assets held, a leverage ratio requirement is easier for regulators and investors to monitor compliance with. This would have a beneficial feedback effect on bank managers' incentives to take risks because better-informed investors and regulators better convey their preferences regarding risk. The proposal of the Financial CHOICE Act provides another benefit; that is, because the denominator would include off-balance-sheet items of structured investment vehicles, it would dampen concerns with the shadow banking system; we discuss this further in Chapter 10.[28] In summary, the proposal of the Financial CHOICE Act is consistent with our bank capital proposal (restricted-equity-more-equity-capital proposal) discussed in Section 9.2; notably, its focus on (1) simplicity, (2) transparency, and (3) requiring the denominator of the leverage ratio be *total assets independent of risk* and include total *balance-sheet and off-balance-sheet assets*.

The *Wall Street Journal* in its July 29, 2016, op-ed noted that both the Republican and Democratic Party platforms called for reinstating the Glass-Steagall Act of 1933 that separates commercial banking and investment banking businesses.[29] In a similar vein, the Volcker Rule of the Dodd-Frank Act attempts to prevent/discourage commercial banks from risky securities trading. As noted earlier, the problem in implementing the Volcker Rule is in defining and identifying trades that are proprietary (where profits/losses accrue to the bank) versus market-making trades a bank makes in its normal course of business to serve a particular client. The *Wall Street Journal* suggests that "[t]he better solution is to shrink the taxpayer safety net, raising capital standards high enough so that banks that take insured deposits can better withstand trading or lending mistakes." We support the *Wall Street Journal* proposal; this proposal is consistent with our bank capital proposal (restricted-equity-more-equity-capital proposal). Under our bank capital proposal of greater equity financing of banks coupled with the restricted equity compensation structure for bank managers (and directors), managers (and directors) would not want to engage in proprietary trades that jeopardize the solvency/financial viability of the bank, for that would also jeopardize the value of the restricted stock and restricted stock options that they own and cannot sell until some years after they leave the bank. Furthermore, greater equity capitalization of the bank would provide a cushion against proprietary trades that do not turn out well for the bank. Regarding the market-making trades – to the extent that the market-making trades were value enhancing for the bank, bank managers would have the incentive to continue to engage in such market-making trades.

10 Why Banks Should Be Mostly Debt Financed

Parade of Non Sequiturs

The restricted equity incentive compensation proposal for bank managers logically leads to a complementary proposal regarding a bank's capital structure: The high leverage implied by debt ratios on the order of 95% (as was the case for many large banks in 2008) will magnify the impact of losses on equity value. As banks' equity values approach zero (as they did for some banks in 2008), equity-based incentive programs lose their effectiveness in motivating managers to enhance shareholder value. Additionally, our evidence suggests that bank CEOs sell significantly greater amounts of their stock as the bank's equity-to-capital ratio decreases. Hence, for equity-based incentive structures to be effective, banks should be financed with considerably more equity than they are being financed currently. Our recommendation for significantly greater equity in a bank's capital structure is consistent with the recent recommendations of Admati and Hellwig (2013) and Fama (2010).

In contrast, proponents of high bank leverage (these proponents include some finance academics, big bank managers, and paid lobbyists of the big banks) have offered a parade of horrible scenarios that would befall the economy if big banks were required to hold significantly more equity capital.[1] For example, bankers and their allies argue that if they were required to hold more equity, they would be forced to curtail their lending. To the extent that this lending would have been to individuals for mortgages and corporations for plant, equipment, and working capital, reduction in such lending would dampen economic growth and employment.[2] This argument is a classic confusion between a bank's investment and financing decisions. Lending activities are a part of a bank's *investment* decisions. Financing this lending with debt or equity is a *financing* decision.

In general, if a bank is engaged in value-enhancing investment activities, its investment activities should not affect how the funds are obtained (through debt or equity). As an illustrative example, consider an auto company that is financed with 45% debt and produces SUVs and sedans in quantities that the company managers think maximizes their profits. If the company were to decrease its financial leverage to 35% debt, would it start producing more SUVs? Probably not. In other words, if a bank were to lower its financial leverage (debt ratio), its lending activities would not be affected.

Another fallacy promoted by bank managers and their allies is that a bank's cost of capital will increase, leading to higher lending costs, if the banks are financed with less debt and more equity. Since cost of debt is less than cost of equity, bank managers and their allies incorrectly argue that greater financing with equity will increase the bank's cost of capital. The reason this argument is incorrect is based on the Noble Prize–winning work of Merton Miller and Franco Modigliani – essentially as the bank is financed with more equity, the equity becomes less risky; hence the cost of equity decreases. In general, the increase in equity financing by itself neither increases nor decreases the bank's cost of capital. This argument is not just a fine theoretical construct. Kisin and Manela (2014) considered the impact of a 10% increase in bank equity capital and estimated an upper bound of 3 basis points (0.03%) in the increase in the bank's cost of capital. Similarly, Kashyap, Stein, and Hanson (2010) considered the impact of a 10% increase in bank capital and estimated a range of 25 to 45 basis points in the increase in the bank's cost of capital. Junge and Kugler (2013) considered a sample of Swiss banks and found that halving their leverage would increase their cost of capital by about 14 basis points. Slovnik and Cournede (2011) and King (2010) considered a sample of Organisation for Economic Cooperation and Development (OECD) banks and documented an increase in the cost of capital of 150 to 160 basis points for a 10% increase in equity capital. For a sample of 13 OECD banks, the Basel Committee on Banking Supervision (2010) computed an increase of

130 basis points in the cost of capital for a 10% increase in equity capital. Miles, Yang, and Marcheggiano (2013) estimated that even if bank equity capital were doubled, bank cost of capital would increase only by 10 to 40 basis points.

From the viewpoint of economic policy, it is not the increase in bank cost of capital per se that is important, but the impact of the increase in bank cost of capital on bank lending. This leads to an even more important question. What is the impact of bank lending on the growth of nonfinancial (both entrepreneurial and larger, more mature) companies? As highlighted in endnote 2, bank lending is about 6% of the total financing for US manufacturing companies, the rest being equity and public debt. Furthermore, Myers (1977) suggested that debt (bank lending is debt) is not an appropriate source of financing for high-growth companies that will have the option to invest in many future projects. (This is one reason why high-tech companies tend not to have much debt in their capital structure.) Finally, the rather modest increase in the bank cost of capital from an increase in bank equity capital should be viewed in the context of the economic and social costs imposed on society by the financial crisis precipitated by the financial distress of the big banks.[3]

A third fallacy is that debt provides a discipline on bank managers: if the bank's debt ratio decreases, this discipline effect would be diluted. Some finance academics have constructed theoretical models to illustrate this argument. However, there is not a single empirical study that documents that debt provides discipline on bank managers in large *publicly held* banks. Indeed, the financial collapse of the "too big to fail" (TBTF) banks (which had debt ratio upwards of 95%) in 2008 is prima facie evidence inconsistent with the argument that debt provides discipline on bank managers. If debt holders in banks with 95% debt ratios could not or would not impose discipline on bank managers, when would debt holders impose such discipline?[4] Kaplan and Stromberg (2008) and Gompers, Kaplan, and Mukharlyamov (2014) documented the discipline effect of debt in *privately held* companies (subsequent to a going-private transaction sponsored by

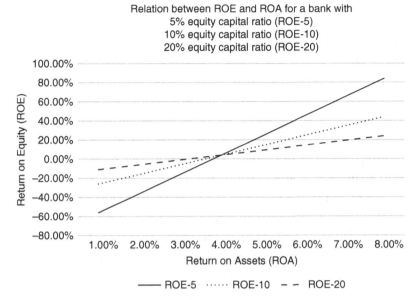

FIGURE 10.1 Return on equity (ROE) has a linear relationship with return on assets (ROA). The linear relationship becomes steeper as the company (bank) is financed with less equity. During good times when ROA is on the high side, for a given ROA, ROE is higher for banks financed with more debt. However, during not-so-good times, when ROA is on the low side, for a given ROA, ROE is lower for banks financed with more debt.

a private equity investor). The equity ownership structure in these newly privately held companies was significantly different from that in large publicly held banks; specifically, subsequent to a going-private transaction, equity is extremely concentrated in the newly privately held company.

The fourth fallacy: the return on equity (ROE) decreases as a bank is financed with more equity capital. A bank's return on assets (ROA) is a value-weighted average of the ROE and the return on debt. Most introductory corporate finance textbooks have a simple proof and illustration of the fact that ROE has a linear relationship with ROA. The linear relationship becomes steeper as the company (bank) is financed with less equity. As Figure 10.1 illustrates, during good times when ROA is on the high side, for a given ROA, ROE is higher for banks financed with more debt. However, during not-so-good times, when ROA is on the low side, for a given ROA, ROE is *lower* for banks financed with more debt. From the shareholder viewpoint, it is ROA that matters, not ROE.[5] Why would banks care about ROE? While bank shareholders might not care, bank managers whose incentive compensation depended on ROE *would* care. The restricted equity proposal noted earlier would focus the manager's attention on creating long-term shareholder value, and not on ROE that reflects short-term performance.

A fifth fallacy is that more banking activities would move to the shadow banking system if banks have to adhere to high equity capital ratio requirements.[6] The *shadow banking system* consists of financial intermediaries that performed functions similar to traditional banks – maturity, credit, and liquidity transformation; money-market mutual funds; and special-purpose vehicles (used for securitization) are examples of such intermediaries. They borrowed short term and invested in long-term illiquid assets; they were also highly leveraged. However, unlike the traditional banks, they did not have access to deposit insurance or central bank liquidity guarantees until 2008. Most of the shadow banks were off-balance-sheet vehicles of the traditional big banks. If the traditional big banks were to bring these off-balance-sheet vehicles onto their balance sheet, they would need additional equity capital to meet their equity capital ratio requirements. Big bank managers whose incentive compensation had a significant ROE component would prefer the high leverage of the off-balance-sheet vehicles because this would magnify the impact of these vehicles' earnings (at the time that these vehicles were created and subsequently) on the ROE of the traditional bank. While the big bank managers could benefit significantly from the off-balance-sheet vehicles, it is unclear how the big bank shareholders might benefit from these off-balance-sheet vehicles; shareholders care about projects/strategies that create and sustain long-term shareholder value, not ROE. Ultimately, as we saw in 2008, these off-balance-sheet vehicles imposed a significant cost on the big bank shareholders and US taxpayers. Under our restricted equity incentive compensation proposal and restricted-equity- more-equity-capital proposal, bank managers can create off-balance-sheet vehicles *if they so choose*; however, they will not have the incentive to create such off-balance-sheet vehicles unless these vehicles are value enhancing (in the positive NPV sense) investment projects that sustain their value in the long run. Our restricted equity incentive compensation proposal, coupled with the restricted-equity-more-equity-capital proposal, provides a powerful disincentive to bank managers to create off-balance-sheet vehicles that may generate some short-term profits but are value destroying (in the negative NPV sense) in the long run.

In essence, the parade of horribles is the parade of non sequiturs.

11 Conclusion

Before stating our conclusions, it is important to note that executive compensation reform and bank capital reform are not a panacea. While some have argued that incentives generated by executive compensation programs led to excessive risk-taking by banks contributing to the 2008 financial crisis, there are more important causes of the financial and economic crisis that started in 2008. For example, as detailed in Chapter 2, public policies regarding home mortgages whose goal was to increase home ownership by those who could not otherwise afford it are perhaps the single most important cause of the financial and economic crisis of 2008 (see Wallison 2015).

Our focus in this book, however, is on the executive compensation structure at the largest US financial institutions during the 2000s. We studied the executive compensation structure in the largest 14 US financial institutions during 2000–8 and compared it with that of CEOs of 37 US banks that neither sought nor received TARP funds. We focused on the CEOs' buys and sells of their banks' stock, purchases of stock via option exercise, and their salaries and bonuses during 2000–8. We considered the capital losses these CEOs incurred due to the dramatic share price declines in 2008. We compared the shareholder returns for these 14 TBTF banks and 37 No-TARP banks. We considered three measures of risk-taking by these banks: the banks' Z-scores, the banks' asset write-downs, and whether or not the banks borrowed capital from various Fed bailout programs and the amount of such capital. Finally, we implemented a battery of robustness checks including construction of a Tobit model of expected CEO trading based on the extant literature on insider and CEO trading; we estimateed abnormal CEO trading based on that Tobit model.

We found that "too big to fail" (TBTF) bank CEOs were able to realize a significantly larger amount on their equity by sales in the precrisis period (2000–7) compared with the large losses the executives experienced on their equity stakes during the crisis (2008). Additionally, stock sales by TBTF bank CEOs was significantly greater than stock sales of No-TARP bank CEOs in the precrisis period in both an absolute and a relative sense (controlling for beginning of period holdings). Finally, several different bank risk-taking measures suggested that TBTF banks were significantly riskier than No-TARP banks. Our results are mostly consistent with and supportive of the findings of Bebchuk, Cohen, and Spamann (2010); that is, managerial incentives matter – incentives generated by executive compensation programs are positively correlated with excessive risk-taking by banks in high-risk but value-reducing investment and trading strategies. Also, our results are generally not supportive of the conclusions of Fahlenbrach and Stulz (2011) that the poor performance of banks during the crisis was the result of unforeseen risk.

Based on our empirical analysis of the compensation structures at 100 of the largest US financial institutions, we recommend the following compensation structure for senior bank executives: executive incentive compensation should only consist of restricted stock and restricted stock options – restricted in the sense that the executive cannot sell the shares or exercise the options for one to three years after his or her last day in office. This will more appropriately align the long-term incentives of the senior executives with the interests of their stockholders. This incentive compensation proposal is developed and detailed in Bhagat and Romano (2009, 2010) and Bhagat, Bolton, and Romano (2014) and is consistent with several recent theoretical papers that suggest that a significant component of incentive compensation should consist of stock and stock options with long vesting periods (e.g., see Edmans et al. 2010; Peng and Roell 2009). If these vesting periods were "sufficiently long," they would be similar to the preceding proposal.

The abovementioned incentive compensation proposal logically leads to a complementary proposal regarding a bank's capital structure: The high leverage implied by debt ratios on the order of 95% (as was the case for many large banks in 2008) will magnify the impact of losses on equity value. As banks' equity values approach zero (as they did for some banks in 2008), equity-based incentive programs lose their effectiveness in motivating managers to enhance shareholder value. Additionally, our evidence suggests that bank CEOs sell significantly greater amounts of their stock as the bank's equity-to-capital ratio decreases. Hence, for equity-based incentive structures to be effective, banks should be financed with considerably more equity than they are being financed currently.

Specifically, our bank capital proposal has two components: First, bank capital should be calibrated to the ratio of tangible common equity to total assets (i.e., to total assets independent of risk). Second, bank capital should be at least 20% of total assets. Our recommendation for significantly greater equity in a bank's capital structure is consistent with the recent recommendations of Admati and Hellwig (2013) and Fama (2010).[1]

Greater equity financing of banks coupled with the abovementioned compensation structure for bank managers and directors will drastically diminish the likelihood of a bank falling into financial distress. This will effectively address two of the more significant challenges facing implementation of the Dodd-Frank Act. The first challenge is the *TBTF problem*. Regulators and their critics have observed that implementation of the Dodd-Frank Act may have institutionalized the TBTF aspect of the largest US banks. Policymakers note that TBTF banks are here to stay and are proposing explicit or implicit taxes on banks above a certain threshold size. The major problem with the TBTF banks is exactly that – they are *too big to fail*. Under our proposal (of greater equity financing of banks coupled with a compensation structure for bank managers and directors that discourages managers from undertaking high-risk investments that are value destroying, instead focusing their attention on creating and sustaining long-term shareholder value), managers (and directors) would not want to grow their banks to a size (or manage a bank of a size) that would jeopardize their solvency/financial viability, for that would also jeopardize the value of their restricted stock and restricted stock options that they own and cannot sell until some years after they leave the bank. Furthermore, greater equity capitalization of the banks would provide a cushion against investments that ex ante were value enhancing but ex post were value reducing. The second challenge is that the *Volcker Rule essentially prohibits/discourages proprietary trading* by TBTF banks. The problem in implementing the Volcker Rule is in defining and identifying trades that are "proprietary" (where profits/losses accrue to the bank) versus trades a bank makes in its normal course of business to serve a particular client. Under our proposal (of greater equity financing of banks coupled with the proposed compensation structure for bank managers and directors), managers (and directors) would not want to engage in proprietary trades that jeopardize the solvency/financial viability of their banks, for that would also jeopardize the value of the restricted stock and restricted stock options they own and cannot sell until some years after they leave the bank. Furthermore, greater equity capitalization of the banks would provide a cushion against proprietary trades that do not turn out well for them.

Two aspects of our incentive compensation proposal need emphasis: this proposal, unlike most other executive compensation reform proposals, does *not* place a ceiling on executive compensation. The proposal only limits the annual *cash* payouts an executive can realize. The *present value* of all salary and stock compensation can be higher than bank managers have received historically because the amount of restricted stock and restricted stock options that can be awarded to a bank manager is essentially unlimited per our proposal, though, in practice, the award amounts should and need to be anchored to the current practices in the particular company. Of course, the higher value would only be realized were the managers to invest in projects that lead to value creation that persists in the long term, in which case we have a win for long-term investors and a win for managers. Also, a focus on creating and sustaining long-term shareholder value would minimize the likelihood of a bailout, which would be a win for taxpayers. Finally, we note that the incentive compensation proposal and the bank equity capitalization proposal rely only on the private incentives and actions of bank managers, bank directors, and bank institutional investors. More specifically, our proposals do *not* rely on additional regulations.

While our focus here is on banks, the incentives generated by the proposed compensation structure would be relevant for maximizing long-term shareholder value in other industries. Hence corporate board compensation committees and institutional investors in firms in other *nonfinancial* industries should also give the abovementioned executive incentive compensation structure serious consideration. Finally, we suggest that *directors* in both financial and nonfinancial companies should adopt a similar incentive compensation structure with regard to their own incentive compensation.

Appendix A
Credit-Rating Agencies and the Subprime Mortgage Securitization Process

Until the turn of the millennium, most mortgage loans were made to borrowers with good credit histories conforming to underwriting standards set by government-sponsored agencies; these loans are referred to as *conforming loans*. However, during 2000–8, subprime and Alt-A loans rapidly increased their market share. *Subprime mortgages* refer to borrowers that have poor credit histories. *Alt-A loans* are made to borrowers with good credit histories but with aggressive underwriting, such as no documentation of income.

Most lending institutions that issue mortgages to homeowners do not carry these mortgages on their balance sheets but sell these mortgages to issuers who, in turn, sell them (eventually) to investors as fixed-income securities. Both subprime loans and Alt-A loans experienced significant increases in the securitization of the loans as a percentage of loans originated. The process of conversion of mortgages to risky fixed-income securities is known as *securitization*. A simplified version of the securitization process is illustrated in Figure A.1.

The securitization process starts when a homeowner/mortgagor finances the purchase of a home or refinances a home. The originator/lender sells the mortgage to a government-backed agency (e.g., Fannie Mae or, Freddie Mac) or an investment bank acting as a mortgage-backed security (MBS) sponsor. The MBS sponsor keeps only a small percentage of the mortgages and pools the rest with similar mortgages and sells them to a bankruptcy-remote trust. The trust issues bonds to institutional investors (e.g., pension funds and hedge funds). The issuer is bankruptcy remote in the sense that if the MBS sponsor goes bankrupt, the assets of the trust/issuer will not be distributed to the creditors of the MBS sponsor. Marketability of the bonds is enhanced by the credit ratings from bond-rating agencies (e.g., Moody's, Standard and Poor's [S&P], and Fitch).

CONFLICT OF INTEREST BETWEEN THE CREDIT-RATING AGENCIES AND THE MBS SPONSOR

The trust/issuer of the mortgage-backed bonds can be viewed as an investment company, as defined in the Investment Company Act of 1940, and hence would be

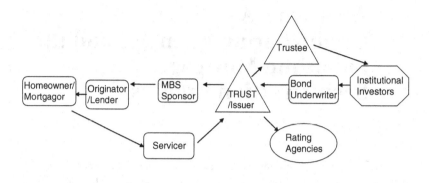

represents flow of dollars.

FIGURE A.I Securitization of mortgage-backed securities.

subject to the extensive requirements of the act (see Bethel, Ferrell, and Hu 2008). However, the trust/issuer can claim exemption from the act if it issues only fixed-income securities that, at issue, received one of the four highest ratings from a nationally recognized rating agency (e.g., S&P, Moody's, and Fitch).

This situation has the potential to create a conflict of interest between the credit-rating agencies and MBS sponsors that set up the trust/issuer because the trust's ability to claim exemption from the 1940 act depends on the ratings provided by the rating agencies. Figure A.2 shows Moody's revenues from rating various securities. While in the first quarter of 2001 Moody's quarterly revenue from rating structured securities (including MBS securities) was slightly greater than from rating corporate securities, by the fourth quarter of 2006, Moody's quarterly revenue from rating structured securities (including MBS securities) was about three times than from rating corporate securities. To the extent that there was a conflict between the credit-rating agencies and MBS sponsors, this was severely exacerbated by 2006.

The aforementioned conflict is similar to the conflict of interest noted in the accounting literature between the auditors and shareholders of firms they were auditing, driven by the large nonaudit fees the auditors were earning from the companies they were auditing in the pre-Sarbanes-Oxley era (see Dhaliwal et al. 2008; Hoitash, Markelevich, and Barragato 2007).

CONFLICT OF INTEREST BETWEEN THE CREDIT-RATING AGENCIES AND INVESTMENT MANAGERS

Until now, credit-rating agencies have used the same rating system to rate mortgage-backed bonds as they do to rate corporate bonds. The methodology to

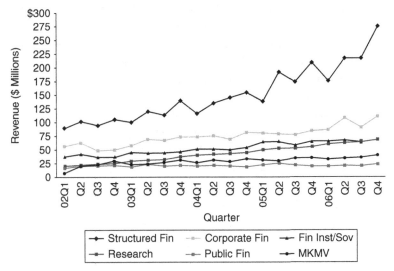

FIGURE A.2 Moody's quarterly revenues from rating various securities. In the first quarter of 2001, Moody's quarterly revenue from rating structured securities (including MBS) was slightly greater than from rating corporate securities. By the fourth quarter of 2006, Moody's quarterly revenue from rating structured securities (including MBS) was about three times that from rating corporate securities. (*Source:* Moody's, http://ir.moodys.com/Mobile/file.aspx? IID=108462&FID=4597523.)

rate corporate bonds is well understood and has been validated by empirical data going back almost a century. Credit-rating agencies are required to and do disclose their criteria and methodology for rating mortgage-backed bonds. However, there are concerns about the complexity and transparency of the models used by the rating agencies (see Mason and Rosner 2007). Perhaps even more important, given the brief existence (less than a decade in some cases) of the ever-more-complex MBS, we do not have the empirical validity of these models to the same level of statistical confidence as for corporate debt.

In 2007, Moody's downgraded several AAA-rated mortgage-backed bonds to junk status within a matter of weeks (see Crouhy and Turnbull 2008). Such a significant drop in rating in such a short period is almost unheard of for corporate bonds (see Hirsch and Bannier 2008). This suggests that AAA-rated mortgage-backed bonds have a higher credit risk than AAA-rated corporate bonds.

Pension funds, hedge funds, and other institutional investors that invest in mortgage-backed bonds usually do so via an investment manager(s) who has discretion over which and how much of various MBS to hold. Part of the incentive compensation of these fund managers depends on the extent to which their portfolios' returns exceeds a benchmark. A mortgage-backed bond portfolio invested in AAA-rated bonds would usually have the AAA return (from investing in a representative basket of AAA-rated corporate and mortgage-backed bonds) as a benchmark. However, as noted earlier, AAA-rated mortgage-backed bonds are riskier than AAA-rated corporate bonds. Hence a portfolio of AAA-rated mortgage-backed bonds would have a higher expected return than a representative basket of AAA-rated corporate and mortgage-backed bonds.

Appendix B
Data Used in This Book: Available Online

We provide the following three databases used in the empirical analysis in this book. They are available online.

1. This database lists insider trading by TBTF bank CEOs and No-TARP bank CEOs during 2000–8 and motivates our recommendation for executive compensation reform:
   http://leeds-faculty.colorado.edu/bhagat/Bhagat-JCF-2014.xlsx
2. This database indicates corporate governance and director ownership and motivates our recommendation for director compensation policy:
   http://leeds-faculty.colorado.edu/bhagat/Bhagat-DirectorOwnershipData.xlsx
3. This database provides an analysis of bank risk and bank size:
   http://leeds-faculty.colorado.edu/bhagat/Bhagat-BankRiskSize.xlsx

Table B.1 *TARP Recipient Information*

	Bank	TARP amount received ($000)	Date received initial TARP funding		Bank	TARP amount received ($000)	Date received initial TARP funding
(1)	Anchor Bancorp, Inc./WI	$110,000	January 30, 2009	(27)	Provident Bankshares Corp.	$151,500	November 14, 2008
(2)	Associated Banc-Corp.	525,000	November 21, 2008	(28)	Regions Financial Corp.	3,500,000	November 14, 2008
(3)	BB&T Corp.	3,133,640	November 14, 2008	(29)	South Financial Group, Inc.	347,000	December 5, 2008
(4)	Boston Private Financial Holdings	154,000	November 21, 2008	(30)	Sterling Bancorp/NY	42,000	December 23, 2008
(5)	Cascade Bancorp	38,970	November 21, 2008	(31)	Sterling Bancshares/TX	125,198	December 12, 2008
(6)	Cathay General Bancorp	258,000	December 5, 2008	(32)	Sterling Financial Corp./WA	303,000	December 5, 2008
(7)	Central Pacific Financial Corp.	135,000	January 9, 2009	(33)	Suntrust Banks, Inc.	4,850,000	November 14, 2008
(8)	City National Corp.	400,000	November 21, 2008	(34)	Susquehanna Bancshares, Inc.	300,000	December 12, 2008
(9)	Comerica, Inc.	2,250,000	November 14, 2008	(35)	SVB Financial Group	235,000	December 12, 2008

No.	Name	Amount	Date
(10)	East West Bancorp, Inc.	306,546	December 5, 2008
(11)	Fifth Third Bancorp	3,408,000	December 31, 2008
(12)	First Bancorp	424,174	January 16, 2009
(13)	First Financial Bancorp, Inc./OH	80,000	December 23, 2008
(14)	First Horizon National Corp.	866,540	November 14, 2008
(15)	First Midwest Bancorp, Inc.	193,000	December 5, 2008
(16)	First Niagara Financial Group	184,011	November 21, 2008
(17)	Firstmerit Corp.	125,000	January 9, 2009
(18)	Flagstar Bancorp Inc.	266,657	January 30, 2009
(19)	Huntington Bancshares	1,398,071	November 14, 2008
(20)	Independent Bank Corp./MI	74,426	December 12, 2008
(36)	Synovus Financial Corp.	967,870	December 19, 2008
(37)	TCF Financial Corp.	361,172	November 14, 2008
(38)	US Bancorp	6,599,000	November 14, 2008
(39)	UCBH Holdings, Inc.	298,737	November 14, 2008
(40)	Umpqua Holdings Corp.	214,181	November 14, 2008
(41)	United Community Banks, Inc.	180,000	December 5, 2008
(42)	Wachovia Corp.	239	July 1, 2009
(43)	Washington Fed Inc.	200,000	November 14, 2008
(44)	Webster Financial Corp.	400,000	November 21, 2008
(45)	Westamerica Bancorporation	83,726	February 13, 2009
(46)	Wilmington Trust Corp.	330,000	December 12, 2008

Table B.1 (cont.)

	Bank	TARP amount received ($000)	Date received initial TARP funding		Bank	TARP amount received ($000)	Date received initial TARP funding
(21)	Keycorp	2,500,000	November 14, 2008	(47)	Wilshire Bancorp. Inc.	62,158	December 12, 2008
(22)	M&T Bank Corp.	600,000	December 23, 2008	(48)	Wintrust Financial Corp.	250,000	December 19, 2008
(23)	Marshall & Ilsley Corp.	1,715,000	November 14, 2008	(49)	Zions Bancorporation	1,400,000	November 14, 2008
(24)	Northern Trust Corp.	1,576,000	November 14, 2008				
(25)	PNC Financial Services Group, Inc.	7,579,200	December 31, 2008		Total	$50,437,016	
(26)	Popular, Inc.	935,000	December 5, 2008				

Note: This table shows how much TARP money each of the 49 L-TARP firms received and when they first received TARP funding.

Table B.2 *CEOs during 2000 and 2008 by Firm*

	Company	2000 CEO	2008 CEO
	TBTF sample		
(1)	AIG	Maurice Greenberg	Edward Liddy
(2)	Bank of America	Ken Lewis	Ken Lewis
(3)	Bank of New York	Thomas Renyi	Robert Kelly
(4)	Bear Stearns	James Cayne	Alan Schwartz
(5)	Citigroup	Sandy Weill	Vikram Pandit
(6)	Countrywide Financial	Angelo Mozilo	Angelo Mozilo
(7)	Goldman Sachs	Henry Paulson	Lloyd Blankfein
(8)	JP Morgan	William Harrison	James Dimon
(9)	Lehman Brothers	Richard Fuld	Richard Fuld
(10)	Mellon Financial	Martin McGuinn	Robert Kelly (2007)
(11)	Merrill Lynch	David Komansky	John Thain
(12)	Morgan Stanley	Philip Purcell	John Mack
(13)	State Street	Marshall Carter	Ronald Logue
(14)	Wells Fargo	Richard Kovacevich	John Stumpf
	L-TARP sample		
(1)	Anchor Bancorp, Inc./WI	Douglas J. Timmerman	Douglas J. Timmerman
(2)	Associated Banc-Corp.	Robert C. Gallagher	Paul S. Beideman
(3)	BB&T Corp.	John A. Allison, IV	John A. Allison, IV
(4)	Boston Private Financial Holdings	Timothy Landon Vaill	Timothy Landon Vaill
(5)	Cascade Bancorp	Patricia L. Moss	Patricia L. Moss
(6)	Cathay General Bancorp	Dunson K. Cheng, Ph.D.	Dunson K. Cheng, Ph.D.
(7)	Central Pacific Financial Corp.	Joichi Saito	Clint Arnoldus
(8)	City National Corp.	Russell Goldsmith	Russell Goldsmith
(9)	Comerica, Inc.	Eugene A. Miller	Ralph W. Babb, Jr.
(10)	East West Bancorp, Inc.	Dominic Ng	Dominic Ng
(11)	Fifth Third Bancorp	George A. Schaefer, Jr.	Kevin T. Kabat

Table B.2 (cont.)

	Company	2000 CEO	2008 CEO
(12)	First Bancorp	Angel Alvarez-Perez	Luis M. Beauchamp
(13)	First Financial Bancorp, Inc./OH	Stanley Pontius	Claude Davis
(14)	First Horizon National Corp.	Ralph Horn	Gerald L. Baker
(15)	First Midwest Bancorp, Inc.	Robert P. O'Meara	John M. O'Meara
(16)	First Niagara Financial Group	William Swan	John R. Koelmel
(17)	Firstmerit Corp.	John R. Cochran	Paul Greig
(18)	Flagstar Bancorp, Inc.	Thomas J. Hammond	Mark T. Hammond
(19)	Huntington Bancshares	Frank G. Wobst	Thomas E. Hoaglin
(20)	Independent Bank Corp./MI	Charles van Loan	Michael M. Magee, Jr.
(21)	Keycorp	Robert W. Gillespie	Henry L. Meyer, III
(22)	M&T Bank Corp.	Robert G. Wilmers	Robert G. Wilmers
(23)	Marshall & Ilsley Corp.	James B. Wigdale	Mark F. Furlong
(24)	Northern Trust Corp.	William A. Osborn	Frederick H. Waddell
(25)	PNC Financial Services Group, Inc.	James E. Rohr	James E. Rohr
(26)	Popular, Inc.	Richard L. Carrion	Richard L. Carrion
(27)	Provident Bankshares Corp.	Peter M. Martin	Gary N. Geisel
(28)	Regions Financial Corp.	Carl E. Jones, Jr.	C. Dowd Ritter
(29)	South Financial Group, Inc.	Mack I. Whittle, Jr.	Mack I. Whittle, Jr.
(30)	Sterling Bancorp/NY	Louis J. Cappelli	Louis J. Cappelli
(31)	Sterling Bancshares/TX	George Martinez	J. Downey Bridgwater

Table B.2 (cont.)

	Company	2000 CEO	2008 CEO
(32)	Sterling Financial Corp./WA	Harold B. Gilkey	Harold B. Gilkey
(33)	Suntrust Banks, Inc.	L. Phillip Humann	James M. Wells, III
(34)	Susquehanna Bancshares, Inc.	Robert S. Bolinger	William John Reuter
(35)	SVB Financial Group	John C. Dean	Kenneth Parmalee Wilcox
(36)	Synovus Financial Corp.	James H. Blanchard	Richard E. Anthony
(37)	TCF Financial Corp.	Bill Cooper	Lynn A. Nagorske
(38)	U S Bancorp	Jerry A. Grundhofer	Richard K. Davis
(39)	UCBH Holdings, Inc.	Thomas S. Wu	Thomas S. Wu
(40)	Umpqua Holdings Corp.	Raymond P. Davis	Raymond P. Davis
(41)	United Community Banks Inc.	Jimmy Tallent	Jimmy Tallent
(42)	Wachovia Corp.	G. Kennedy Thompson	G. Kennedy Thompson
(43)	Washington Fed, Inc.	Guy C. Pinkerton	Roy Whitehead
(44)	Webster Financial Corp.	James C. Smith	James C. Smith
(45)	Westamerica Bancorporation	David L. Payne	David L. Payne
(46)	Wilmington Trust Corp.	Ted Thomas Cecala	Ted Thomas Cecala
(47)	Wilshire Bancorp, Inc.	Soo Bong Min	Joanne Kim
(48)	Wintrust Financial Corp.	Edward Joseph Wehmer	Edward Joseph Wehmer
(49)	Zions Bancorporation	Harris H. Simmons	Harris H. Simmons
No-TARP sample			
(1)	Astoria Financial Corp.	George L. Engelke, Jr.	George L. Engelke, Jr.
(2)	Bank Mutual Corp.	Michael T. Crowley, Jr.	Michael T. Crowley, Jr.

Table B.2 (*cont.*)

	Company	2000 CEO	2008 CEO
(3)	Bank of Hawaii Corp.	Lawrence M. Johnson	Al Landon
(4)	Brookline Bancorp, Inc.	Richard P. Chapman, Jr.	Richard P. Chapman, Jr.
(5)	Chittenden Corp.	Paul A. Perrault	Paul A. Perrault (2007)
(6)	Colonial Bancgroup	Robert E. Lowder	Robert E. Lowder
(7)	Commerce Bancorp, Inc./NJ	Vernon W. Hill, II	Vernon W. Hill, II (2007)
(8)	Compass Bancshares, Inc.	D. Paul Jones Jr.	D. Paul Jones Jr. (2006)
(9)	Corus Bankshares, Inc.	Robert J. Glickman	Robert J. Glickman
(10)	Cullen/Frost Bankers, Inc.	Richard W. Evans, Jr.	Richard W. Evans, Jr.
(11)	Dime Community Bancshares	Vincent F. Palagiano	Vincent F. Palagiano
(12)	Downey Financial Corp.	Daniel D. Rosenthal	Daniel D. Rosenthal
(13)	First Commonwealth Financial Corp./PA	Joseph E. O'Dell	John J. Dolan
(14)	First Indiana Corp.	Marni McKinney	Robert H. Warrington (2007)
(15)	Firstfed Financial Corp./CA	Babette E. Heimbuch	Babette E. Heimbuch
(16)	Franklin Bank Corp.	Anthony J. Nocella	Anthony J. Nocella (2006)
(17)	Fremont General Corp.	James A. McIntyre	James A. McIntyre (2007)
(18)	Glacier Bancorp, Inc.	Michael J. Blodnick	Michael J. Blodnick
(19)	Greater Bay Bancorp	David L. Kalkbrenner	Byron A. Scordelis (2007)
(20)	Hanmi Financial Corp.	Chung Hoon Youk	Jay Seung Yoo
(21)	Hudson City Bancorp, Inc.	Leonard Gudelski	Ronald E. Hermance, Jr.

Table B.2 (*cont.*)

	Company	2000 CEO	2008 CEO
(22)	Indymac Bancorp, Inc.	Michael W. Perry	Michael W. Perry
(23)	Investors Financial Services Corp.	Kevin J. Sheehan	Kevin J. Sheehan (2007)
(24)	Irwin Financial Corp.	William I. Miller	William I. Miller
(25)	Jefferies Group, Inc.	Frank E. Baxter	Richard B. Handler
(26)	MAF Bancorp, Inc.	Allen H. Koranda	Allen H. Koranda (2007)
(27)	Mercantile Bankshares Corp.	H. Furlong Baldwin	Edward J. Kelly, III (2007)
(28)	National City Corp	David A. Daberko	Peter E. Raskind
(29)	New York Community Bancorp, Inc.	Joseph R. Ficalora	Joseph R. Ficalora
(30)	Prosperity Bancshares, Inc.	David Zalman	David Zalman
(31)	SLM Corp.	Albert L. Lord	Albert L. Lord
(32)	Sovereign Bancorp Inc.	Jay S. Sidhu	James Campanelli
(33)	TD Banknorth, Inc.	William J. Ryan	William J. Ryan (2007)
(34)	Trustco Bank Corp/NY	Robert A. McCormick	Robert J. McCormick
(35)	Unionbancal Corp.	Takahiro Moriguchi	Masaaki Tanaka
(36)	United Bankshares, Inc./WV	Richard M. Adams	Richard M. Adams
(37)	Washington Mutual, Inc.	Kerry K. Killinger	Kerry K. Killinger

Table B.3 *Net CEO Payoffs, 2000–8, L-TARP and No-TARP Firms*

L-TARP sample	Value of stock holdings, first available year	Total net trades, 2000–8 (A)	Total cash compensation, 2000–8 (B)	CEO payoff, 2000–8 (A) + (B)	Estimated value lost, 2008 (C)	Net CEO payoff,; 2000–8 (A) + (B) + (C)	Estimated value remaining, last available year
(1) Anchor Bancorp, Inc./WI	$26,883,312	$3,798,047	$5,192,086	$8,990,133	($23,352,645)	($14,362,512)	$4,023,879
(2) Associated Banc-Corp.	8,874,040	(30,001,135)	10,036,279	(19,964,856)	(2,514,926)	(22,479,782)	10,651,717
(3) BB&T Corp.	21,728,513	(192,218)	19,920,237	19,728,019	(9,082,332)	10,645,687	69,856,043
(4) Boston Private Financial Holdings	2,967,297	5,267,959	9,584,909	14,852,868	(1,786,159)	13,066,709	3,043,417
(5) Cascade Bancorp	954,474	2,306,853	4,382,294	6,689,147	(871,749)	5,817,398	1,658,455
(6) Cathay General Bancorp	7,674,180	(980,910)	12,863,900	11,882,990	5,729,173	17,612,163	51,744,861
(7) Central Pacific Financial Corp.	945,087	(301,657)	6,214,516	5,912,859	(2,520,893)	3,391,966	2,872,846
(8) City National Corp.	156,887,269	(37,714,990)	16,117,173	(21,597,817)	(3,985,288)	(25,583,105)	242,211,301

(9)	Comerica, Inc.	37,008,078	3,280,726	18,839,384	22,120,110	(15,280,838)	6,839,272	24,624,024
(10)	East West Bancorp Inc.	1,418,168	56,001,460	14,864,316	70,865,776	(2,120,623)	68,745,153	18,937,545
(11)	Fifth Third Bancorp	94,954,671	16,004,385	18,070,201	34,074,586	(7,763,859)	26,310,727	7,031,606
(12)	First Bancorp	45,775,262	(2,501,250)	15,018,008	12,516,758	2,187,039	14,703,797	23,368,066
(13)	First Financial Bancorp, Inc./OH	2,873,880	(413,182)	4,816,840	4,403,658	(244,623)	4,159,035	6,270,294
(14)	First Horizon National Corp.	23,241,420	375,598	11,880,415	12,256,013	(501,156)	11,754,857	2,948,692
(15)	First Midwest Bancorp, Inc.	14,742,812	(862,537)	8,189,626	7,327,089	(5,912,611)	1,414,478	3,319,214
(16)	First Niagara Financial Group	1,327,892	514,706	7,965,734	8,480,440	683,777	9,164,217	5,739,089
(17)	Firstmerit Corp.	17,860,203	(6,003,165)	8,860,208	2,857,043	(9,467)	2,847,576	6,337,911
(18)	Flagstar Bancorp, Inc.	45,270,316	11,201,395	19,186,296	30,387,691	(43,717,085)	(13,329,394)	6,764,771
(19)	Huntington Bancshares	52,930,054	(1,083,970)	10,556,604	9,472,634	(5,627,131)	3,845,503	10,083,762

Table B.3 (cont.)

L-TARP sample	Value of stock holdings, first available year	Total net trades, 2000–8 (A)	Total cash compensation, 2000–8 (B)	CEO payoff, 2000–8 (A) + (B)	Estimated value lost, 2008 (C)	Net CEO payoff,: 2000–8 (A) + (B) + (C)	Estimated value remaining, last available year
(20) Independent Bank Corp./MI	1,465,205	1,090,134	3,786,875	4,877,009	(1,625,078)	3,251,931	452,215
(21) Keycorp	24,300,354	4,695,583	20,237,912	24,933,495	(36,317,124)	(11,383,629)	24,788,625
(22) M&T Bank Corp.	265,037,489	90,350,005	9,085,770	99,435,775	(113,182,135)	(13,746,360)	268,105,332
(23) Marshall & Ilsley Corp.	45,209,703	15,672,931	15,648,886	31,321,817	(8,294,696)	23,027,121	15,274,236
(24) Northern Trust Corp.	70,233,651	14,326,627	24,018,750	38,345,377	(9,471,342)	28,874,035	38,157,929
(25) PNC Financial Services Group, Inc.	23,326,198	27,578,906	25,155,677	52,734,583	(34,503,496)	18,231,087	121,397,696
(26) Popular, Inc.	24,550,247	(2,617,270)	8,197,988	5,580,718	(21,051,901)	(15,471,183)	16,843,164
(27) Provident Bankshares Corp.	5,652,313	993,635	5,673,032	6,666,667	(279,756)	6,386,911	2,782,014
(28) Regions Financial Corp.	12,396,381	(565,296)	17,301,072	16,735,776	(43,953,037)	(27,217,261)	34,317,749

(29)	South Financial Group Inc.	2,191,101	452,030	10,437,874	10,889,904	(3,703,946)	7,185,958	3,913,017
(30)	Sterling Bancorp/NY	5,879,775	2,575,267	11,518,086	14,093,353	(1,681,301)	12,412,053	12,935,239
(31)	Sterling Bancshares/TX	7,054,247	838,199	4,590,931	5,429,130	(564,560)	4,864,570	1,126,229
(32)	Sterling Financial Corp./WA	1,567,650	803,276	6,372,000	7,175,276	(3,712,860)	3,462,416	5,864,179
(33)	Suntrust Banks, Inc.	34,081,567	(8,221,733)	15,774,785	7,553,052	(18,290,432)	(10,737,380)	23,110,708
(34)	Susquehanna Bancshares, Inc.	334,207	547,821	5,346,337	5,894,158	(467,600)	5,426,558	2,053,472
(35)	SVB Financial Group	4,622,784	12,635,192	8,174,164	20,809,356	(4,567,862)	16,241,494	6,498,273
(36)	Synovus Financial Corp.	54,912,811	(117,344)	11,148,955	11,031,611	(6,262,324)	4,769,287	19,362,713
(37)	TCF Financial Corp.	49,462,373	10,610,158	14,014,293	24,624,451	(15,840,669)	8,783,782	57,282,527
(38)	US Bancorp	52,502,559	48,810,074	27,831,430	76,641,504	(23,469,447)	53,172,057	86,149,221
(39)	UCBH Holdings, Inc.	2,883,021	3,589,388	13,110,000	16,699,388	(3,450,231)	13,249,157	27,597,035

Table B.3 (cont.)

L-TARP sample	Value of stock holdings, first available year	Total net trades, 2000–8 (A)	Total cash compensation, 2000–8 (B)	CEO payoff, 2000–8 (A) + (B)	Estimated value lost, 2008 (C)	Net CEO payoff,: 2000–8 (A) + (B) + (C)	Estimated value remaining, last available year
(40) Umpqua Holdings Corp.	1,978,915	2,718,719	5,515,478	8,234,197	(490,928)	7,743,269	7,758,148
(41) United Community Banks, Inc.	11,171,789	(2,653,737)	6,006,000	3,352,263	(2,806,476)	545,787	12,054,871
(42) Wachovia Corp.	11,549,139	(2,665,951)	36,960,000	34,294,049	(96,106,292)	(61,812,243)	120,916,584
(43) Washington Fed, Inc.	453,935	(2,906,287)	3,529,059	622,772	(1,728,100)	(1,105,328)	3,488,208
(44) Webster Financial Corp.	22,512,768	4,112,804	10,912,779	15,025,583	(19,151,297)	(4,125,714)	14,699,167
(45) Westamerica Bancorporation	32,713,282	12,314,172	7,093,024	19,407,196	(3,391,607)	16,015,589	113,824,504
(46) Wilmington Trust Corp.	14,322,737	2,028,626	10,462,281	12,490,907	(8,649,788)	3,841,119	23,807,253
(47) Wilshire Bancorp, Inc.	7,715,768	3,251,684	1,846,397	5,098,081	110,822	5,208,903	1,116,477
(48) Wintrust Financial Corp.	4,561,083	11,834,959	5,931,149	17,766,108	(6,792,709)	10,973,399	9,959,418
(49) Zions Bancorporation	101,414,151	9,741,440	8,930,000	18,671,440	(55,425,946)	(36,754,506)	66,172,980

No-TARP sample	Value of stock holdings, first available year	Total net trades, 2000–8 (A)	Total cash compensation, 2000–8 (B)	CEO payoff, 2000–8 + (B)	Estimated value lost, 2008 (C)	Net CEO payoff, 2000–8 + (B) + (C)	Estimated value remaining, last available year
(1) Astoria Financial Corp.	$27,725,496	$15,733,993	$14,191,675	$29,925,668	($41,424,965)	($11,499,297)	$68,517,281
(2) Bank Mutual Corp.	1,646,859	(5,266,976)	6,316,900	1,049,924	1,864,654	2,914,578	28,731,969
(3) Bank of Hawaii Corp.	20,187,172	25,347,162	7,835,004	33,182,166	(1,811,046)	31,371,120	17,983,848
(4) Brookline Bancorp, Inc.	1,779,179	(1,160,977)	5,533,125	4,372,148	(1,393,151)	2,978,997	17,888,741
(5) Chittenden Corp.	7,233,448	233,727	5,495,261	5,728,988	—	5,728,988	24,840,332
(6) Colonial Bancgroup	64,473,910	(9,627,753)	13,072,593	3,444,840	(54,926,318)	(51,481,478)	17,154,148
(7) Commerce Bancorp, Inc./NJ	55,200,152	54,401,611	16,040,000	70,441,611	—	70,441,611	206,000,731
(8) Compass Bancshares Inc.	23,469,767	20,771,960	14,913,707	35,685,667	—	35,685,667	101,927,174
(9) Corus Bankshares Inc.	116,412,613	194,701	8,375,000	8,569,701	(107,251,980)	(98,682,279)	14,057,012
(10) Cullen/Frost Bankers Inc.	9,887,202	11,471,908	9,224,000	20,695,908	(1,459,412)	19,236,496	34,520,378

Table B.3 (cont.)

No-TARP sample	Value of stock holdings, first available year	Total net trades, 2000–8 (A)	Total cash compensation, 2000–8 (B)	CEO payoff, 2000–8 + (B)	Estimated value lost, 2008 (C)	Net CEO payoff, 2000–8 + (B) + (C)	Estimated value remaining, last available year
(11) Dime Community Bancshares	5,404,096	10,720,836	7,688,600	18,409,436	(6,197,389)	12,212,047	19,427,150
(12) Downey Financial Corp.	2,163,080	(40,631)	6,955,575	6,914,944	(1,820,244)	5,094,700	1,993,807
(13) First Commonwealth Financial Corp./PA	735,782	(317,201)	3,871,755	3,554,554	46,832	3,601,386	768,179
(14) First Indiana Corp.	64,066,536	646,975	2,673,667	3,320,642	—	3,320,642	4,115,535
(15) Firstfed Financial Corp./CA	4,890,072	(472,417)	7,065,740	6,593,323	(12,944,373)	(6,351,050)	922,131
(16) Franklin Bank Corp.	3,535,558	(997,565)	1,970,624	973,059	—	973,059	8,530,947
(17) Fremont General Corp.	50,683,705	68,189,404	8,400,500	76,589,904	—	76,589,904	200,727,074
(18) Glacier Bancorp Inc.	1,757,644	(841,617)	3,234,718	2,393,101	(63,707)	2,329,394	8,355,277

(19)	Greater Bay Bancorp	4,937,347	1,344,217	6,465,697	7,809,914	—	7,809,914	5,129,375
(20)	Hanmi Financial Corp.	642,744	(454,846)	4,110,290	3,655,444	(533,000)	3,122,444	739,000
(21)	Hudson City Bancorp, Inc.	8,052,291	37,915,698	19,819,233	57,734,931	(10,918,115)	46,816,816	80,729,111
(22)	Indymac Bancorp, Inc.	8,257,405	(3,640,208)	12,920,100	9,279,892	(13,700,529)	(4,420,637)	15,657,748
(23)	Investors Financial Services Corp.	33,339,912	65,389,925	18,442,898	83,832,823	—	83,832,823	99,301,219
(24)	Irwin Financial Corp.	161,347,080	25,713	8,598,961	8,624,674	(45,732,991)	(37,108,317)	14,639,366
(25)	Jefferies Group, Inc.	37,132,782	(7,065,004)	42,246,707	35,181,703	(19,092,724)	16,088,979	154,881,740
(26)	MAF Bancorp Inc.	17,555,668	5,856,942	4,065,879	9,922,821	—	9,922,821	48,126,603
(27)	Mercantile Bankshares Corp.	11,278,785	(5,307,271)	9,099,300	3,792,029	—	3,792,029	15,079,013
(28)	National City Corp	30,274,819	10,491,812	16,753,095	27,244,907	(6,026,823)	21,218,084	7,366,940
(29)	New York Community Bancorp, Inc.	16,142,005	22,282,297	9,240,000	31,522,297	(36,516,665)	(4,994,368)	71,064,299

Table B.3 (cont.)

No-TARP sample	Value of stock holdings, first available year	Total net trades, 2000–8 (A)	Total cash compensation, 2000–8 (B)	CEO payoff, 2000–8 + (B)	Estimated value lost, 2008 (C)	Net CEO payoff, 2000–8 + (B) + (C)	Estimated value remaining, last available year
(30) Prosperity Bancshares, Inc.	6,083,402	3,742,015	5,378,094	9,120,109	602,724	9,722,833	19,925,077
(31) SLM Corp.	16,556,546	79,675,704	24,466,057	104,141,761	(36,440,126)	67,701,635	52,049,817
(32) Sovereign Bancorp, Inc.	22,092,853	1,708,739	10,053,423	11,762,162	(4,768,162)	6,994,000	7,009,348
(33) TD Banknorth, Inc.	9,990,045	6,898,869	8,994,186	15,893,055	—	15,893,055	28,212,482
(34) Trustco Bank Corp/NY	30,788,697	1,226,977	12,199,558	13,426,535	838,685	14,265,220	10,817,321
(35) Unionbancal Corp.	165,375	(45,144)	3,703,454	3,658,310	48,680	3,706,990	98,160
(36) United Bankshares, Inc./WV	4,022,832	(1,266,544)	8,301,138	7,034,594	5,399,778	12,434,372	27,328,167
(37) Washington Mutual, Inc.	59,532,727	29,805,336	28,452,000	58,257,336	(77,199,025)	(18,941,689)	77,199,025

Table B.4 *Variable Definitions and Data Sources for Chapter 8 Analysis*

Variable	Definition	Original sources
Risk measures		
Z-score	Equals $(ROA + CAR)/\sigma(ROA)$, where ROA is return on assets and CAR = E/A, where E = (total assets – total liabilities) and A is total assets. Higher Z-score implies more stability.	Compustat
Merton Distance to Default (DD)	The market value of the firm minus the face value of the firm's debt divided by the volatility of the firm value. The estimates of firm value and volatility are obtained by applying the Merton (1974) option valuation model. Higher Merton DD implies more stability.	
ROA	Return on assets, Net income divided by total assets. Higher value implies more stability.	Compustat
CAR	Capital asset ratio = equity divided by total assets. Higher value implies more stability.	Compustat
$\sigma(ROA)$	Standard deviation of ROA, rolling five-year periods.	Compustat
$\sigma(RET)$	Standard deviation of daily stock returns.	CRSP
Write-down	Sum of accounting write-downs for 2007 and 2008.	Bloomberg and 10-K, 10-Q
Controls		
Size	Natural logarithm of total assets.	Compustat
Revenue	Natural logarithm of total revenue.	Compustat
Market-to-book	Market value of equity divided by the book value of equity.	Compustat
Director ownership	Natural logarithm of the median director dollar stockholding as of the beginning of the year.	RiskMetrics and proxy statement

Table B.4 (*cont.*)

Variable	Definition	Original sources
CEO ownership	Percentage of CEO stock ownership as of the beginning of the year.	RiskMetrics and proxy statement
Firm age	Calculated as the difference between the sample year and the year that firm's first appearance in the CRSP monthly stock return database.	CRSP, Compustat
Leverage	Total liabilities divided by total assets.	Compustat
Investment bank	A dummy variable that equals 1 if investment bank and 0 otherwise	Compustat
Insurance company	A dummy variable that equals 1 if insurance company and 0 otherwise	Compustat
Crisis period dummy	A dummy variable that equals 1 if the observation occurs during the financial crisis years of 2007, 2008, or 2009 and 0 otherwise.	Compustat

Notes

I INTRODUCTION

1. For example, see Charles Calomiris and Allan Meltzer, "How Dodd-Frank Doubles Down on 'Too Big to Fail,'" *The Wall Street Journal*, February 18, 2014, A13. More recently, on June 2, 2016, two Federal Reserve Board governors signaled that big banks will be required to hold more equity. "Mr. Powell said that the Fed's move would go beyond existing rules to make big banks 'fully internalize the risk' they pose to the economy. While some critics want to break up these large banks, the Fed has instead sought to force them to tighten capital and other rules they must follow, effectively taxing their size. The rules have sent a clear message to big banks: Staying large will be costly" (www.wsj.com/articles/feds-tarullo-warns-banks-of-significant-increase-in-capital-in-future-stress-tests-1464870270).

2. In 2009, the Group of Twenty (G-20) adopted principles on banks' incentive compensation emphasizing deferral and clawbacks. Financial Stability Forum, "Principles for Sound Compensation Practices" (April 2, 2009), available at www.financialstabilityboard.org/list/fsb_publica tions/from_01012007/index.htm. These principles were incorporated into the supervisory guidelines of the Basel Committee on Banking Supervision and implemented in the United States and European Union. The G-20 consists of the finance ministers and central bankers of 19 industrial and emerging-market countries plus the European Union. The Basel Committee was created by the central bankers of the G-10 nations to coordinate supervisory standards, with membership expanded to the G-20 in 2009. Most recently, the European Union has restricted bankers' incentive compensation to 100% of total fixed pay, with some exceptions for shareholder-approved packages. For a summary of the legislation, which is known as Capital Requirements Directive (CRD) IV, see Davis Polk & Wardwell, "Client Memorandum: Recent European Compensation Developments: Financial Institutions and Beyond," April

23, 2013, available at www.davispolk.com/sites/default/files/files/Publi cation/f3691634-6c28-4c9a-bbbd-bba7a8ad07e0/Preview/PublicationAtt achment/2679f2aa-634f-4093-9a35-c44b9c147edb/04.23.12.European.Co mpensation.pdf. More recently, the SEC has announced plans to implement an expanded clawback provision regarding executive compensation: "SEC Eyes Broadened 'Clawback' Restrictions," June 2, 2015, available at www.wsj.com/articles/sec-eyes-broadened-clawback-r estrictions-1433285178.

3. Bhagat and Romano (2009, 2010).

4. In the global financial crisis, for example, the US government protected creditors and even shareholders in the largest financial institutions, such as the insolvent Citigroup, by bolstering firms with cash infusions for preferred stockholdings, although it did not bail out shareholders of other large institutions that failed, such as Washington Mutual. Gandhi, Lustig, and Plazzi (2016) provide evidence of the implicit guarantees provided by US taxpayers to the big bank investors.

5. For one of the few formal models considering the interaction of different regulatory tools – capital requirements, supervision, and market discipline – which provides counterintuitive results, such as supervision and market discipline are complements not supplements and that under restrictive conditions capital requirements can be reduced if subordinated debt is mandated, see Rochet (2008).

6. See, e.g., *The Wall Street Journal* op-ed of August 7, 2014, "Dodd-Frank Goes 0 for 11."

2 MORTGAGE PUBLIC POLICIES AND THE FINANCIAL CRISIS

1. The causes of the global financial crisis of 2008 will no doubt be analyzed and debated by economists for generations. Factors that have been identified as contributing to this crisis range from misguided government policies to an absence of market discipline by financial institutions that had inadequate or flawed risk monitoring and incentive systems; see, e.g., Calomiris (2009), Diamond and Rajan (2009), and French et al. (2010). Such government policies included monetary policy (low interest rates by the Federal Reserve) and the promotion of subprime risk-taking by government-sponsored entities dominating the residential mortgage market so as to increase home ownership by those who could not otherwise afford it. Sources of inadequate market discipline included ineffective

prudential regulation, such as bank equity capital requirements in the Basel Accords that favored securitized subprime loans over more conventional assets and that relied on inflated credit ratings of biased and possibly corrupt credit-rating agencies, as detailed in Appendix A. Internal organizational factors contributing to the crisis included business strategies that depended on high leverage and short-term financing of long-term assets, reliance on risk and valuation models with grossly unrealistic assumptions, and poorly designed incentive compensation. These factors, taken as a whole, encouraged what, with the benefit of hindsight, can be characterized as excessive risk-taking.

2. The increase in GSE housing goals for low- and moderate-income borrowers likely fueled the subprime mortgage originations during 2000–6. The Community Reinvestment Act of 1977 (CRA) may have added to this. The CRA directed the federal banking regulatory agencies to use their supervisory authority to encourage insured depository institutions to meet the credit needs of low- and moderate-income areas. Unlike the GSE housing goals, the CRA did not specify numerical goals. Agarwal et al. (2012) document that the CRA did contribute to risky lending during 2004–6 by banks undergoing CRA examinations.

3. As noted earlier, these "profits" were not profits in the traditional net-present-value sense but were merely an accounting artifact of the difference between the AAA tranche yield and the LIBOR.

3 PRECRISIS EXECUTIVE COMPENSATION AND MISALIGNED INCENTIVES

1. Lehman Brothers, for example, in 2005, paid executive officers with both cash and equity incentive compensation under its Short-Term Executive Compensation Plan, as well as stock options, with base pay making up a small portion of total compensation. Lehman Bros. Holdings, Inc., Proxy Statement 16 (February 27, 2006). The equity component was in the form of restricted stock units (RSUs), of which 35% vested over three years and the remainder over five years, subject to certain forfeiture provisions. *Id.* at 17. The stock options could be exercised in two years if the stock price increased by 28%; otherwise, they could not be exercised for four and a half years, with an expiration date of five years. In addition to the annual incentive plan, there was also a long-term incentive plan that awarded

performance stock units that convert to transferrable shares vesting on a staggered basis over three years. *Id.* That year, its CEO received 58% of his total compensation in equity, but of the 42% in cash compensation, virtually all was a cash bonus that vested automatically, and that bonus, $13.75 million, was roughly equal to the value of his awarded RSUs ($14.9 million). *Id.* at 19. In 2007, the CEO received a much larger percentage in equity than cash, with the cash bonus equal to only slightly more than 10% of his total compensation and only about one-tenth of awarded RSUs. Lehman Bros. Holdings, Inc., Proxy Statement 26–27 (March 5, 2008). The firm also paid nonexecutive employees annual cash and equity bonuses, with the latter ranging from 1% to 50% of total compensation, the percentage increasing as total compensation increased. Lehman Bros. Holdings, Inc., Amendment to 2005 Stock Incentive Plan, in Proxy Statement Addendum (March 30, 2007) (describing the company Equity Award Program because shareholders were asked to approve an amendment to the plan).

2. See, e.g., Sepe and Whitehead (2013).

3. Ellul and Yerramilli (2014) created a risk management index for bank holding companies that measures the strength and independence of the risk management function, which includes both individual and organization features, such as whether the chief risk officer is an executive officer of the holding company or among the five highest compensated employees (true in only 20% of the firm-year observations but with increasing frequency, e. g., 43.5% in 2009) and whether the board risk management committee has an independent director with banking or finance expertise or meets more frequently than average over a year. The index measure varies considerably across firms, as do the individual components of the index. Firms that had a higher index (better risk management) precrisis had lower tail risk (performed better) during the financial crisis.

4. Simplified cash flows and probabilities have been used for illustrative purposes to clarify the intuition of the analysis. The project's *expected* cash flows, as in the numerical illustration, need only have the pattern that early on there are positive expected cash flows and later on they turn negative so that the NPV is negative. In this stylized example, the expected cash flows would be positive for the first four years, zero in year five, and negative for all subsequent years. Because the six outcomes have equal probability, in year one cash flow expected by both

the bank executives and the investing public are ($500 million × 5/6) + (–$500 million × 1/6) = $333 million in each year. For the investing public, $333 million is the expected cash flow in every year because they are not aware of the risk of increasing losses over time associated with outcome 6. However, the bank executives are aware that these potential losses increase over time. For year three, the bank executives' expected cash flow are ($500 million × 5/6) + (–$500 million × 3 × 1/6) = $167 million. For year four, the bank executives' expected cash flows are ($500 million × 5/6) + (–$500 million × 4 × 1/6) = $83 million. By year six, the expected cash flow is –$83 million; by year 12, the expected cash flow is –$583 million. Taking the present value of this series of 12 annual cash flows using a 10% discount rate yields an expected value of the project of –$152 million based on what the bank executives know. Because the investing public believes that the expected cash flows are $333 million each year, their expected project value over the same 12 years and with the same 10% discount rate is $2.27 billion. Under the assumption of a 10% discount rate, the NPV is negative if the cash flows last for 12 years or longer, which is not an unreasonable time horizon for bank investments.

5. Griffin, Lowery, and Saretto (2014) construct a model with similar implications.

6. In an efficient market, the share price would rise by the expected value of the trading strategy were it announced in advance because it is a positive NPV project according to the publicly available information. Accordingly, the stock price would not rise that much on the subsequently realized positive cash flows, affecting the matching of the size of the payout of an incentive compensation system based on annual stock price increases. For the purpose of simplifying the example, we ignore that timing issue by making the plausible assumption that the trading strategy is not public information when adopted and that the public valuation (stock price) depends only on the realized cash flow each year.

7. Commercial banks are not permitted to go bankrupt in the United States: insolvent banks are taken over by banking regulators, and the assets and depositor liabilities are sold to another bank or liquidated.

8. The behavioral psychology literature finds that individuals are overly self-confident and optimistic, often referred to as the *better-than-average effect*. For a corporate finance application in which optimistic managers

perceive negative NPV projects as positive NPV projects (they overestimate the probability of positive cash flows and thereby underestimate the probability of losses), which fits with empirical patterns of corporate financing and free cash flow usage; see Heaton (2002). The literature provides empirical support for such posited behavior, e.g., Malmendier and Tate (2005). For the classic review of behavioral finance (application of the psychological literature to financial decision making), see DeBondt and Thaler (1996).

9. As with the original example, simplified cash flows and probabilities have been used for illustrative purposes. The project's expected cash flows need only be different from actual NPV. In this example, this difference is caused by the differences between the expected and actual probabilities of outcomes. But the difference could be caused by other errors in expectation, such as the executives not accurately forecasting the cash flows or the growth of potential loss in outcome 6 over time. In addition, as before, the public is not better informed than the bank insiders and also perceives the project's NPV as positive; for the purpose of the example, it does not matter whether or not the reason for the public's miscalculation is that it makes the same estimation error as the managers.

10. Based on the aforementioned stylized cash flow and probability assumptions, the expected cash flows do not become negative until the tenth year of the project. In year one, the bank managers expect the cash flow to be ($500 million × 90%) + (–$500 million × 10%) = $400 million each year. In year three, when the loss in outcome 6 increases, the managers' expected cash flow is ($500 million × 90%) + (–$500 million × 3 × 10%) = $300 million. For year four, the expected cash flow is $250 million; by year 10, the expected cash flow is –$50 million, and by year 30, the expected cash flow has decreased to –$1,050 million. Taking the present value of these 30 years of cash flows, using a 10% discount rate, the expected present value becomes –$42 million in the thirtieth year. If the project lasts fewer than 30 years, it has a positive expected value. However, these expectations are much different from the actual probabilities. In year one, the cash flow associated with the actual probabilities is ($500 million × 75%) + (–$500 million × 25%) = $250 million, considerably lower than the executives' expected value of $400 million. By year 10, the cash flow associated with the actual probability is –$875 million, and it is –$3,375 million by year 30. Taking the present value of the cash flows over the 30-year period yields an actual value of –$7.2 billion.

The actual value becomes negative much more quickly than the executives expect: after only seven years, the actual present value is –$275 million, while the executives expect the present value through seven years to be a positive $1,350 million. The actual cash flow becomes negative in the fourth year of the project, and again assuming a 10% discount rate, the NPV becomes negative if the cash flows persist for seven years.

4 MANAGERIAL INCENTIVES HYPOTHESIS VERSUS UNFORESEEN RISK HYPOTHESIS

1. Of the 14 firms in our "too big to fail" sample, the vesting period for long-term incentive compensation ranged from zero to five years based on their 2006 compensation. The average vesting period was less than two and a half years. Several CEOs received only fully vested shares. In all cases, any restricted stock holdings immediately vested on the CEO's retirement; in some cases, the restricted stock was awarded as cash when the vesting period ended.
2. There is substantial evidence in the finance literature that insiders have an informational advantage and use it to generate superior returns; for example, see Ben-David and Roulstone (2010).

5 BANK CEOS' BUYS AND SELLS DURING 2000–8

1. Bank of America reached an agreement to acquire Merrill Lynch on September 15, 2008; the acquisition was completed on January 1, 2009. As such, Merrill Lynch is analyzed as an independent institution in this study.
2. It is common practice for insiders to exercise stock options only to immediately sell the stock in the open market. By making both trades simultaneously, the insider avoids using any cash to exercise the options. These two transactions are frequently disclosed on the same day. For example, in 2007, Angelo Mozilo of Countrywide filed more than 30 Form 4s in which he disclosed exercising exactly 70,000 options and then immediately selling exactly 70,000 shares of common stock. In the same year, he filed another 30 Form 4s in which he disclosed the same pair of trades on exactly 46,000 options and shares. By simultaneously exercising options and selling shares, he was able to minimize cash outlay.
3. The beneficial ownership we consider includes common-stock equivalents that the individuals have immediate access to. This generally includes

common stock, in-the-money and vested options, and vested restricted stock received through incentive plans. It does not include options that are not exercisable and restricted stock that has not vested. Options may not be exercisable because the market price of the stock is below the option exercise price or because the option has not vested.

4. Even the 24 CEO "buys" in 2008 worth over $32 million can be misleading: only two of these trades, worth about $11.3 million, occurred prior to the mandatory TARP investments being announced on October 14, 2008. All others occurred after October 20, 2008.

5. Mellon Financial CEOs actually gained just over $1 million; however, this does not include the 2008 crisis. Mellon Financial merged with Bank of New York in mid-2007, so this gain is for 2007, not 2008.

6. This ignores the possibility that the CEOs were able to renegotiate and restructure stock and option holdings during 2008. Boards frequently reissue new options with new exercises for stock options that are substantially out-of-the-money. See, e.g., Chen (2004). In reality, the value lost after restructuring their beneficial ownership was likely less than $2,013 million.

7. Statistical tests confirm that the median ratio of the CEOs' net trades during 2000–8 to the CEOs' holdings in 2000 for the TBTF banks is significantly greater than the corresponding ratio for the No-TARP bank CEOs.

8. Statistical tests confirm that the median ratio of the CEOs' net trades during 2002–8 (2004–8) to the CEOs' holdings in 2002 (2004) for the TBTF banks is significantly greater than the corresponding ratio for the No-TARP bank CEOs.

9. This note of caution may not actually apply to the nine original TARP firms. The US Treasury essentially forced all nine firms to accept TARP assistance, whether they were performing well or not, because the Treasury did not want the financial markets to identify some of these firms as "weak" and others as "strong."

10. Fahlenbrach and Stulz (2011). The CEOs averaged sales of 2% of their holdings per quarter during 2007–8, except during the quarter of Lehman Brothers' bankruptcy, when they sold a much larger (~10%) of their holdings. Combining the sales data with equity and option grants over the period, they state that CEO ownership stayed around the same throughout.

11. This conclusion is therefore distinctly different from that of Fahlenbach and Stulz (2011). In Fahlenbach and Stulz's view, bank CEOs and senior executives could not or did not foresee the extreme risk of some of the banks' investment and trading strategies, and the poor performance of these banks during the crisis is attributable to an extreme negative realization of the high-risk nature of their investment and trading strategy. Their perspective can be analogized to the bank executives' expected probabilities of cash flows in our second stylized example, summarized in Example 3.2, being equal to the actual probabilities. But even if Fahlenbach and Stulz's characterization of events – by disregarding precrisis stock transactions – is accurate, a proposition that we do not concede, it does not follow that the precrisis compensation structure was optimal and cannot be improved on to reduce the probability of accepting investments with large negative tail events.

12. Acharya et al. (2013) (finding in sample of 77 banks that (a) in precrisis years 2003–6 nonexecutive compensation incentives are more sensitive to revenues than quality or sustainability of earnings; (b) the more sensitive nonexecutive compensation policies are to short-term bank performance (proxied by how firms readjust total cash and stock compensation with variations in performance), the higher the risk taken by banks on a variety of measures – aggregate risk, tail risk, implied volatility of stock returns, and Z-score – during the crisis years of 2007–9; and (c) incentive-induced excessive risk-taking was associated with significant declines in firm value during the crisis.

6 EXECUTIVE COMPENSATION REFORM

1. A recent *Wall Street Journal* article notes almost exactly the three criteria noted next. See "Activists' New Target: Executive Pay," *The Wall Street Journal*, June 12, 2015, p. C1. "Some activists argue that ill-designed plans encourage the wrong kinds of growth – for example, boosting revenue at the expense of profitability . . . One factor teeing up the issue for activists is the complexity of compensation, experts say. 'I've seen bonus plans that would take a Ph.D. in physics to figure out,' said Kevin McManus, vice president at proxy advisor Egan-Jones Ratings Co."

2. See Diebold (2010).

3. Dodd-Frank Wall Street Reform and Consumer Protection Act of 2010, Pub. L. No. 111–203, 124 Stat. 1376, § 951 (2010) (extending to all US firms a

requirement that shareholders vote, in an advisory capacity, on CEO compensation). Other countries, such as the United Kingdom and Australia, had already such a requirement in place, and additional countries, such as Germany, have adopted the requirement since then.

4. See, Rose (2011).

5. Unprofitable over the long-term trading strategy is a negative net present value (NPV) trading/investment strategy. Long-term profitability is synonymous with positive NPV trading/investment strategy.

6. Rock Center for Corporate Governance (2016).

7. We would also leave to the board whether the number of shares or options to be received under the plan should depend on a performance target, although we are wary of the efficacy of performance targets because managers focused on meeting a target may make decisions that negatively affect long-term value, such as decreasing margins to attain a sales target. While such an effect would be mitigated by the long-term horizon of restricted stock, if the number of performance-based shares is set too high, the immediate goal of receiving shares might offset attention to the long-term value effect of a decision.

8. See Bhagat and Bolton (2013) and DeYoung, Peng, and Meng (2013).

9. Some have suggested that if bank managers were concerned about maintaining bank reputation, then such long-term vesting periods might not be necessary. The evidence in Griffin, Lowery, and Saretto (2014) is inconsistent with the argument that investment bankers' actions during 2000–10 reflected a serious concern for their banks' reputations.

10. See Metrick and Yasuda (2011) and Litvak (2004).

11. Currently (and historically), most restricted stock that is granted to officers and directors becomes completely vested when the individual leaves the firm, except for cause or specific details of the employment agreement, such as noncompete requirements.

12. The restricted equity proposal is further consistent with several recent theoretical papers that suggest that a significant component of incentive compensation should consist of stock and stock options with long vesting periods. If these vesting periods were "sufficiently long," they would be similar to our proposal. See Edmans et al. (2010) and Peng and Roell (2009).

13. Hall and Murphy (2002).

14. There are constraints on executives' ability to hedge stock and option positions under tax and securities laws. See, e.g., Schizer (2000).

15. The Internal Revenue Code limits the current deduction to $1 million. 26 USC § 162(m)(1).
16. Kaplan and Rauh (2010).
17. Kaplan and Rauh (2013).
18. DeYoung et al. (2013).
19. FSB (2009).
20. The motivation for greater specification of the agreed-on compensation principles was not solely to enhance the stability of the global financial system but also to establish a "level playing field" across international banks' compensation practices. By limiting discretion regarding the principles' content, the expectation was that supervisory demands would be more uniform and that international banks' compensation practices would more readily converge.
21. The FSB principles, by contrast, simply stated that bonuses should diminish or disappear on poor performance, without specifying amounts subject to specific clawback.
22. American Recovery and Reinvestment Act of 2009, Pub. L. No. 11-5, 7001,123 Stat. 115 (2009); Sarbanes-Oxley Act of 2002, Pub. L. No. 107–204, § 304, 15 USC § 7243 (2006).
23. www.sec.gov/rules/proposed/2015/33-9861.pdf.
24. See, e.g., Hughes (2013). For instance, companies adopting clawback policies to comply with Dodd-Frank face the prospect of uncertain litigation costs because under most states' law, wages "once earned" cannot be clawed back. Therefore, companies will not be able to exercise "self-help" and achieve a clawback by not paying part or all of a current salary or bonus but will have to sue an individual who does not voluntarily repay the amount in question for the funds. Additionally, there is the prospect of costly litigation in the SEC's enforcement of the Sarbanes Oxley clawback provision. A few nonculpable executives, rather than settle, have challenged being subjected to a clawback without individual wrongdoing or knowledge. Although two district courts have rejected executives' motions to dismiss on that ground – *SEC* v. *Baker*, No. A-12-CA-285-SS (W.D. Tex., November 13, 2012); *SEC* v. *Jenkins*, No. 2:09-CV-1510-GMS (D. Ariz. June 9, 2010) – the issue is still unsettled. This is because one of the courts also found that the statute could raise constitutional issues of "severe and unjustified" deprivation but that such issues could not be decided on a motion to dismiss – *SEC* v. *Jenkins*.

Finally, there are also tax complications with clawbacks: under the "claim of right" doctrine, an individual has to pay tax on compensation received in a given year, even if he or she may "later be required to repay it." None of these additional complications would arise under the restricted equity proposal, while the executive would also not be able to reap inapposite gains from incentive compensation.

25. See, e.g., Hirsch, Reichert, and Sohn (2013), who advance a further objection to clawbacks – that they may have the unintended consequence of increasing risk-taking. They hypothesize that clawbacks will have a differential impact on decision making depending on a firm's financial position and that where the investment outcome only affects the size of a loss, the manager with a clawback will select the riskiest project, as with a higher variance, it offers a possibility of reducing the extent of the loss and hence the amount of compensation clawed back. These authors provide findings from a laboratory experiment that supported the hypothesis: as in the setting of a loss position, individuals with clawback compensation contracts opted more frequently for the riskier of two projects than those without clawbacks.

26. For example, Holmstrom (1979, 1999).

27. Evidence can be adduced of the perverse effects of government efforts to restrict the amount of executive compensation. For example, after US corporate tax-deductible pay was limited to $1 million for fixed compensation but not for performance-based pay, firms altered the mix of compensation to reduce cash salaries and increase incentive compensation. See Perry and Zenner (2000). Some commentators attribute the mushrooming of equity incentive compensation and hence executive pay in the 1990s, along with the excessive risk-taking of the 2000s, to that reform. For example, Bruce Bartlett, "Not So Suite: Clinton Tax Law Is the Problem, Not Greedy Execs," available at www.national review.com/nrof_barlett/bartlett092502.asp. A similar reaction appears to be occurring in Europe: 65% of UK financial services companies increased the base salary of their employees by over 20% in anticipation of the incoming cap. See, e.g., Daniel Schäfer, "Salaries Lifted to Beat Bonus Cap," *Financial Times*, August. 20, 2013, available at www.ft.com/cms/s/ 0/0ff854c2-08e4-11e3-ad07-00144feabdc0.html. As noted earlier, we recognize that the restricted equity proposal may have this type of effect and suggest means by which it can be mitigated – increasing award

amounts to compensate for increased underdiversification and permitting modest liquidation of annual awards.

28. For example, Bolton, Mehran, and Shapiro (2010) (recommending tying compensation to changes in the spread on credit default swaps, which are contracts written on debt securities that insure the holder against the debt's default); Gordon (2012) (advocating conversion of financial institutions' senior management's equity-based compensation into subordinated debt at a discount to the equity value, when a firm experiences financial difficulty); Bebchuk and Spamann (2010) (recommending compensation package of a proportionate mix of financial institutions' senior securities – debt and preferred stock – and equity); and Tung (2011) (recommending compensation in the form of subordinated debt of the bank subsidiary).

29. Option theory (Black and Scholes 1973; Merton 1977) suggests that, all else being equal, the value of an option increases with volatility of the underlying asset. Since a company's shareholders are essentially holding a call option with the total value of the company as the underlying asset and the value of debt as the exercise price, it follows that the more volatile the company's cash flow is, the more valuable the call option is. Thus the value of common stock increases with the volatility of the company's cash flow.

30. Some proposals advocate pegging compensation to a specific debt security, such as credit default swaps, rather than a proportionate package of the capital structure. This, while seemingly avoiding complexity, will not satisfactorily avoid the problem because those securities are also typically not publicly traded. Besides the lack of transparency from the absence of market pricing, because credit default swap spreads are computed using accounting figures that are partially under managers' control, they may also be subject to manipulation because managers will have increased incentives to misrepresent figures used in swap pricing when it immediately will affect their compensation. Although credit default swaps have historically traded in private over-the-counter markets, Dodd-Frank requires regulators to implement rules to establish the use of centralized clearing exchanges to trade these products, which could increase the transparency of prices but will not eliminate the need for accounting data to calculate the spreads because the underlying debt is infrequently traded. The convertible security proposed by Gordon (2012)

has further valuation difficulties: because management's stock differs significantly from that of outside stockholders (i.e., their shares will become debt securities, which are senior to the outstanding shares of the stockholders when the firm experiences financial difficulty), their stock will not be equivalent in value, nor will its value move in tandem with the value of the outstanding common stock. Moreover, determining the value of management's equity will be complicated because it depends on the likelihood of conversion and the rate that will be applicable (which under the proposal requires a further probability calculation of the value of the common stock at an unknown point in time that is prior to the moment at which conversion occurs). Finally, the possible conversion into debt at a discount reduces the value of stock compensation to an executive, and consequently, the executive will require a higher amount of equity to offset the lower valuation (i.e., the increased risk). Furthermore, credit default swaps are also issued by only the largest financial institutions and therefore are not suitable for executive compensation in medium- and small-sized financial institutions. Finally, determining the appropriate formula with which to relate changes in default spreads to executive compensation bonuses or clawbacks would undoubtedly be challenging, for the calculation of swap prices is complex because values do not change linearly with changes in other economic variables. For example, in discussing the formal model underlying their proposal to tie bank executives' compensation to credit default swap spreads, the optimal compensation contract consists of debt and equity in a ratio equal to the "rate of return promised to bondholders at the optimal risk level," which, as Bolton et al. (2010) note, "may be difficult to calculate."

31. Stock in a levered firm, from a finance perspective, is equivalent to an option on the firm, in which the equity holder obtains the upside of future risky projects but can walk away from the firm without repaying creditors if the firm's downside value is less than its liabilities. Lambert, Larcker, and Verecchia (1991) model when stock option compensation results in managers taking less or more risk (which depends on how "in the money" – that is, by how much the exercise price is below the stock price – the options are). The model indicates that managers are more likely to take on risk when the probability of the option finishing in-the-money is low, as in the scenario in the text, and thus of greatest concern to the fisc. With restricted

stock, the longer horizon increases the probability that an option will finish in-the-money, which, in the Lambert et al. model, increases the manager's aversion to risk.

32. See Alces and Galle (2012) (critiquing debt-based bank executive incentive compensation proposals that emphasizes behavioral economic difficulties).

33. See Hansmann (1988) (expositing the well-known difficulty of collective choice and the reason for corporate law's restriction of managers' fiduciary duty to shareholders).

34. For example, Wei and Yermack (2011). Deferred compensation and pension benefits are referred to in the literature as "inside debt." For a further critique of relying on research on inside debt to advocate debt-based compensation, see Alces and Galle (2012).

35. See, for example, www.forbes.com/2005/03/15/cx_da_0315ebbers guilty.html; "Appeals Court Restores Qwest Insider Trading Conviction," available at www.nytimes.com/2009/02/26/business/26q west.html. Jeffrey Skilling's indictment in the Second District of Texas is particularly illustrative; *United States of America* v. *Jeffrey K. Skilling and Richard A. Causey*, Cr. No. H-04–25. Also see www.acco unting-degree.org/scandals/.

36. The case of Towers Watson provides a more recent example. "Towers CEO Sold Stock Ahead of Big Deal. As Towers Watson & Co was negotiating a merger earlier this year *that would later cause its stock to fall*, Chief Executive John Haley netted nearly $10 million from selling the consulting company's shares." *The Wall Street Journal*, September 24, 2015, p. C1.

37. www.sec.gov/rules/proposed/2016/34–77776.pdf.

38. www.sec.gov/rules/proposed/2016/34–77776.pdf, p. 136: "Neither would the proposed definition include dividends paid and appreciation realized on stock or other equity-like instruments that are owned outright by a covered person."

39. www.theglobeandmail.com/report-on-business/newly-minted-british-p m-takes-aim-at-corporate-governance-proposes-reform/article31062949/.

40. Larcker et al. (2012) provide an informative commentary on "say on pay."

41. See Larcker et al. (2012).

7 DIRECTOR COMPENSATION POLICY

1. See Gilson and Kraakman (1991), who call for institutional investors to organize a core of professional directors who would sit on corporate boards to ensure effective management.
2. Cox (1984) has argued for the application of a stronger, more rigorous duty of care.
3. See Black (1992) and Coffee (1991).
4. See "Archer-Daniels Faces Informal SEC Inquiry into Executive Pay," *The Wall Street Journal*, October 10, 1995, p. C18; "Bad Chemistry: W. R. Grace Is Roiled by Flap over Spending and What to Disclose, Departed CEO Makes Issue of the Chairman's Perks, Son's Use of Grace Funds," *The Wall Street Journal*, March 10, 1995; "William Agee Will Leave Morrison Knudsen," *The Wall Street Journal*, February 2, 1995, p. B1; www.forbes.com/2005/03/15/cx_da_0315ebbersguilty.html; "Appeals Court Restores Qwest Insider Trading Conviction," available at www.nytimes.com/2009/02/26/business/26qwest.html.
5. See Elson (1995, 1996); Bhagat, Carey, and Elson (1999); Bhagat and Bolton (2008); Bhagat, Bolton, and Romano (2008).
6. See Bhagat and Tookes (2012).
7. *Ibid.* Table 7-2 indicates that industry practice varies considerably regarding mandatory director stock ownership in the largest US corporations.
8. See Bhagat and Bolton (2013).
9. *Ibid.*
10. Unlike for executives, we are not recommending any cash compensation for directors. Most directors are successful professionals who have other sources of income – other than serving on the board of the company in question. Conflict of interest between the director and long-term shareholders will become acute if a director is reliant on retainer fees for his or her livelihood.

8 ARE LARGE BANKS RISKIER?

1. For example, see the recent book by former Treasury Secretary Timothy Geithner (2014).
2. For example, the SAFE Banking Act of 2012 was introduced in the US Senate on May 9, 2012. Among other restrictions, it proposes a strict 10%

cap on any bank's share of the total amount of deposits of all insured banks in the United States and a limit of 2% of the US gross domestic product (GDP) of the nondeposit liabilities of a bank holding company. The SAFE Banking Act was not enacted, however.

3. Flannery (2014) and Pennacchi (1987a, 1987b) argue that the adequacy of bank capital depends on both portfolio risk and the period of time for which that bank capital must protect liability holders from loss.

4. Merton (1974) builds on the Black and Scholes (1973) option pricing model to value corporate bonds. Another area where Merton's (1974) framework is widely applied is the pricing of deposit insurance (see Merton 1977; Pennacchi 1987a, 1987b; Ronn and Verma 1986).

5. See Chesney, Stromberg, and Wagner (2010) for a discussion of the rationale underlying this risk-taking variable.

6. See Nike, Inc.'s 2013 DEF 14A proxy statement for details.

7. As a robustness check, we consider alternative measures of corporate governance, such as the G-index (Gompers, Ishii, and Metrick 2003) in our analysis. Governance, as measured by these indices, is not related to firm risk-taking; the relationships between all other explanatory variables and risk-taking are qualitatively similar to our main results.

8. However, it is in sharp contrast to Cheng, Hong, and Scheinkman (2010), who used alternative governance measures such as the G-index and found that these governance indices have no effect on financial firms' risk-taking. We also found that governance measures such as the G-index have no effect on financial firms' risk-taking (in untabulated results); a possible reason is that these indices are mostly measures of antitakeover provisions. Theoretically, it is difficult to make a direct connection between antitakeover provisions and bank risk-taking.

9 BANK CAPITAL STRUCTURE AND EXECUTIVE COMPENSATION

1. For example, if a bank made a loan to a business of $1 million, given the 100% risk weight for such assets, the bank would need capital in the amount of 8% × 100% × $1 million = $80,000. By contrast, if it used the same $1 million to buy a US Treasury bond, given the 0% risk weight for sovereign debt, it would not need to hold any capital against that asset, despite total assets remaining unchanged.

2. IRB was intended to address regulatory arbitrage opportunities created by the arbitrary requirements of the standardized approach, such as, for instance, banks cherry picking assets within a category to increase their yield, that is, the riskiest assets, without incurring an increased capital charge because the standardized risk categories were insensitive to the risk of specific borrowers or assets within the class. For example, see Tarullo (2008) (discussing regulatory arbitrage opportunities afforded by Basel I).

3. Regulators refer to bank capital as the sum of Tier 1 capital and Tier 2 capital. Tier 1 capital includes common stock, retained earnings, capital surplus from the sale of common or preferred stock above par and disclosed capital reserves such as cash dividends not yet declared. Tier 2 capital includes loan loss provisions, preferred stock of maturity of at least 20 years, subordinated equity and debt obligations with maturity of at least seven years, undisclosed capital reserves, and hybrid capital, such as contingent convertible debt. Per the Basel Accords, bank regulators consider Tier 1 capital or Tier 1 capital and Tier 2 capital as the numerator (in measuring bank capital). The denominator is risk-weighted total assets, which has been and continues to be under considerable controversy. The risk weights are ad hoc and can be easily manipulated and gamed. For example, sovereign debt has a weight of 20%, whereas corporate debt has a weight of 100%; this does not make sense when considering AAA-rated corporate debt and sovereign debt from countries such as Greece and Italy.

4. Tangible common equity includes common stock plus retained earnings (both via the income statement and unrealized value changes on cash flow hedges). We do not include intangible assets in common equity (for the purposes of measuring bank equity capital ratio) because when a bank's equity capital ratio becomes a binding constraint (i.e., when the bank is approaching financial distress), intangible assets lose a significant part of their value. There is another reason for using tangible common equity when measuring bank capital. Anginer and Demirguc-Kunt (2014) studied the relation between different types of bank capital and their impact on systemic risk of the banking industry. They found that Tier 1 capital, especially tangible capital, was correlated with reductions in systemic risk. However, Tier 2 capital has the opposite, destabilizing effect. Furthermore, these effects are accentuated during the crisis years and for the larger banks.

5. Vice Chairman Hoenig voted against the Basel III rule implementation as inadequate without a binding leverage constraint (Statement by Thomas Hoenig, Basel III Capital Interim Final Rule and Notice of Proposed Rulemaking, FDIC, July 9, 2013, available at www.fdic.gov/about/learn/board/hoenig/statement7-9-2013.html) and has advocated that the United States take the lead and abandon Basel III in favor of the ratio of tangible equity (i.e., excluding goodwill, tax assets, and other accounting entries) to tangible assets (assets less intangibles) (Alan Zibel, "FDIC's Hoenig: U.S. Should Reject Basel Accord," *The Wall Street Journal*, September 14, 2012, available at http://online.wsj.com/news/articles/SB10000872396390443524904577651551643632924). Haldane has called for simplifying Basel's capital requirements to eliminate IRB and reemphasize standardized weights for broad asset classes and for applying a stricter leverage ratio. Andrew G. Haldane, "The Dog and the Frisbee," August 31, 2012, available at www.bis.org/review/r120905a.pdf). See also Brooke Masters, "Haldane Calls for Rethink of Basel III," *Financial Times*, August 31, 2012. For a cogent summary of both regulators' positions, see Alex J. Pollock, "Hoenig and Haldane Are Right about Basel III," *American Banker*, October 15, 2012, available at www.aei.org/article/economics/financial-services/banking/hoenig-and-haldane-are-right-about-basel-iii/. A recent *Wall Street Journal* article, "The Banker Who Cried 'Simplicity,'" December 21–22, 2013, p. A13, highlights Haldane's central arguments.
6. For Hoenig's and Haldane's detailed critiques of Basel III, see "Basel III Capital: A Well-Intended Illusion," Remarks by FDIC Vice Chairman Thomas M. Hoenig to the International Association of Deposit Insurers 2013 Research Conference in Basel, Switzerland, FDIC, April 9, 2013, available at www.fdic.gov/news/news/speeches/spapr0913.html.
7. Haldane (2009).
8. *The Wall Street Journal*, November 13, 2012, p A20. "The FDIC's own director, Thomas Hoenig, sees in Basel III the same complicated system for judging risk that failed in Basel II 'but with more complexity.' Using theoretical models that have failed in practice, the rules assign 'risk weights' to different assets, divined by an almost endless series of calculations. For the largest banks with the resources to spend on regulatory arbitrage, this is an opportunity to get risky assets officially designated as safe." *The Economist*, September 19, 2015, "Whose Model Is It Anyway?" "The models used to gauge the riskiness of a loan book were

once provided by regulators, with fixed weightings for categories such as business credit or loans to other banks. But an update to the global regulatory guidelines, known as Basel II and adopted just before the crisis, encouraged banks to come up with their own risk models … The models are often fiendishly complicated, as well as being numerous … Repeated studies have found that putting the same pool of loans and securities through different banks' formulae lead to wildly different outcomes." Belatedly, Basel has also realized that there might be a problem in letting banks decide the risk weights of the assets they own. *The Wall Street Journal*, March 24, 2016, available at www.wsj.com/articles/basel-com mittee-proposes-curbs-on-bank-risk-models-1458833654?tesla=y. "Global regulators moved to further tighten the reins on banks, proposing limits on the discretion institutions have to measure how much risk they can take. The compromise plan reached Thursday by the Basel Committee on Banking Supervision wouldn't allow banks to calculate their own credit risk from exposure to other banks, large corporations and stocks … Regulators, especially those in the U.S., consider it problematic to allow banks to measure their own credit risk and determine how much capital they need to guard against a possible default by a counterparty and the individual firm's exposure if there is a loss."

9. Basel III requires that 6% of the total 8% capital requirement be Tier 1 capital, and of that, 4.5% must be equity. The minimum capital requirements are to be phased in by 2015, while the phase-in of the conservation buffer and leverage ratio requirements will not be completed until 2019 and 2018, respectively. Basel Committee on Banking Supervision, "Basel III: A Global Regulatory Framework for More Resilient Banks and Banking Systems," June 2011, p. 69, available at www.bis.org/publ/bcbs189.htm. The Basel III minimum capital and conservation buffer requirements are said to have been determined by the loss experience of large banks over the past decade and in the 2008 crisis, respectively. Daniel K. Tarullo, Member, Board of Governors of the Federal Reserve System, "Remarks at the Peter G Peterson Institute for International Economics: Regulating Systemically Important Financial Firms," June 3, 2011, p. 8, transcript available at www.federalreserve.gov/newsevents/speech/tarullo20110 603a.htm.

10. Continuing with the example, under the leverage ratio requirement, the bank must hold the same amount of capital against a $1 million asset, whether it is a corporate loan or a Treasury bond, of 4% × $1 million = $40,000 (or under Basel III, 3% × $1 million = $30,000).

11. Basel Committee on Banking Supervision (2013). The additional capital must be Tier 1 capital. The Basel Committee document states that national regulators may impose higher requirements on their G-SIBs, which is the implicit understanding for all Basel requirements and no doubt was an acknowledgment that members of the committee were intending to do so. US banking regulators, for instance, have proposed a leverage ratio of 5% for the largest bank holding companies and 6% for their bank subsidiaries. US Treasury Department, FDIC, "Regulatory Capital Rules: Regulatory Capital, Enhanced Supplementary Leverage Ratio Standards for Certain Bank Holding Companies and their Subsidiary Insured Depository Institutions" (July 2013). They were directed by Congress to impose an additional leverage requirement on such institutions. See Dodd-Frank, §165.

12. The G-SIB surcharge is subject to as long a phase-in as the capital buffer by 2019. See Basel Committee on Banking Supervision (2013).

13. See Kalemli-Ozcan, Sorensen, and Yesiltas (2012). Because they are derived from publicly disclosed information, these data are simple leverage ratios, not Basel risk-weighted ratios. They also do not include off-balance-sheet assets (given the limitation of the data), but those assets were, for the most part, also not included in the Basel risk-weight calculation. The average level of debt was considerably higher at the former investment banks and European banks (firms that were not subject to a leverage ratio). See Andrew G. Haldane, Executive Director, Financial Stability, Bank of England, "Remarks at the Federal Reserve Bank of Chicago Twelfth Annual International Banking Conference on 'The International Financial Crisis: Have the Rules of Finance Changed': Banking on the State," September 25, 2009, transcript available at www.bis.org/review/r091111e.pdf) (connecting this discrepancy to leverage ratio requirements).

14. Basel advocates could no doubt contend that the precrisis ratios were misleading because in retrospect it is clear that both banks and regulators inadequately measured the risk of assets such as securitized mortgages

and that Basel III has sorted that out. But, while this may be so, there is no reason to believe that the methodology is now sufficiently accurate that some other asset's future risk will not prove to be greater than the weight that has been currently assigned, creating another crisis. It is true that banks will tend to hold more capital than the minimum requirement in order to avoid being pushed below the minimum by a minor market shock and thereby be subjected to regulatory corrective action, but the regulatory objective should be to establish a sufficient minimum against the tail risk, independent of whether banks might hold a cushion of capital above that minimum.

15. Darrell Duffie (2010, p. 48). Citigroup illustrates the problem. Its Tier 1 capital ratio never fell below 7% during the financial crisis, yet its stock market capitalization declined to approximately 1% of its total accounting assets.

16. See, e.g., Haldane 2009, p. 14; Tarullo 2008, p. 31. There is striking suggestive evidence that the market priced the probability of the moral hazard problem caused by limited liability in relation to bank capital: in states where bank shareholders had liability for a proportion of a bank's debt beyond what they had invested (referred to as *double liability*), the average capital ratios were lower at 18.2% compared to 22.9% for banks in states where shareholders did not have such liability; Macey and Miller (1992). "The obvious explanation for the disparities in capital ratios is that creditors did not demand as high a level of capitalization in double liability states as they did in states without double liability because they believed they could obtain repayment of some or all of their deposits by means of assessment in the event a bank failed."

17. Thomas M. Hoenig, FDIC Vice Chairman, "Speech to the American Banker Regulatory Symposium, Washington, DC: Back to Basics: A Better Alternative to Basel Capital Rules," September 14, 2012, available at www.fdic.gov/news/news/speeches/archives/2012/spsep1412_2.html. Allan H. Meltzer: "In the 1920s, capital ratios for large New York banks (engaged in both commercial and investment banking under the pre–Glass-Steagall regime then in place) ranged from 15% to 20% of assets. Stockholders took losses, but none of the major New York banks failed during the Great Depression." "Banks Need More Capital, Not More Rules," available at www.wsj.com/articles/S B10001424052702304192704577405821765336832.

18. Tarullo (2008, p. 29).
19. Miles et al. (2013, pp. 3–4); see also Haldane (2009, p. 14), explaining that capital ratios for UK banks were over 10% until around World War I.
20. It should also be noted that European banks, which have been more highly levered than US banks, have issued large amounts of *covered bonds*, in which creditors have claims on specific collateral for repayment.
21. Admati and Hellwig (2013): "[E]quity capital ratios equivalent to 10% of unweighted assets, and possibly higher, should be seriously considered"; Miles, Yang, and Marcheggiano (2013): Results of a model empirically estimating the benefit of reducing financial crises against the cost of increasing borrowing costs "suggest that the optimal amount of capital is likely to be around twice as great," as Basel III's capital requirements for largest banks of "just under 10% of risk-weighted assets," further specified as in the range of 16% to 20%.
22. See *The Economist*, February 13, 2016, "Deutsche Bank's unappetizing cocos"; and *Bloomberg Business*, February 9, 2016.
23. See *The Economist*, November 14, 2015, "Buttonwood, Born to Run"; and the *Wall Street Journal*, March 3, 2016, "The Perverse Effects of Crisis-Prevention Bonds."
24. "Adding leverage to the banking system in the hope that this will prove to be stabilizing is a gamble. There is considerable evidence that strategies that encourage increasing leverage within the banking industry have in past crises only exacerbated losses. The goal is resilience and, if necessary, resolution without government or taxpayer assistance. That is best achieved not by increasing leverage, but by requiring the right balance of debt and added equity for each firm and the industry as a whole." "The Relative Role of Debt in Bank Resiliency and Resolvability," remarks by FDIC Vice Chairman Thomas M. Hoenig, presented to the Peterson Institute for International Economics, Washington, DC, January 20, 2016, available at www.fdic.gov/news/news/speeches/spjan2016.html.
25. http://web.stanford.edu/~johntayl/2015_pdfs/Testimony_Senate_Banking-SCFICP-July-29-2015.pdf: "Chapter 14 would operate faster – ideally over a weekend – and with no less precision than Chapter 11. Unlike Chapter 11, it would leave all operating subsidiaries outside of bankruptcy entirely. It would do this by moving the original financial firm's operations to a new bridge company that is not in bankruptcy. This bridge company would be recapitalized by leaving behind long-term unsecured

debt – called the 'capital structure debt.' The firm's long-term unsecured debt would bear the losses due to the firm's insolvency and any other costs associated with bankruptcy. If the amount of long-term debt and subordinated debt were sufficient, short-term lenders would not have an incentive to run, and the expectation of Chapter 14's use will reduce ex ante uncertainty about runs."

26. www.wsj.com/articles/feds-tarullo-warns-banks-of-significant-increase-in-capital-in-future-stress-tests-1464870270.

27. http://financialservices.house.gov/uploadedfiles/financial_choice_act_comprehensive_outline.pdf.

28. www.wsj.com/articles/fixing-american-finance-1468017759.

29. www.wsj.com/articles/glass-steagall-trump-clinton-act-1469746827.

10 WHY BANKS SHOULD BE MOSTLY DEBT FINANCED: PARADE OF NON SEQUITURS

1. Admati et al. (2013) provide a very comprehensive and persuasive discussion of why banks should be financed with considerable more equity than they are being financed currently.

2. Bank-based financing is not a major source for funds for the vast majority of firms in the US manufacturing sector. The shareholders' equity for the entire US manufacturing sector in 2016 was $3,976 billion; total liabilities were $5,638 billion, of which bank debt accounted for $568 billion; see http://census.gov/econ/qfr/mmws/current/qfr_pub.pdf. Hence bank debt accounts for less than 6% of the financing for the US manufacturing sector. It is possible that bank debt financing might be more significant for smaller firms that have less access to public equity and public debt markets. The shareholders' equity for firms with assets under $25 million in the US manufacturing sector in 2016 was $159 billion; total liabilities were $147 billion, of which bank debt accounted for $43 billion. Hence bank debt accounted for about 14% of the financing of firms with assets under $25 million in the US manufacturing sector in 2016.

3. As noted in Chapter 1, the financial crisis that started in 2007 has inflicted a large cost on the US economy and an even larger cost on US workers and families. Hall (2014) estimated the shortfall of output at the end of 2013 as 13.3%, or $2.2 trillion. The labor force participation rate is currently at 62.8% – the lowest it has been for more than three decades. Hall (2014) estimated that the labor force participation rate in 2013 was 1.9% below the

1990–2007 trend. This 1.9% figure translates to 4.4 million additional US adults who were unemployed as of 2013.

4. Of course, if debt holders in these TBTF banks were fairly confident of being bailed out by public taxpayers, they would not have any incentive to monitor or impose discipline. The question is, Do debt holders in banks smaller than the TBTF banks provide monitoring and impose discipline on bank managers, and can they do it more effectively than *shareholders* in these smaller banks? We are not aware of any empirical evidence that directly addresses this question.

5. For example, see Barber and Lyon (1996).

6. Gorton and Metrick (2010) and Pozsar et al. (2013) provide an excellent description of the institutional features of the shadow banking system.

11 CONCLUSION

1. Also, in several op-eds (e.g., October 24, 2011, and August 7, 2014), the *Wall Street Journal* has recommended significantly higher equity capital requirements for banks.

Bibliography

Acharya, V., and M. Richardson. 2009. *Restoring Financial Stability: How to Repair a Failed System.* Hoboken, NJ: Wiley.

Acharya, V., H. Mehran, and A. Thakor. 2011. "Caught between Scylla and Charybdis? Regulating Bank Leverage When There Is Rent Seeking and Risk Shifting." Federal Reserve Bank of New York working paper.

Acharya, V., et al. 2013. "Non-Executive Incentives and Bank Risk-Taking," available at http://fic.wharton.upenn.edu/fic/papers/13/13–18.pdf.

Acharya, V., D. Anginer, and A. J. Warburton. 2015. "The End of Market Discipline? Investor Expectations of Implicit Government Guarantees." SSRN, available at http://ssrn.com/abstract=1961656.

Admati, A., and M. Hellwig. 2013. *The Bankers' New Clothes: What's Wrong with Banking and What to Do about It.* Princeton, NJ: Princeton University Press.

Admati, A., P. DeMarzo, M. Hellwig, and P. Pfleiderer. 2013. "Fallacies, Irrelevant Facts, and Myths in the Discussion of Capital Regulation: Why Bank Equity Is Not Socially Expensive." Stanford University working paper.

Adrian, T., and H. Shinn. 2009. "Money, Liquidity, and Monetary Policy." Federal Reserve Bank of New York staff report.

Agarwal, S., E. Benmelech, N. Bergman, and A. Seru. 2012. "Did the Community Reinvestment Act (CRA) Lead to Risky Lending?" NBER working paper.

Aggarwal, R. K., and A. A. Samwick. 1999. "The Other Side of the Trade-Off: The Impact of Risk on Executive Compensation." *Journal of Political Economy* 107 (February), 65–105.

Agrawal, A., and G. N. Mandelker. 1987. "Managerial Incentives and Corporate Investment and Financing Decisions." *Journal of Finance* 42, 823–37.

Alces, K., and B. Galle. 2012. "The False Promise of Risk-Reducing Incentive Pay: Evidence from Executive Pensions and Deferred Compensation." *Journal of Corporation Law* 38, 53.

Allen, F., E. Carletti, and R. Marquez. 2011. "Credit Market Competition and Capital Regulation." *Review of Financial Studies* 24, 983–1018.

American International Group. 2004. "Proxy Statement," available at: www.sec.gov/Archives/edgar/data/5272/000095011704001279/a37136.htm.

Amihud, Y., and B. Lev. 1981. "Risk Reduction as a Managerial Motive for Conglomerate Mergers." *Bell Journal of Economics* 12, 605–17.

Anderson, T. W., and H. Rubin. 1949. "Estimation of the Parameters of a Single Equation in a Complete System of Stochastic Equations." *Annals of Mathematical Statistics* 20, 46–63.

Anginer, D., and A. Demirguc-Kunt. 2014. "Has the Global Banking System Become More Fragile over Time?," *Journal of Financial Stability* 13, 202–13.

Anginer, D., and A. Demirguc-Kunt. 2014. "Bank Capital and Systemic Stability." World Bank working paper.

Ashcraft, A. B., and T. Schuermann. 2007. "Understanding the Securitization of Subprime Mortgage Credit." Federal Reserve Bank of New York working paper.

Avdjiev, S., P. McGuire, and P. Woolridge. 2015. "Enhanced Data to Analyse International Banking." *BIS Quarterly Review* 2015, 53–68.

Baker, G. P., and B. J. Hall. 2004. "CEO Incentives and Firm Size." *Journal of Labor Economics* 22, 767–98.

Baker, D., and T. McArthur. 2009. "The Value of the 'Too Big to Fail' Big Bank Subsidy." Center for Economic and Policy research paper.

Balachandran, S., B. Kogut, and H. Harnal. 2010. "The Probability of Default, Excessive Risk, and Executive Compensation: A Study of Financial Services Firms from 1995 to 2008." Columbia Business School Research Paper Series (manuscript at 34), available at http://ssrn.com/astract=1914542.

Barber, B., and J. Lyon. 1996. "Detecting Abnormal Operating Performance: The Empirical Power and Specification of Test Statistics." *Journal of Financial Economics* 41, 359–400.

Barth, J., T. Li, T. Phumiwasano, and G. Yago, 2008. *Perspectives on the Subprime Market*. Santa Monica, CA: Milken Institute.

Basel Capital Accord. 1998. *International Convergence of Capital Measurement and Capital Standards*. Basel: Bank for International Settlements.

Basel Committee on Banking and Supervision, 2010. "An Assessment of the Long-Term Economic Impact of Stronger Capital and Liquidity Requirements."

Basel Committee on Banking and Supervision, 2013. "Global Systemically Important Banks: Updated Assessment Methodology and the Higher Loss Absorbency Requirement." Available at www.bis.org/publ/bcbs255.htm.

Bebchuk, L., and A. Cohen. 2003. "Firms' Decisions Where to Incorporate." *Journal of Law and Economics* 46, 383–425.

Bebchuk, L., A. Cohen, and H. Spamann. 2010. "The Wages of Failure: Executive Compensation at Bear Stearns and Lehman 2000–2008." *Yale Journal on Regulation* 27, 257–82.

Bebchuk, L., and H. Spamann. 2010, "Regulating Bankers' Pay." *Georgetown Law Journal* 98, 247.

Bebchuk, L. and J. M. Fried. 2010. "Paying for Long-Term Performance." *University of Pennsylvania Law Review* 158, 1915–57.

Beltratti, A., and R. M. Stulz. 2010. "The Credit Crisis around the Globe: Why Did Some Banks Perform Better?," Fisher College of Business working paper no. 2010-03-005.

Beltratti, A., and R. M. Stulz. 2012. "The Credit Crisis around the Globe: Why Did Some Banks Perform Better?," *Journal of Financial Economics* 105(1), 1–17.

Ben-David, I., and D. Roulstone. 2010. "Idiosyncratic Risk and Corporate Transactions." Unpublished working paper, Ohio State University.

Berger, A., and C. Bouwman. 2013. "How Does Capital Affect Bank Performance during Financial Crisis?," *Journal of Financial Economics* 109, 146–76.

Bernanke, B. S. 1983. "Nonmonetary Effects of the Financial Crisis in the Propagation of the Great Depression." *American Economic Review* 73, 257–76.

Bethel, J. E., A. Ferrell, and G. Hu. 2008. "Law and Economic Issues in Subprime Litigation." Harvard Law School working paper.

Bhagat, S., and B. Bolton. 2008. "Corporate Governance and Firm Performance." *Journal of Corporate Finance* 14, 257–73

Bhagat, S., and B. Bolton. 2013. "Director Ownership, Governance and Performance." *Journal of Financial and Quantitative Analysis* 48, 105.

Bhagat, S., and B. Bolton. 2014. "Financial Crisis and Bank Executive Incentive Compensation." *Journal of Corporate Finance* 25, 313–41.

Bhagat, S., B. Bolton, and J. Lu. 2015. "Size, Leverage, and Risk-Taking of Financial Institutions." *Journal of Banking and Finance* 59, 520–37.

Bhagat, S., and R. Romano. 2009. "Reforming Executive Compensation." *Yale Journal on Regulation* 26(2), 359–72.

Bhagat, S., and R. Romano. 2010. "Reforming Executive Compensation: Simplicity, Transparency and Committing to the Long-Term." *European Company and Financial Law Review* 7, 273–96.

Bhagat, S., and H. Tookes. 2012. "Voluntary and Mandatory Skin in the Game: Understanding Outside Directors' Stock Holdings." *European Journal of Finance* 18, 191.

Bhagat, S., B. Bolton, and R. Romano. 2008. "The Promise and Perils of Corporate Governance Indices." *Columbia Law Review* 108, 1803–82.

Bhagat, S., B. Bolton, and R. Romano. 2014. "Getting Incentives Right: Is Deferred Bank Executive Compensation Sufficient?" *Yale Journal of Regulation* 31, 523–64.

Bhagat, S., D. Carey, and C. Elson. 1999. "Director Ownership, Corporate Performance, and Management Turnover." *The Business Lawyer*, 54.

Bharath, S., and T. Shumway. 2008. "Forecasting Default with the Merton Distance to Default Model." *Review of Financial Studies* 21, 1339–69.

Bhattacharyya, S., and A. Purnanandam. 2011. "Risk-Taking by Banks: What Did We Know and When Did We Know It?" University of Michigan working paper, available at http://ssrn.com/abstract=1619472.

Black, F., and M. Scholes. 1973. "The Pricing of Options and Corporate Liability." *Journal of Political Economy* 81, 637–54.

Black, B. S. 1990. "Is Corporate Law Trivial? A Political and Economic Analysis." *Northwestern Law Review* 84, 542–97.

Black, B. 1992. "Agents Watching Agents: The Promise of Institutional Investor Voice." *UCLA Law Review* 39, 811.

Bolton, P., H. Mehran, and J. Shapiro. 2010. "Executive Compensation and Risk Taking." Federal Reserve Bank of New York staff report no. 456.

Bound, J., D. A. Jaeger, and R. M. Baker. 1995. "Problems with Instrumental Variables Estimation When the Correlation between the Instruments and the Endogenous Explanatory Variable Is Weak." *Journal of the American Statistical Association* 90(430), 443–50.

Boyd, J. H., G. De Nicolo, and A. M. Jalal. 2006. "Bank Risk-Taking and Competition Revisited: New Theory and New Evidence." IMF working paper no. WP/06/297.

Boyd, J. H., R. Jagannathan, and S. Kwak. 2009. "What Caused the Current Financial Mess and What Can We Do about It?" *Journal of Investment Management* 7, 1–17.

Boyd, J. H., and D. E. Runkle. 1993. "Size and Performance of Banking Firms: Testing the Predictions of Theory." *Journal of Monetary Economics* 31, 47–67.

Brewer, E., III, and J. Jagtiani. 2009. "How Much Did Banks Pay to Become Too-Big-to-Fail and to Become Systemically Important?" Federal Reserve Bank of Philadelphia working paper.

Cai, J., and R. A. Walkling. 2011. "Shareholders' Say on Pay: Does It Create Value?" Journal of Financial and Quantitative Analysis 46, 299–339.

Calice, G., C. Ioannidis, and J. Williams. 2012. "Credit Derivatives and the Default Risk of Large Complex Financial Institutions." *Journal of Financial Services Research*, 42(1–2), 85–107.

Calomiris, C. 2009. "The Subprime Turmoil: What's Old, What's New, and What's Next." Unpublished working paper, Columbia Business School.

Calomiris, C. W., and C. M. Kahn. 1991. "The Role of Demandable Debt in Structuring Optimal Banking Arrangements." *American Economic Review* 81, 497–513.

Calomiris, C. W., and J. R. Mason. 2003a. "Consequences of US Bank Distress during the Depression." *American Economic Review* 93, 937–47.

Calomiris, C. W., and J. R. Mason. 2003b. "Fundamentals, Panic and Bank Distress during the Depression." *American Economic Review* 93, 1615–47.

Calomiris, C. W., and J. R. Mason. 1997. "Contagion and Bank Failure during the Great Depression: The Chicago Banking Panic of June 1932." *American Economic Review* 87, 863–84.

Carhart, M., 1997. "On Persistence in Mutual Fund Performance." *Journal of Finance* 52, 57–82.

Carletti, E., and P. Hartmann. 2003. "Competition and Stability: What's Special about Banking?" European Central Bank working paper no. 146.

Chen, R.-R., N. K. Chidambaran, M. B. Imerman, and B. J. Sopranzetti. 2014. "Liquidity, Leverage, and Lehman: A Structural Analysis of Financial Institutions in Crisis." *Journal of Banking and Finance*, 45, 117–39.

Cheng, I.-H., H. Hong, and J. A. Scheinkman. 2010. "Yesterday's Heroes: Compensation and Creative Risk-Taking." NBER working paper.

Chen, M. 2004. "Executive Option Repricing: Incentives and Retention." *Journal of Finance* 59, 1167–99.

Chesney, M., J. Stromberg, and A. Wagner. 2010. "Risktaking Incentives, Governance, and Losses in the Financial Crisis." Unpublished working paper, University of Zurich.

Coffee, J. 1991. "Liquidity versus Control: The Institutional Investor as Corporate Monitor." *Columbia Law Review* 91, 1277.

Cox, J. 1984. "Compensation, Deterrence, and the Market as Boundaries for Derivative Suit Procedures." *George Washington Law Review* 52, 762–3.

Crouhy, M., and S. M. Turnbull. 2008. 'The Subprime Credit Crisis of 07." University of Houston working paper.

Cziraki, P. 2015. "Trading by Bank Insiders before and during the 2007–2008 Financial Crisis." University of Toronto working paper.

Daines, R. 2001. "Does Delaware Law Improve Firm Value?" *Journal of Financial Economics* 62, 525–58.

De Nicolo, G. 2000. "Size, Charter Value and Risk in Banking: An International Perspective." International Finance Discussion Paper 689, Board of Governors of the Federal Reserve System.

DeBondt, W. F. M., and R. H. Thaler. 1996. "Financial Decision-Making in Markets and Firms: A Behavioral Perspective." In Robert Jarrow et al. eds., *Handbook in Operations Research and Management Science*.

Demirguc-Kunt, A., E. Detragiache, and O. Merrouche. 2013. "Bank Capital: Lessons from the Financial Crisis." *Journal of Money, Credit and Banking* 45, 1147–64.

Demirguc-Kunt, A., and H. Huizinga. 2011. "Do We Need Big Banks? Evidence on Performance, Strategy and Market Discipline." European Banking Center Discussion Paper No. 2011-005.

Demsetz, R. S., M. R. Saidenberg, and P. E. Strahan. 1997. "Agency Problems and Risk-Taking at Banks." Federal Reserve Bank of New York working paper.

Demsetz, R. S., and P. E. Strahan. 1997. "Diversification, Size, and Risk at Bank Holding Companies." *Journal of Money, Credit, and Banking* 29, 300–13.

Dermine, J., and D. Schoenmaker. 2010. In Banking, Is Small Beautiful? *Financial Markets, Institutions and Instruments* 19, 1–19.

DeYoung, R., E. Peng, and M. Yan. 2013. "Executive Compensation and Business Policy Choices at U.S. Commercial Banks." *Journal of Financial and Quantitative Analysis* 48, 165.

Dhaliwal, D. S., C. A. Gleason, S. Heitzman, and K. Melendrez. 2008. "Auditor Fees and Cost of Debt." *Journal of Accounting, Auditing and Finance.*

Diamond, D. W., and R. G. Rajan. 2009. "The Credit Crisis: Conjectures about Causes and Remedies." *American Economic Review: Papers & Proceedings* 99(2), 606–10.

Diebold, F. X., N. A. Doherty, R. J. Herring, editors. 2010. The Known, the Unknown, and the Unknowable in Financial Risk Management: Measurement and Theory Advancing Practice. Princeton, NJ: Princeton University Press.

Duffie, D. 2010. *How Big Banks Fail and What to Do about It.* Princeton, NJ: Princeton University Press.

Duffie, D., L. Saita, and K. Wang. 2007. "Multi-Period Corporate Default Prediction with Stochastic Covariates." *Journal of Financial Economics* 83. 635–65.

Eckbo, E., and K. Thorburn. 2012. *Foundations and Trends in Finance.*

Edmans, A., X. Gabaix, T. Sadzik, and Y. Sannikov. 2010. "Dynamic Incentive Accounts." Unpublished working paper, Wharton School, University of Pennsylvania.

Ellul, A., and V. Yerramilli. 2014. "Stronger Risk Controls, Lower Risk: Evidence from U.S. Bank Holding Companies." *Journal of Finance* (in press), available at http://papers.ssrn.com/sol3/papers.cfm?abstract_id=1550361.

Elson, C. 1995. "The Duty of Care, Compensation, and Stock Ownership." *University of Cincinnati Law Review* 63, 649.

Elson, C. 1996. "Shareholding Directors Create Better Corporate Performance." *Issue Alert*, May 1996.

Fahlenbrach, R., and R. Stulz. 2011. "Bank CEO Incentives and the Credit Crisis." *Journal of Financial Economics* 99, 11–26.

Fama, E. 2010. Interview, available at www.bloomberg.com/video/64476076/ (accessed December 2013).

Fama, E. F., and K. R. French. 1992. "The Cross-Section of Expected Stock Returns." *Journal of Finance* 47, 427–65.

Federal Reserve Bank of Chicago. 2010. "Profitwise News and Views: Default Rates on Prime and Subprime Mortgages: Differences & Similarities."

Ferri, F., and D. A. Maber. 2013. "Say on Pay Votes and CEO Compensation: Evidence from the UK." Review of Finance 17, 527–63.

FHFA (US Housing and Finance Agency). 2010. "Mortgage Note 10–2: The Housing Goals of Fannie Mae and Freddie Mac in the Context of the Mortgage Market: 1996 – 2009."

FCIC (Financial Crisis Inquiry Commission). 2011. *FCIC Report* Washington: US Government Printing Office.

Financial Stability Board. 2009. *FSB Principles for Sound Compensation Practices: Implementation Standards 3*, available at www.financialstabilityboard.org/publications/r_090925c.pdf.

Fisch, J. E. 2000. "The Peculiar Role of the Delaware Courts in the Competition for Corporate Charters." *University of Cincinnati Law Review.*

Flannery, M. J. 2014. "Maintaining Adequate Bank Capital." *Journal of Money, Credit and Banking.* 46(1), 157–80.

French, K., et al. 2010. *The Squam Lake Report.* Princeton, NJ: Princeton University Press.

Galloway, T. M., W. B. Lee, and D. M. Roden. 1997. "Banks' Changing Incentives and Opportunities for Risk-Taking." *Journal of Banking and Finance* 21, 509–27.

Gande, A., and S. Kalpathy. 2011. "CEO Compensation at Financial Firms." Unpublished working paper, Southern Methodist University.

Gandhi, P., H. Lustig, and A. Plazzi. 2016. "Equity Is Cheap for Large Financial Institutions: The International Evidence." Stanford University working paper.

Geithner, T. 2014. *Stress Test: Reflections on the Financial Crisis.* New York: Crown Publishers.

Gilson, R., and R. Kraakman. 1991. "Reinventing the Outside Director: An Agenda for Institutional Investors." *Stanford Law Review* 43, 883–92.

Gompers, P., J. Ishii, and A. Metrick. 2003. "Corporate Governance and Equity Prices." *Quarterly Journal of Economics* 118, 107–55.

Gompers, P., S. N. Kaplan, and V. Mukharlyamov. 2014. "What Do Private Equity Firms Do?" Harvard University working paper.

Gordon, J. 2012. "Executive Compensation and Corporate Governance in Financial Firms: The Case for Convertible Equity-Based Pay." *Columbia Law Review* 834.

Gorton, G., and A. Metrick. 2010. "Regulating the Shadow Banking System." Yale University working paper.

Goyal, V. K. 2005. "Market Discipline of Bank Risk: Evidence from Subordinated Debt Contracts." *Journal of Financial Intermediation* 14, 318–50.

Griffin, J., R. Lowery, and A. Saretto. 2014. "Complex Securities and Underwriter Reputation: Do Reputable Underwriters Produce Better Securities?" *Review of Financial Studies* 27, 2872–925.

Hahn, J., and J. A. Hausman. 2002. "A New Specification Test for the Validity of Instrumental Variables." *Econometrica* 70, 163–89.

Haldane, A. G. 2009. "Banking on the State." Available at www.bis.org/review/r091111e.pdf.

Hall, R. E. 2014. "Quantifying the Lasting Harm to the U.S. Economy from the Financial Crisis." Available at www.nber.org/papers/w20183.

Hall, B. J., and K. J. Murphy. 2002. "Stock Options for Undiversified Executives." *Journal of Accounting and Economics* 33, 3–42.

Hansen, L. P. 1982. "Large Sample Properties of Generalized Method of Moments Estimators." *Econometrica* 50(4), 1029–54.

Hausman, J. A. 1978. "Specification Tests in Econometrics." *Econometrica* 46, 1251–71.

Heaton, J. B. 2002. "Managerial Optimism and Corporate Finance." *Financial Management* 31.

Hirsch, B., B. Reichert, and M. Sohn. 2013. "Can Clawback Provisions in Management Incentive Contracts Backfire and Lead to More Risk Taking?" Available at http://ssrn.com/abstract=2312487.

Hirsch, C., and C. E. Bannier. 2008. "The Economics of Rating Watchlists: Evidence from Rating Changes." Frankfurt School of Finance and Management working paper.

Hoenig, T. 2013. "Basel III Capital Interim Final Rule and Notice of Proposed Rulemaking." Available at www.fdic.gov/about/learn/board/hoenig/statement7-9-2013.html.

Hoitash, R., A. Markelevich, and C. Barragato. 2007. "Auditor Fees and Audit Quality." *Managerial Accounting Journal* 22(8), 761–86.

Holmstrom, B. 1979. "Moral Hazard and Observability." *Bell Journal of Economics* 10, 74.

Holmstrom, B. 1999. "Managerial Incentive Problems: A Dynamic Perspective." *Review of Economic Studies* 66, 169.

Holmstrom, B. and J. Tirole. 1997. "Financial Intermediation, Loanable Funds, and the Real Sector." *Quarterly Journal of Economics* 112, 663–91.

Houston, J. F., C. Lin, P. Lin, and Y. Ma. 2010. "Creditor Rights, Information Sharing, and Bank Risk-Taking." *Journal of Financial Economics* 96:3, 485–512.

Hu, B. 2009. "AIG Shouldn't Have Paid Unit Bonuses, Greenberg Says." Available at www.bloomberg.com/apps/news?pid=20601087&sid=aM1tb.djytxs&¬refer=home (accessed December 2013).

HUD (US Department of Housing and Urban Development). 2008. *Profiles of GSE Mortgage Purchases in 2005–2007.* Washington, DC: US Government Printing Office.

Hughes, M. 2013. "Clawbacks Gain Favor, Raise Issues in Absence of Guidance, Speakers Say." *Corporate Accountability Report* 11, 685.

Jensen, M., and W. Meckling. 1976. "Theory of the Firm: Managerial Behavior, Agency Costs, and Ownership Structure." *Journal of Financial Economics* 3, 305–60.

Jessen, C., and D. Lando. 2014. "Robustness of Distance-to-Default." *Journal of Banking and Finance* (in press).

Jenter, D. 2005. "Market Timing and Managerial Portfolio Decisions." *Journal of Finance* 60, 1903–49.

Kose, J., L. Litov, and B. Yeung. 2008. "Corporate Governance and Risk-Taking." *Journal of Finance* 4, 1679–1728.

Jokivuolle, E., and J. Keppo. 2013. "Bankers' Compensation: Sprint Swimming in Short Bonus Pools?" Available at http://papers.ssrn.com/sol3/papers.cfm?abstract_id=2346602.

Junge, G., and P. Kugler. 2013. "Quantifying the Impact of Higher Capital Requirements on the Swiss Economy." *Swiss Journal of Economics and Statistics* 149, 313–56.

Kalemli-Ozcan, S., B. Sorensen, and S. Yesiltas. 2012. "Leverage across Firms, Banks, and Countries." *Journal of International Economics* 88.

Kaplan, S. N., and P. Stromberg. 2008. "Leveraged Buyouts and Private Equity." NBER working paper.

Kaplan, S. N., and J. Rauh. 2010. "Wall Street and Main Street: What Contributes to the Rise in the Highest Incomes?" *Review of Financial Studies* 23, 1004.

Kaplan, S. N., and J. Rauh, 2013. "It's the Market: The Broad-Based Rise in the Return to Top Talent." *Journal of Economic Perspectives* 27, 35.

Kashyap, A. K., J. C. Stein, and S. Hanson. 2010. "An Analysis of the Impact of 'Substantially Heightened' Capital Requirements on Large Financial Institutions." University of Chicago working paper.

Keely, M. C. 1990. "Deposit Insurance, Risk, and Market Power in Banking." *American Economic Review* 80, 1183–2000.

King, M. 2010. "Mapping Capital and Liquidity Requirements to Bank Lending Spreads." Basel: Bank of International Settlements, WP 324.

Kisin, R., and A. Manela. 2014. "The Shadow Cost of Bank Requirements." Washington University working paper.

Lambert, R., D. Larcker, and R. Verrecchia. 1991. "Portfolio Considerations in Valuing Executive Compensation." *Journal of Accounting Research* 29, 129.

Larcker, D. F., A. L. McCall, G. Ormazabal, and B. Tayan. 2012. "Ten Myths of 'Say on Pay.'" Rock Center for Corporate Governance at Stanford University Closer Look Series: Topics, Issues and Controversies in Corporate Governance No. CGRP-26. Available at SSRN: http://ssrn.com/abstract=2094704.

Laeven, L. and Levine, R. 2009. "Bank Governance, Regulation and Risk-Taking." *Journal of Financial Economics* 93, 259–75.

Litvak, K. 2004. "Venture Capital Limited Partnership Agreements: Understanding Compensation Arrangements." University of Texas Law and Economics Research Paper.

Macey, J. R., and G. P. Miller. 1992. "Double Liability of Bank Shareholders: History and Implications." *Wake Forest Law Review* 27.

Malmendier, U., and G. Tate. 2005. "CEO Overconfidence and Corporate Investment." *Journal of Finance* 60, 2661–700.

Mason, J. R., and J. Rosner. 2007. "Where Did the Risk Go? How Misapplied Bond Ratings Cause Mortgage Backed Securities and Collateralized Debt Obligation Market Disruptions," May 3, available at SSRN: https://ssrn.com/abstract =1027475 or http://dx.doi.org/10.2139/ssrn.1027475.

McDonald, R. 2010. "Contingent Capital with a Dual Price Trigger." Unpublished working paper, Northwestern University.

Mehran, H., and A. Thakor. 2011. "Bank Capital and Value in the Cross-Section." *Review of Financial Studies* 24, 1019–67.

Metrick A., and A. Yasuda. 2011. "Venture Capital and the Finance of Innovation."

Merton, R. C. 1974. "On the Pricing of Corporate Debt: The Risk Structure of Interest Rates." *Journal of Finance* 29(2), 449–70.

Merton, R. C. 1977. "An Analytic Derivation of the Cost of Deposit Insurance and Loan Guarantees: An Application of Modern Option Pricing Theory." *Journal of Banking and Finance* 1(1), 3–11.

Milanovic, B. 2004. "Do More Unequal Countries Redistribute More? Does the Median Voter Hypothesis Hold?," World Bank Policy Research Working Paper Series.

Miles, D., J. Yang, and G. Marcheggiano. 2013. "Optimal Bank Capital." *Economic Journal* 123, 1–37.

Molyneux, P., K. Schneck, and T. M. Zhou. 2010. "Too-Big-to-Fail and Its Impact on Safety Net Subsidies and Systemic Risk." University of Bocconi working paper.

Murphy, K. J. 2010. "Executive Pay Restrictions for TARP Recipients: An Assessment." Testimony before US Congress, available at http://ssrn.com /abstract=1698973.

Murphy, K. J. 2012. "The Politics of Pay: A Legislative History of Executive Compensation." In Jennifer Hill and Randall Thomas (eds.), Research Handbook on Executive Pay. London: Edgar Elgar.

Murphy, K. M., and A. Shleifer 2004. "Persuasion in Politics." American Economic Review 94(2), 435–9.

Myers, S. C., 1977. "Determinants of Corporate Borrowing." Journal of Financial Economics 5, 147–75.

OFHEO (US Office of Federal Housing Enterprise Oversight). 2008. "Mortgage Markets and Enterprises in 2007."

Peng, L., and A. Roell. 2009. "Managerial Incentives and Stock Price Manipulation." Unpublished working paper, Columbia University.

Paletta, D., D. Solomon, and D. Enrich. 2010. "White House's Tax Proposal Targets Big Banks' Risks." The Wall Street Journal, January 14.

Pennacchi, G. G., 1987a. "Alternative Forms of Deposit Insurance: Pricing and Bank Incentive Issues." Journal of Banking and Finance 11(2), 291–312.

Pennacchi, G. G. 1987b. "A Reexamination of the Over-(or Under-) Pricing of Deposit Insurance." Journal of Money, Credit and Banking 19(3), 340–60.

Perry, T., and M. Zenner. 2000. "Pay for Performance? Government Regulation and the Structure of Compensation Contracts." Available at http://papers.ssrn.com /sol3/papers.cfm?abstract_id=60956.

Pozsar, Z., T. Adrian, A. Ashcraft, and H. Boesky. 2013. "Shadow Banking." FRBY Economic Policy Review, December 2013.

Raboy, D. 2009. "Economics Behind the Subprime Crisis." In Emergency Economic Stabilization Handbook. Eagan, MN: West Thompson Reuters.

Rajan, R.G. 2006. "Has Finance Made the World Riskier?" European Financial Management 12, 499–533.

Repullo, R. 2004. "Capital Requirements, Market Power, and Risk-Taking in Banking." Journal of Financial Intermediation 13(2), 156–82.

Rice, T., and P. E. Strahan. 2010. "Does Credit Competition Affect Small-Firm Finance?" Journal of Finance 65(3), 861–89.

Rime, B. 2005. "Do "Too Big to Fail" Expectations Boost Large Banks Issuer Ratings?" Swiss National Bank research paper.

Romano, R. 1985. "Law as a Product: Some Pieces of the Incorporation Puzzle." Journal of Law, Economics and Organization 1, 225–83.

Ronn, E., and A. Verma. 1986. "Pricing-Risk-Adjusted Deposit Insurance: An Option-Based Model." *Journal of Finance* 41(4): 871–95.

Rochet, J. 2008. "Why Are There So Many Banking Crises?" In *The Politics and Policy of Bank Regulation*. Princeton, NJ: Princeton University Press.

Rock Center for Corporate Governance. 2016. *CEOs and Directors on Pay: 2016 Survey on CEO Compensation*. Palo Alto, CA: Stanford University.

Rose, P. 2011. "On the Role and Regulation of Proxy Advisors." *Michigan Law Review* 109, 62.

Rozeff, M. S., and M. A. Zaman. 1998. "Overreaction and Insider Trading: Evidence from Growth and Value Portfolios." *Journal of Finance* 53, 701–16.

Sargan, J. D. 1988. *Lectures on Advanced Econometric Theory*. Oxford: Basil Blackwell.

Saunders, A., E. Strock, and N. G. Travlos. 1990. "Ownership Structure, Deregulation, and Bank Risk-Taking." *Journal of Finance* 45, 643–54.

Schizer, D. M. 2000. "Executives and Hedging: The Fragile Legal Foundation of Incentive Compatibility." *Columbia Law Review* 100.

Sepe, S. M., and C. K. Whitehead. 2013. "Risky Business: Competition, Compensation and Risk-Taking." Cornell Legal Studies Research Paper No. 13–87, available at http://ssrn.com/abstract=2307216.

Seyhun, N. 1986. "Insiders' Profits, Cost of Trading and Market Efficiency." *Journal of Financial Economics* 16, 189–212.

Slovnik, P., and B. Cournede. 2011. "Macroeconomic Impact of Basel III." OECD Economics working paper.

Smith, C. W., and R. M. Stulz. 1985. "The Determinants of Firms' Hedging Policies." *Journal of Financial and Quantitative Analysis* 20, 391–405.

Smith, C. W., and J. B. Warner. 1979. "On Financial Contracting: An Analysis of Bond Covenants." *Journal of Financial Economics* 7, 117–61.

Stern, G. H., and R. Feldman. 2009. "Addressing TBTF by Shrinking Financial Institutions: An Initial Assessment." *The Region*.

Stiroh, K. J. 2006. "New Evidence on the Determinants of Bank Risk." *Journal of Financial Services Research* 30, 237–63.

Stock, J. H., and M. Yogo. 2005. "Testing for Weak Instruments in Linear IV Regression." In Donald W. K. Andrews, James H. Stock (eds.), *Identification and inference for econometric models: Essays in honor of Thomas Rothenberg*, pp. 80–108. Cambridge University Press.

Swiss Confederation Federal Department of Finance. 2013. "Strengthening Financial Sector Stability." Available at www.efd.admin.ch/themen/wirt schaft_waehrung/02315/.

Taylor, J., and E. Kapur. 2015. "How Bankruptcy Reform Can Address 'Too Big to Fail,'" available at http://web.stanford.edu/~johntayl/2015_pdfs/Testimony _Senate_Banking-SCFICP-July-29-2015.pdf.

Tarullo, D. K. 2008. "Banking on Basel." Peterson Institute for International Economics.

Tsesmelidakis, Z., and R. C. Merton. 2012. "The Value of Implicit Guarantees." MIT working paper, available at SSRN: http://ssrn.com/abstract=2231317.

Tung, F. 2011. "Pay for Banker Performance: Structuring Executive Compensation for Risk Regulation." *Northwestern University Law Review* 105, 1205.

Vallascas, F., and K. Keasey. 2012. "Does Bank Default Risk Increase with Information Asymmetry? Evidence from Europe." University of Leeds working paper.

Vyas, D. 2011. "The Timeliness of Accounting Write-Downs by U.S. Financial Institutions during the Financial Crisis of 2007–2008." *Journal of Accounting Research* 49(3), 823–60.

Wallison, P. 2015. *Hidden in Plain Sight: What Really Caused the World's Worst Financial Crisis and Why It Could Happen Again.* New York: Encounter Books.

Wei, C., and D. Yermack. 2011. "Investor Reactions to CEOs' Inside Debt Incentives." *Review of Financial Studies* 24, 3813.

Index

abnormal CEO trading, 71, 174
Admati, 5, 120, 168, 176, 225, 226, 228

bank capital, 155
bank capital reform programs, 154, 158
bank's cost of capital, 169
Basel III, 155, 156, 157, 158, 159, 221, 222, 223, 224, 225, 235
Bebchuk, Cohen and Spamann, 44, 175
Berle and Means, 102
Bhagat and Bolton, 6, 119, 120, 127, 128, 152, 212, 218
Bhagat and Romano, 165, 175, 204
Brexit, 97

carried interest, 76
CEO turnover, 112, 113
clawbacks, 1, 87, 88, 89, 90, 96, 203, 214, 216
CoCo bonds, 160
compensation committees, 81, 85, 88, 94, 115, 116, 178
corporate boards, 3, 82, 85, 116, 127, 218
corporate governance measure, 6, 119, 152
Cziraki, 70, 232

debt-based compensation, 1, 2, 7, 91, 93, 94, 217
deferred compensation, 76, 88, 93
deposit insurance, 3, 91, 92, 159, 172, 219, 236, 238, 239
derivative contracts, 81
derivative transactions, 78
director compensation, xiv, 6, 9, 101, 113, 114, 116, 120, 153, 183
director dollar stockholding, 6, 119, 120, 127, 134, 152, 201
director ownership, 36, 104, 112, 114, 128, 144, 145, 152, 183
diversification, xiii, 6, 33, 53, 54, 67, 77, 78, 92, 115, 116, 118, 119, 121, 152, 215
Dodd-Frank Act, xiii, xiv, 1, 4, 88, 176

endogeneity, 5, 119, 138, 139, 140, 141, 142, 152
equity capital to total assets ratio (EAR), 125
Estimated Value Lost, 39, 46, 47, 48, 50, 83, 84, 196, 200
excessive risk-taking, xiii, 1, 2, 5, 6, 24, 30, 31, 67, 69, 70, 72, 87, 88, 89, 90, 119, 122, 152, 154, 163, 174, 175, 205, 211, 214
executive compensation reform policies, 73

Fahlenbrach and Stulz, 30
Fama, 57, 62, 108, 120, 168, 176, 233
Fannie Mae, 12, 14, 16, 17, 179, 234
financial crisis, xiii, 1, 3, 6, 9, 12, 19, 27, 33, 34, 35, 39, 70, 89, 91, 121, 130, 145, 146, 147, 157, 158, 159, 160, 161, 170, 174, 202, 204, 206, 224, 226, 230, 232, 234, 235, 240
Freddie Mac, 12, 14, 16, 17, 179, 234

GSE Act, 12

Incentive-based Compensation Arrangements, 95
independent director, 103, 206
insider trading, 30, 36, 64, 67, 70, 94, 163
institutional investors, xiii, 1, 10, 20, 178, 179, 181, 218

labor force participation rate, 1, 226
leverage, 5, 9, 118, 119, 127, 152, 155, 156, 157, 158, 159, 168, 172, 176, 205, 221, 222, 223, 225, 228
liquidity, xiii, 16, 33, 53, 54, 67, 77, 78, 80, 114, 115, 172
long-term shareholder value, 4, 7, 31, 33, 34, 73, 74, 94, 101, 155, 158, 162, 172, 177, 178
L-TARP, 36

Managerial Incentives Hypothesis, vii, 30, 31, 32, 33, 34, 43, 45, 52, 53, 54, 67

Merton DD, 5, 118, 125, 126, 134, 141, 152, 201

mid-level managers, 116

moral hazard, 2, 91, 92, 93, 138, 224

mortgage backed securities (MBS), 19

Net CEO Payoff, 33, 45, 46, 48, 50, 52, 53, 82, 83, 84, 85, 87, 192, 196, 200

Net Trades, 33, 34, 38, 39, 40, 42, 43, 46, 48, 50, 54, 55, 56, 57, 58, 60, 61, 64, 67, 68, 79, 83, 84, 114, 163, 164, 196, 200

non-financial companies, 113, 178

No-TARP, 36

Prime Minister May, 97

prime mortgages, 16

private equity, 76

proprietary trading, 4, 177

Regulatory Hybrid Security, 161, 162

Restricted Equity proposal, 2, 3, 7, 9, 74, 75, 77, 79, 81, 82, 85, 87, 89, 91, 92, 93, 96, 101, 113, 115, 154, 160, 172, 212, 214

Restricted-Equity-More-Equity-Capital, 157, 160, 161, 162, 166, 173

retainer, 101, 104, 105, 106, 107, 108, 114, 127, 218

return on assets (ROA), 125

risk-taking, 5

risk-weighted, 155

say on pay, 97

securitization, 18, 19, 22, 23, 172, 179, 229

shadow banking, 172, 227

standard deviation of asset returns (σ(ROA), 125

subprime mortgages, 16

succession planning, 76

TBTF, 1

TLACs (total-loss-absorbing-capacity), 161

too-big-to-fail, xiii, xiv, 1, 4, 6, 27, 37, 114, 170, 176, 227, 231

total shareholder return, 75

Troubled Assets Relief Program (TARP), 35

undiversified, 33, 53, 235

Unforeseen Risk Hypothesis, vii, 30, 31, 32, 33, 34, 43, 45, 52, 53, 54

vesting, 24, 25, 31, 76, 77, 88, 175, 206, 209, 212

Volcker Rule, xiv, 4, 177

Wallison, 12, 174, 240

write-downs, 64

Z-score, 5, 63, 65, 71, 118, 119, 121, 125, 130, 131, 132, 134, 135, 136, 140, 141, 145, 146, 147, 148, 149, 150, 152, 174, 201, 211

Printed in the United States
By Bookmasters